To

To celebrate our
15 years of
collaboration and
work.

With love

Neil

November 2011

Evolution of Gestalt Series
Volume II

Robert G. Lee and
Neil Harris, Editors
••••••••••••••••••

Relational Child, Relational Brain

● ● ● ● ● ● ● ● ● ● ● ●

Development and Therapy in Childhood and Adolescence

A GestaltPress Book

**published and distributed by
Routledge, Taylor & Francis Group
New York**

All rights reserved. No part of this publication may be reproduced, stored in a retrieval system, or transmitted, in any form or by any means, electronic, mechanical, photocopying, recording, or otherwise without the prior written permission of the publisher:

Copyright 2011 by: GestaltPress
                      127 Abby Court
                      Santa Cruz, CA 95062

    and   165 Route 6A
                  Orleans, MA 02653

Email: gestaltpress@aol.com, gestaltpress@comcast.net

Distributed by: **Routledge, Taylor & Francis Group**
                             711 Third Avenue
                             New York, NY 10017

Library of Congress Cataloging-in-Publishing Data
   1. Gestalt therapy, 2. psychology, 3. children, 4. brain,
   5. adolescents, 6. field theory, 7. relational process,
   8. intersubjectivity, 9. Robert G. Lee, 10. Neil Harris

ISBN: 978-0-415-80776-0

for Debbie

and our collective

children and grandchildren,

with love (from Robert)

and for Jo,

George and Martha,

home ground (from Neil)

Contents

Preface x
Acknowledgments..xvii
The Editors xxii
The Contributors..xxiv

Theory

1. Who Are We?
   Narrative, Evolution, & Development:
   Our Stories and Ourselves
   Gordon Wheeler 5

2. Shame & Belonging in Childhood: The Interaction
   Between Relationship and Neurobiological
   Development in the Early Years of Life
   Robert G. Lee 55

3. Attachment and Mindfulness: Paths of the
   Developing Brain
   Daniel Siegel 77

Support

4. Something in the Air: Conditions that Promote
   Contact when Meeting Young People Who Have
   Stories of Early Trauma and Loss
   Neil Harris 119

5. The Tiger Girl: A Story of Committed, Coordinated,
   Multilevel Support
   Anna-Maria Norén...139

6. The Adolescent Male: Shame, Support, and
   Developmentally Effective Psychotherapy
   Bronagh Starrs 163

7. Relational Modes and the Evolving Field of Parent-Child Contact: A Contribution to a Gestalt Theory of Development
   Mark McConville 175

Applications

8. Zig Zag Flop and Roll: Creating an Embodied Field for Healing and Awareness when Working with Children
   Denise Tervo 199

9. A Different Kind of Contact for Boys: Understanding the Influences of Nature and Nurture on a Boy's Relational Style
   Peter Mortola, Howard Hiton, & Stephen Grant 229

10. Working with Adolescents from a Catholic Background in Northern Ireland: A Generation-Long Accumulation of Shame
    Bronagh Starrs 259

11. Disordered Eating: A Tapestry of Relational Themes and Creative Adjustment
    Marlene Blumenthal 285

12. Am I Bovvered? A Gestalt Approach to Working with Adolescents
    Jon Blend 305

13. You, Me, and the Parts of Myself I'm Still Getting to Know: An Interview with Violet Oaklander on the Role of the Relational Triangle in Her Approach to Therapeutic Work with Children and Adolescents
    Peter Mortola 339

Appendix 350

Preface

• • • • • • • • • • • • • • • • •

Our children are our future.

This often-cited, simple, yet profound, truth is at the heart of the motivation for compiling this volume.

This is the second book in the Evolution of Gestalt Series, each emanating from a study conference at Esalen Institute, Big Sur, California. The first study conference, in October, 2005, focused on our relational nature as humans. While Western culture has brought us much, it also rests on an assumption which dates from at least as far back as ancient Greece – that we are isolated individuals. Of course, if this is true, then in-depth connection with others is limited if not impossible, and the motivation for living ultimately becomes greed, material acquisition, and achieving power over others. The stark, ubiquitous examples that have punctuated recent history, which flow from this understanding of our human condition, include Enron, MCI, the US mortgage crisis, food monopolies that among other consequences have promoted the rise of obesity, and the world banking crisis. The sentiment behind this position was succinctly expressed by a high level banking executive in a statement he recently made to a US congressional committee, "You can't blame us that people were stupid enough to trust us."

But is this really our human nature or is it a statement of the condition of the larger field in which we find ourselves?

The first Esalen Evolution of Gestalt conference explored how interconnected we are – how our complex embodied minds provide us with a sense of others' experience and how our energy fields affect one another. In addition, it explored how our sense of whether our voice and our caring for others is heard as well as our sense of inclusion/exclusion, our sense of belonging, affects our sense of self, the decisions we make, and the actions we take.

From its beginnings, the essence of Gestalt theory has been relational – from the original Gestalt psychologists' Law of Prägnanz, which holds that percepts are organized configurations, the quality of which are dependent on prevailing environmental conditions, to Lewin's field theory and his sense that the need in the field organizes the field, to Goodman's statement that there is no organism without its surrounding environment, to Buber's I-Thou, to current explorations and understandings that our sense of self is intersubjectively co-created. Thus, it is fitting that this sort of exploration, around how we are interconnected as humans, would be at the center of interest and study at a Gestalt conference.

Not only was the first Evolution of Gestalt Conference a huge success, but it gave us *CoCreating the Field: Intention and Practice in the Age of Complexity* (Ullman & Wheeler, 2010), an exquisitely crafted collection of writings on our interconnected condition and the implications for working with clients and living our personal lives.

But what does all this mean for childhood and adolescent development? And what does that mean for those of us who work with children, adolescents and their families? How can we add to the pioneering work of Oaklander, McConville, Frank, Wheeler and others who have looked at development and therapy with children and adolescents through a Gestalt, relational lens?

Extending one of the thrusts of the first conference, what can the explosion of information over the last fifteen years or more from neurobiological and related research, tells us about and add to Gestalt's relational stance in viewing development and therapy in childhood and adolescence?

With this mandate, the second evolution of Gestalt conference, Relational Child, Relational Brain, took place at Esalen Institute in

February, 2007. It followed the model of the first conference with whole community plenaries in the mornings that focused on neurobiology, childhood and adolescent development, and the complexity of intersubjective interaction with the surrounding fields of family, culture, gender, socio-political atmosphere and more. The afternoons were filled with workshops exemplifying Gestalt relational approaches to working with children and adolescents and their families. And in the evenings there were special presentations by honored guests such as Dan Siegel, Peter Levine, and Violet Oaklander, focussing further on neurobiology, development, and relational Gestalt practice.

As with the first evolution of Gestalt conference, this second conference exceeded expectations. There were two themes that evolved as the conference unfolded. First, from a number of sources, bio-neurological and related research tells us that, from infancy, relationship enables and directly influences brain growth – thus supporting Gestalt's relational stance in viewing development and in conducting therapy. Second, was an exploration of the operation of Gestalt process in a relational paradigm and its applications to our work with children and adolescents and their families in various contexts.

Our attempt here, in organizing this volume, is to bring this conference to you, the reader. All of the authors, except for one, were present at the conference. Most of the chapters came from presentations at the conference, often evolving further as a result of the conference. Some of the chapters were inspired by the authors' experience attending the conference.

We have divided the chapters into three sections – Theory, Support, and Applications. A number of the chapters could have been placed in more than one of these sections. In the first section, Theory, we have included three chapters that focus primarily on the interconnection between relationship and brain size, brain development, and brain capacity. The second section, Support, is comprised of four chapters that speak, in various ways, to the importance of the relational connection in the larger field. Six chapters make up the Applications section. These chapters present Gestalt relational approaches to working with children and adolescents and their families in various contexts.

We begin the section on Theory, in Chapter 1, as the conference began, with the convenor of the conference, Gordon Wheeler addressing the question of our relational makeup from the perspective of the story that we tell ourselves about the beginnings of our species. In a chapter entitled "Who Are We? Narrative, Evolution, & Development: Our Stories and Ourselves," Wheeler takes apart the old myths that the development of our larger brain size, as a species, was due to our need to become hunters and warriors and shows instead that it was because of our survival need to embrace the complexity of relationship.

In Chapter 2, "Shame & Belonging in Childhood: The Interaction Between Relationship and Neurobiological Development in the Early Years of Life," Robert Lee, the second presenter at the conference, continues the exploration of the connection between brain development and relationship. In non-technical language, he presents a summary of the neurobiological research that has identified the underpinnings of shame and belonging in the first two years of life. In the process, he brings a Gestalt understanding to what research says are relationally driven processes, clarifying further two important relational milestones in early development and the subsequent, implied relational paths for healing in therapy.

Reading Chapter 3, "Attachment and Mindfulness: Paths of the Developing Brain," by Dan Siegel, is a delightful experience. In this edited version of his presentation at the conference, Siegel's breadth of experience and gracious solidity are palpable as he discusses two relational paths for the developing brain – via attachment and via mindfulness.

Chapter 4 starts the section on Support. In a chapter entitled "Something in the Air: Conditions that Promote Contact when Meeting Young People Who Have Stories of Early Trauma and Loss," Neil Harris focuses on the importance of environmental support from literally the ground up. He shares with us poignant accounts of how, in working with troubled youngsters, mistrust, suspicion, and potential ruptures in the field are eased and avoided through attunement to what might otherwise be considered background issues in the field – issues ranging from attention to structuring the physical environment, to support of therapists and significant others.

Chapter 5, "The Tiger Girl: The Power of Coordinated, Multilevel Support," exemplifies a refinement of an old saying. Anna-Maria Norén shares with us the heartwarming account of how it took a commited, coordinated village to raise a kindergarten age child and her family in rural Sweden. In the process we are privileged to witness not only Norén's wisdom and thoroughness in establishing a "good enough" field for this child and her family but also Norén's incredible attunement to the fragile, unformed voices in the field.

Bronagh Starrs introduces another dimension to our conversation on support here. In Chapter 6, "The Adolescent Male: Shame, Support, and Developmentally Effective Psychotherapy," she shares how using the resources of support within her own body helped her attune to the needs of an adolescent's parents, in the process reestablishing an all important parental connection for this young man. She then describes how these multilevel sources of support enabled a journey of discovery and healing in her young client.

Finally, in our section on Support, Mark McConville brings light to a common way that parental support can go unintentionally and unknowingly awry. Chapter 7, "Relational Modes and the Evolving Field of Parent-Child Contact: A Contribution to a Gestalt Theory of Development" exemplifies a developmental principle that McConville helped form, namely that there is no child development without field development.

The section on Applications opens with Chapter 8 – Denise Tervo's "Zig Zag Flop and Roll: Creating an Embodied Field for Healing and Awareness when Working with Children." Tervo masterfully combines her sense of compassion, her attunement to embodiment, and her breadth of experience and knowledge in working with the effects of trauma in three of her young clients and their families.

Peter Mortola, Howard Hiton, and Stephen Grant give us a different look at boys and their troubles in Chapter 9, "A Different Kind of Contact for Boys: Understanding the Influences of Nature and Nurture on a Boy's Relational Style." With a decade of experience behind them, these authors unravel the gender-based mysteries of boys' struggles to make connection with themselves and others.

Chapter 10, "Working with Adolescents from a Catholic Background in Northern Ireland: A Generation's-Long Accumulation of Shame," presents an intimate look into what it takes to be with, understand, and respond to traumatized adolescents and their families in Northern Ireland. Bronagh Starrs, using McConville's stages of adolescent development and Lee's concept of ground shame, weaves a story of sensitivity, anguish, and discovery as she relationally navigates the survival realities of four young Northern Irish adolescents.

Next, Marlene Blumenthal addresses the mushrooming phenomenon of working with young women with eating problelms and disorders. In Chapter 11, "Disordered Eating: A Tapestry of Relational Themes and Creative Adjustment," we see, through her skilled hands, how relationship is the necessary crucible in which the underlying often hidden lessons of and adjustments to the past can be discovered, processed and healed.

Meeting adolescents to a large degree is an art. In Chapter 12, "Am I Bovvered? A Gestalt Approach to Working with Adolescents," Jon Blend appreciatively describes the creativity that can make-up adolescents' contact styles. He shares his resourcefulness, including his background in music and drama, in developing relational connections with his adolescent clients, whose worlds he seeks to understand and join. In the process we get a look at how he is with them as he and they together discover more satisfying paths.

Peter Mortola's interview with Violet Oaklander concludes this volume. No collectively authored book on working with children could be complete without Oaklander's presence. And as Violet says in the introduction to this chapter, Peter Mortola, a former student, long-time colleague, and researcher of her style and work with children, is the perfect person to interview her. The subject of this interview is Oaklander's concept of the "relational triangle" in her work with children and adolescents.

This book is the continuing, evolving child of the original conference. We launch it in the same spirit from which it came: with a hope of a continued dialogue on our relational understanding of children, adolescents, and their families and what it means to work with them in a way that honors them. Enjoy!

January, 2011

Robert G. Lee
Newton, Massachusetts
USA

Neil Harris
Bransgore, Dorset
UK

Acknowledgments

• • • • • • • • • • • •

The collective effort and care it takes to organize and run a conference of this quality and then to write a book that conveys the experience of the conference to you, the reader, is considerable. There are many who need to be acknowledged.

Let us start with Esalen Institute itself. With its breathtaking beauty, momentous history, comfortable acommodations, attentive staff, and incredible food, it is the perfect place to offer a Gestalt study conference. Nancy Lunney-Wheeler, her staff, and the entire staff at Esalen Institute deserve our deepest appreciation for the magnificent job they did in providing a nourishing conference environment.

It was Gordon Wheeler who first envisioned this conference at the end of the Evolution of Gestalt I Conference. He invited Deb Ullman, Marlene Blumenthal, Denise Tervo, Mary Ann Kraus, Peter Mortola and the two of us, Robert Lee and Neil Harris, to join him in co-chairing a committee to organize this conference. It is a credit to the tireless efforts of this committee that the conference ran so smoothly and that the conference design provided such high quality opportunities to learn in an interactive, relational format.

This kind of study conference is to a large extent dependent on the participation of its attemdees to be successful. The people who attended this conference brought with them a host of experience in being with children and adolescents, which produced rich engagements. In addition, the attendees had a capacity to be interested in and to hold the experience of others, possibly linked to what it takes to be drawn to working with children and adolescents. This made a perfect fit with a major theme of the conference and added significantly to what the conference was able to achieve.

We express a special thank you to Dan Siegel and Peter Levine who donated their time to speak to the conference. Their breadth of knowledge of neurobiological and related research and practice, as well as their comfortability with speaking and interacting with an audience gave us all a fuller, richer grounding in the significance of our relational interconnections.

As for the writing of this book, first we wish to thank our authors for the depth of the stories they have to tell and the creativity, groundedness, and eloquence with which they have written. There were a number of stories that didn't get into these pages, both because of life happenings and space limitations. We wish to thank those authors as well, and we hope their work will find print in subsequent publications.

As for me, Robert, this conference and book represent a long, privileged journey in working with children, adolescents and their families. On the first leg of that journey, in working with boys and their families in the Buffalo ghetto, in the mid 1970s, I learned so much about what it took for these boys and their families to survive in a hostile world in which guns and violence were ever-present.

The second leg of that journey was an internship in my PhD training which focused on working with children, adolescents and their families. I am indebted to my supervisor, Lou Levine, who shared his wisdom and love for this population.

Over the years in my private practice and at a clinic here in Boston I have been blessed with the opportunity of witnessing and influencing the paths of many children, adolescents and their families. Thank you to all of them for what they have given my life.

In 1987 I began to be more deeply aware of the workings of shame, through my own experience and the then-current literature attempting

Acknowledgments ... xix

to deal with this crucial hidden organizer of the field when there is insufficient support and connection. I subsequently conducted research related to the concept of shame. Then together with Gordon Wheeler, I explored the nuances of shame and belonging from a Gestalt perspective (Lee & Wheeler, 1996). I applied these discoveries in my work with young people. Still I did not have an appreciation of the full potential of this approach until my experiences in helping to design and teach the The Advanced Children and Adolescent Program at the Gestalt Institute of Cleveland. I owe my colleagues on that faculty, Mark McConville, Marlene Blumenthal, Denise Tervo, Gordon Wheeler, Debra Dunkle, and Mark Warren, a large debt of gratitude for their competence, connective ability, and the opportunities we have given each other to learn. I also wish to express my appreciation collectively to the talented, experienced, and heart-rich students that we have had the honor of teaching through this program over the years.

This volume would not have been possible if it was not for the support that I have received from my colleagues at GestaltPress, Gordon Wheeler and Deb Ullman. A special thanks goes to Sarah Toman for all that she contributed in the early stages of this project.

Thank you also to Elena Sidorova for her artistic skills in crafting another increcible cover for GestaltPress. Also a special thank you to the kids and people who participated in the cover photo shoot – the kids: Solon, Quince, and Nigela Anderson and Natalie and Brendon Chin; photographers/organizers: Jasmine Inglesmith (whose photo graces the cover), Nicholas Chin, Julia Berazneva, and Tara, Jannah, and Tagan Murray. Thank you also to Don, Jean, Tara, Jannah, and Tagan Murray for use of their gorgeous Vermont farm for the site of the photo shoot. On a slightly drizzly day, a great deal of good will and a group of photogenic kids produced a magnificent image .

Like usual, two people have been a continuous source of support for me in my personal life. I could not have done this project without the love of my wife, Debbie, and the grounding presence of my friend and colleague, Lee Geltman.

Finally, it has been such a treat to work with my coeditor, Neil Harris.

For me, Neil, the route to the conference, and then to co-editing this book has been one of serendipity and surprises. My first encounters with the field of child and adolescent psychiatry, and with Gestalt therapy happened almost simultaneously, back in the late 1980s, a particularly rich patch of my life. My training as a Gestalt therapist, with Gestalt South West in England, and my further training in child psychiatry in the south of England went hand and hand. I want to name and appreciate Gaie Houston, Malcolm Parlett, Marianne Fry, Peter Hardwick and Paul Sepping in particular. They lit the path and accompanied me along the way. My colleagues in the Child and Adolescent Mental Health team on Guernsey in the beautiful Channel Islands, and those working with Family Futures Consortium in Islington, London, have been my teachers and companions in difficult, challenging and hugely rewarding work with many, many children and their families.

Always I am nourished, replenished, and held by my family: my wife Jo, and my children George and Martha.

Though the tension between the medical model, with invitations to linear reductionism, and my life as a Gestalt therapist has at times felt like a wrestling match, working with Robert Lee on this volume has marked another step towards integration. Robert has taught me new skills in the art of the editor; he has been kindly and encouraging, and patient.

January, 2011

Robert G. Lee
Newton, Massachusetts
USA

Neil Harris
Bransgore, Dorset
UK

The Editors

•••••••••••

Robert G. Lee, Ph.D., a psychologist in private practice in Newton, Massachusetts, USA, has written extensively and presented widely on shame and belonging as regulator processes of the relational field. He applies his intersubjective, constructivist insights to a wide range of clinical populations, including working with individuals, couples, families, children, adolescents, and brain-injured folks as well as to the topics of self process, development, field theory, ethics, culture, gender, neurobiological underpinnings of shame and belonging, chronic illness, and trauma. Robert's books include *The Voice of Shame: Silence and Connection in Psychotherapy.* (co-editor, Jossey-Bass, 1996), *The Values of Conneciton: A Relational Approach to Ethics* (editor, GestaltPress/The Analytic Press, 2004*), and The Secret Language of Intimacy: Releasing the Hidden Power in Couple Relationships* (GestaltPress/Routledge, Taylor & Francis Group, 2008). He is an editor at GestaltPress, a faculty member for the Advanced Child and Adolescent Program at the Gestalt Institute of Cleveland and a visiting faculty member of a number of Gestalt training programs in Australia, Canada, Europe, Mexico, and the USA. Other interests in his life include dancing, snorkeling, watercolor painting, and being with and enjoying his wife and their collective children.

Correspondence address: rlee@dr.com

Neil Harris, M.A.(Oxon), M.B., Ch.B, M.R.C.Psych., is a Gestalt therapist registered with the United Kingdom Council for Psychotherapy, and has a private psychotherapy and supervision practice in Bransgore, Dorset, UK. He is also in practice as a Consultant Child and Adolescent Psychiatrist with a particular interest in attachment, trauma and abuse. He works with the Child and Adolescent Mental Health Service on Guernsey in the Channel Islands, with a focus on delivering services to foster children. He is Consultant Child Psychiatrist for Family Futures Consortium, London, UK, an organization working with the issues of trauma and attachment in adoptive and long-term foster families.

Address for correspondence: neilph@aol.com

The Contributors

• • • • • • • • • • • • • • • •

Jon Blend, MA Dip Psych, CQSW, trained as a psychotherapist at The Gestalt Centre, London where he tutors on child and adolescent therapy and is a non-executive Director. His background includes over twenty-five years' experience working in community psychiatry, social work and performing arts. Since 1995 Jon has counselled children and parents at a Family Consultation Service in Southern England. He also maintains a psychotherapy practice in London. He is resident musician with Playback South, an improvizational theatre company and enjoys being married and being a stepparent.

Correspondence address: life-changes@ntlworld.com

Marlene Moss Blumenthal, PhD, trained as a clinical psychologist and practices as a licensed school psychologist and Gestalt psychotherapist. She has worked with adolescents, their families, and their teachers in day treatment, residential, and school settings, both individually and in groups, as well as in private practice. She has published research on mother/adolescent daughter relationships, conflict modes and Gestalt resistances. Marlene is a former director of clinical training at the Gestalt Institute of Cleveland, developed and co-chairs GIC's Advanced Child and Adolescent Training Program, and teaches internationally.

Correspondence address: marloblum@yahoo.com

Stephen Grant, LCSW, is a Licensed Clinical Social Worker in private practice and also a seasoned provider of boys groups in elementary and middle school. He is also the parent of two school age boys.

Correspondence address: buckmansteve@yahoo.com

Howard Hiton, LPC, MS, is a Licensed Professional Counselor in private practice who specializes in working with boys. He is also the parent of two school age boys.

Correspondence address: hiton@speakeasy.net

Mark McConville, PhD, is a Clinical Psychologist in private practice in Beachwood, Ohio, specializing in adult, adolescent, emerging adult, and family psychology. He is a senior faculty member at the Gestalt Institute of Cleveland, and has taught and published widely on the subjects of child development, parenting, and counselling methodology. His books include the award-winning *Adolescence: Psychotherapy and the Emergent Self* (Jossey-Bass, 1995) and T*he Heart of Development: Gestalt Approaches to Childhood and Adolescence*, vols. I & II, (The Analytic Press, 2001, co-editor). His current project, on the transition from adolescence to adulthood, is *Getting a Life: a Parent's Guide to the 'Failure to Launch' Syndrome*. He serves as Consulting Psychologist to several prominent schools in the Cleveland area.

Correspondence address: markmcc1127@sbcglobal.net

Peter Mortola, PhD, is associate professor of counseling psychology and coordinator of the school psychology program at Lewis and Clark College in Portland, Oregon. He is the author of *Windowframes* (2006) and, with colleagues Howard Hiton and Stephen Grant, *BAM! Boys' Advocacy and Mentoring: A Guidebook for Leading Boys' Preventative Groups*. Mortola and his colleagues believe in the ability of boys to be healthy, happy individuals who are positive contributors to community and family life. See more at *bamgroups.com*.

Correspondence address: pmortola@lclark.edu

Anna-Maria Norén has worked in Child Psychiatry for more than 30 years. She earned her academic degree from the University of Gothenburg, Sweden, Department of Social Work and trained at the

Gestalt Academy of Scandinavia where later she became a teacher and still later was Headmaster for almost ten years. For a number of years she has been the quality development manager and assisting head at the Child Psychiatry Clinic in the county of Dalarna, Sweden. She has spent considerable time in Africa where her husband for many years was engaged in economic development projects, an experience which has given her a deep appreciation and respect for others.

Correspondence address: ami@mora.mail.telia.com

Daniel Siegel, MD, is a clinical professor of psychiatry at the UCLA School of Medicine where he is also on the faculty of the Center for Culture, Brain, and Development and the Co-Director of the Mindful Awareness Research Center at UCLA. He is a Distinguished Fellow of the American Psychiatric Association, the co-editor of a handbook of psychiatry and the author of numerous articles and chapters. Dan's internationally acclaimed text, *The Developing Mind: Toward a Neurobiology of Interpersonal Experience* (Guilford, 1999), introduced the idea of interpersonal neurobiology. His other books include *Parenting from the Inside Out: How a Deeper Self-Understanding Can Help You Raise Children Who Thrive* (Tarcher/Penguin, 2003, co-authored with Mary Hartzell, M.Ed.), *The Mindful Brain: Reflection and Attunement in the Cultivation of Well-Being* (Norton, 2007), *Mindsight: The New Science of Personal Transformation* (Bantam Books, 2010), *The Mindful Therapist: A Clinician's Guide to Mindsight and Neural Integration* (Norton, 2010), *The Whole-Brain Child* (DelacortePress, 2012), and *The Pocket Guide to Interpersonal Neurobiology: An Integrative Handbook of the Mind* (Norton, 2012). He lives in southern California with his family.

Bronagh Starrs maintains a private practice in Omagh, Northern Ireland, as a psychotherapist and trainer, specializing in working with children, adolescents and their families, and with people who are coming to terms with the legacy of "The Troubles" in their lives. Bronagh has a particular interest in tracking the impact of psychological trauma through childhood and adolescence and how this trauma can continue to impact the adult self. She has authored various articles and chapters on the subject. She teaches and presents internationally on the developmental implications of trauma on the adolescent journey.

Correspondence address: bronaghstarrs@gmail.com

Denise A Tervo, PhD, is a licensed psychologist, supervisor and trainer in Pittsburgh, PA. She has worked with adults, children, adolescents, families, and clinical groups for more than thirty-five years. Denise is a faculty member of the Gestalt Institute of Pittsburgh and the Gestalt Institute of Cleveland. In Cleveland she teaches in the Gestalt Therapy, Working with Physical Process, and Advanced Child and Adolescent Training Programs. A national and international trainer, she integrates body process and energy awareness in her Gestalt practice. See more at DeniseTervo.com.

Correspondence address: dtervo1@aol.com

Gordon Wheeler, PhD, is President of Esalen Institute in California, offering over 600 residential programs each year in moving through personal growth and healing into transformational service in the world. The author of over a dozen books and more than 100 articles in the field of relational psychology, Gordon teaches and trains widely around the world, with particular emphasis on working with intimacy, self-theory and development, support and shame, lifelong personal development, men's issues, and relationship and social activism as spiritual practice. Gordon's current project is a new interpretation of Homer's *Iliad* as a map of radical alternatives in achieving men's identity. Gordon and his wife, Nancy, are blessed with eight children and a growing number of grandchildren. They make their home in Big Sur and Santa Cruz, California.

Correspondence address: gordonmwheeler@gmail.com

Relational Child, Relational Brain

Theory

Editors' Note:
From birth through childhood, adolescence, and into adulthood, what is our basic nature as humans – isolated individuals who grow-up to become autonomous, independent, and self-reliant, who are driven by what has become known in some circles as "the selfish gene?" Or are we relational in character, developing agency in the service of an interdependent and interconnective existence and mind? Gordon Wheeler opened the 2007 Esalen conference on children and adolescents, addressing this most basic question of our human condition. He approaches this inquiry from the perspective of the story that we tell ourselves of our beginnings as a species and of the development of our larger brain size. Our capacity to register, manage and integrate the mass of sensory data that our social existence generates rests in the complexity of our physical selves, and particularly in the development of the marvel that is our social mind. For Gordon, the emergence of this highly evolved capacity is a recursive process, driven by the basic mechanisms and dictates of survival, and arising from the structured ground that is our relational existence. The essence of the human mind is the relational capacity for narrative, the nuanced and continuous thread of our individual and collective stories. Yet, it is now evident that there is no individual story, only those that we tell each other, and create and tell together. This is the paradigm shift that Gordon describes so clearly, provoking us to grasp the new possibilities for community, relationship and change that emerging neuroscience helps us understand, and which open doors for our survival as a species in the future.

1

Who Are We?

Narrative, Evolution, & Development: Our Stories and Ourselves

Gordon Wheeler

Part One – Changing Our Story: The Power of Narrative

Humans are the storytelling animal. This is not just an observation, or a figure of speech: it is basic to the very prosocial process structures of our brain/minds, which are organized flexibly and associatively in communicable units of narration. The layered and holistic structure of the brain/mind *is* narrative structure, context-event-sequence or relatedness. This is the basic "first/next" or "if/then" patterning required for generating imaginal scenarios and thus dealing with variable contingency, which gives our species its remarkable adaptability and range.

6 ... RELATIONAL CHILD, RELATIONAL BRAIN

This is what narrative is: a meaningful gestalt, or relational whole, sequenced in a "first/next" or "if/then" pattern over time. First this, then this, then this, with the events standing in some relationship of contingency to each other (if some elements have no contingent relationship, even as context, then we say they're "just background," or "not part of the story "). Story is elements plus meaningful connections among them. Meaning is pattern with contingency. Narrative is how we hold meaning, which is to say, contingency patterning – and how we communicate it to others (which is then the same thing). It is this ability to communicate meaning in the form of story to our fellow beings that is key to our species survival in and as complexly social groups. Without this complex social capacity, we could never have migrated beyond our original evolutionary environment in Africa and dealt with the infinitely variable conditions humans encounter and deal with (more and less well) around the globe. How this capacity arose in the brain – what needs and niche drove this remarkable development – is part of the story of this essay.

Most fundamental of all our narratives are the stories we tell about our own origins as human beings: how the world began, how we emerged from something primordial that went before, and therefore what the essence is of our shared human nature and experience. Did humans appear in a single moment of creation, or was the process more progressive and emergent; and if so, was it guided by some unfolding intention or just by "blind" material conditions? In either case do we *belong to* nature, or are we inherently *apart from* it? If apart, are we the masters or the supplicants of nature? Was our early history a Golden Age, a peaceful Eden from which we have fallen, or have we rather progressed and improved along the way? All these are questions posed by fundamental origins stories of various cultures, at various times, with varying degrees of explicitness or implication in other belief elements.

Clearly the answers to these questions and others like them – the stories we share and tell about ourselves and our origins and thus our nature – will then have a deeply formative impact on what we experience as meaningful and fulfilling in life, and how we should best go about the business of living. What kind of life is worth living, and what kind of ethical code will support getting us there? Our basic "who are we?" stories will provide the criteria and frame for satisfying or unsatisfying answers to this kind of question.

And what of our relations with our fellow humans? Cooperative, competitive, or both: and then which is primary? Do we *care* about others, really – or is that just a strategic pose, not really part of our nature, as Nietzsche, Freud, the Social Darwinists and others (but not Darwin himself) have suggested? Left "to ourselves" in a "state of nature," would we fall naturally back into a life of loving harmony, or would it be murderous competition – or perhaps some other condition, and if so, then what would that look like? Were our earliest "natural" days an Age of Gaia where peace and cooperation reigned, the Great Age of the Feminine, as some imagine it – or do we rather descend from "killer apes," as popular anthropology and many scientific models insisted just a generation ago – and often still do imply in unexamined ways?

These are far from just academic matters. Our failure to agree on the basic terms of our origins and nature is the source and expression of a *primary fault line in our modern Western culture,* as well as other contemporary cultures – a fault line which is then exploited, here and elsewhere, by forces and interests of unrestrained power and greed. Are we fundamentally *prosocial, civil* beings – or are we in need of constant policing, without any "help" from our basic evolved nature?

These are political questions, as well as scientific and narrative ones. It is no accident that a so-called "Conservative" political position often tends to be aligned with a Hobbesian worldview and narrative of human nature as basically selfish and exclusively, ruthlessly competitive (not that people *should* act that way, at least in many conservative views, but that it is their nature to do so, when unconstrained. Thus a human nature story may align with a compassionate ethical perspective; or – as in many monotheistic perspectives, these two may be fundamentally opposed, and always in tension. In which case prosocial and compassionate impulses, however desirable, are seen as running against our natural grain, and available only through divine intervention, or authoritarian rule). This Hobbesian, hyper-individualistic ideology is then a view that tends to support authoritarian religious and political structures (as our only hope of social stability), and justify existing social differences in wealth and power with corresponding neglect of social problems (which may in this view be seen as hopeless and unavoidable, even if tragic). Under such a worldview of our origins and nature, community welfare and opportunity programs may be seen as hopelessly quixotic or even destructive: well-meaning, but they just don't fit with "human nature," or "who we are."

Now to say this much is to say that power needs and fierce competition are at least *part of* our human capacity and therefore of our human nature (or else how could they emerge at all, even under provocative social conditions?) But are they all of it, or the core? In a different narrative, authors as diverse as Rousseau, Marx, Kropotkin, Goodman, Riane Eisler and many others have all argued in various ways that the worst abuses of violence, exploitation, and war are not really endemic to our species nature, but are consequences of *faulty social arrangements*, and thus at least potentially meliorable by more progressive social policies. Here too, it's no accident that in a political conservative you will often find a "nature" partisan in the old "nature-nurture" debate: if environment is less relevant, then differences of achievement and privilege are due more to the luck of the genetic draw (perhaps expressed as "character")[1], and there's really nothing you can or should do about it. Thus an extreme "nature" position often goes with a narrative of ruthless competition, survival of the fittest, and stark, "social Darwinist" individualism. Among religious conservatives

---

[1] In Shakespeare, for example, a pessimistic conservative statist, we find that bad people are pretty much just bad, by their nature. No environmental condition is adduced to account for their badness. Occasionally illegitimate, disadvantaged birth, or physical deformity will seem to be a malign predictor, but in general not much is offered by way of explanation for socially destructive impulses and acts.

this fundamental savagery may also be held as "sin" or otherwise evil; but it is still posited, sadly, as our basic human nature, through and through, with punitive authority essentially the only remedy.

All this then speaks to the crucial role of narrative – and in particular, shared social metanarrative, such as our origins stories – in personal, social, and political life. Such narratives and metanarratives are equally determinative in science as well – the sciences themselves being examples of complex controlling narratives in this sense.[2] In our own field of psychology for instance, including the humanistic domains of developmental and clinical psychology, even today emergent field perspectives such as a radical Gestalt relational model or the fertile developments in intersubjective psychoanalysis may sit uneasily with our inherited concepts and tools in personality and clinical thinking. We carry, and are sustained and oriented by, an inherited cultural narrative of paradigmatic individualism which insists that the individual is in some sense *prior* to the relational context, clinically, experientially, and ontologically. Relationship and connective impulses are then seen as secondary, instrumental to achieving individual ends, but not really part of our inborn nature. Many of us no longer believe in that story, which contradicts both research and experience, yet the

---

[2] To say this is not to make the facile "post-modernist" claim that there is no such thing as facts, or the physical/energetic universe "is" just whatever we wish it is at any moment – or even that all possible ways of interpreting data are "equal." Rather, it is to point out that correspondence or pattern – what we call perception, measurement, comparison, the basic "stuff" of science (and of coping with life) become *data* only in a context, only as part of a whole. This is our basic Gestalt precept – the whole gives the *meaning* of the parts. Gestalts (such as scientific narratives) are "best-available" syntheses; always there are outlying events and data that fit uneasily in the current story, or not at all. That narrative itself is then under pressure to fit as a dynamic element in a larger gestalt of meaning – a "worldview," including our story of human nature and origins. At times when the human econiche changes radically, those metastories will begin to shift. We are now living in such times.

narrative still permeates and informs our language, our categories, and thus our own thinking.

Likewise in biology, in the face of cascading evidence from neurology, paleontology, anthropology, and other disciplines that contradicts the old, rigidly individualistic picture of isolated "organisms" battling each other for dominance, the prevailing narrative in the field still remains the "selfish gene" story – a story of atomized "bits" of genetic information – genes -- competing and combining, freely and temporarily, into fundamentally atomized organisms or individuals, who then compete to propagate on behalf of their respective genetic material. Not only are the individuals the sum in this view of their genetic "bits" and thus essentially cut off from each other by genetic competition, but they really have only a sort of derivative existence themselves, being no more than vehicles for the self-propagation of independent genes, and largely under the control of inborn programs for that propagation. In extreme forms of this narrative the relationship of mother to fetus, for example, is depicted as one of deadly competition: the fetus is "out to get" (ie, programmed by genes to get) as much nutrition from the mother as is physically possible; while the "goal" of the mother (ie, the controlling program of her genes) is to preserve herself at the fetus's expense, giving only the absolute minimum of a zero-sum nutritional resource to the aggressive intruder in her own body.[3]

In the extreme, to be sure, the logic of this narrative completely breaks down even in its own terms. What would be the survivability of a fetal genetic makeup whose effects were to make its carrier destroy

---

[3] And note here that Perls (and his wife Lore) both tended to see the relationship of mother to infant as fundamentally antagonistic in much this sense: abrupt and punitive weaning was posited by Perls (1947) as both necessary for the selfish interest of the mother, *and* key to all subsequent development and all subsequent neurosis for the child. We're alone in the world and at odds with others, in the "flavor" of this view – not just by trauma or distorted social stress, but by the *basic existential terms of our reality* (terms shared of course by Freud, and the mainstream of late Victorian and then High Modernist culture at large).

its own host (and remember that the human infant, born a fetus really, needs "hosts" for one to two decades or more)? And what would be the genetic point of a Medea-like mother whose nature was to destroy the very genetic products which the same story tells us are the sole point of her existence, and the sole goal of those same genes? On the contrary, plainly in terms of "gene selection," neither party to this relationship has much of a future without some *fundamentally inborn commitment to the survival and welfare of the other*. I.e., the bias of each of us is fundamentally relational by nature, and has to be: without your well-being, I cannot survive or thrive, and vice versa. Without your deeply innate bias toward interest in my welfare, I have little chance, as infant or adult (even a dominant tyrant is ever exposed to assassination – even among chimpanzees [see de Waal, 1982, 2005]). Without that "altruistic" commitment at the most basic genetic level, then that particular mosaic of genetic makeup will necessarily be selected out, that group will not cohere enough to prevail, and that genetic pattern and will recede in the shared gene pool of the species. "Selfish gene" pro-ponents may argue that this is altruism merely for the sake of one's own welfare; but isn't that what altruism *is*: the identification of another person's welfare with my own, so that some part of the care I invest in the shared field is directed toward them?

Even in the center of the "selfish gene" argument the rational base is equally shaky. By focusing so exclusively on "the gene" in isolation as the driver of survival and evolution, and reducing both organism and society to side-effects (in the way the old Behaviorist model did with motivation and experience), Dawkins (1976) and other writers in this vein posit a monadic biological world made up of self-contained little genetic "units," each of them essentially separate and essentially im-mortal (and stable), and each operating independently and competi-tively in the jungle of life under the principle of survival of the fittest single gene. This of course is a perfect mirror of the Western cultural metanarrative or paradigm of ideological individualism – the position that the individual is ontologically primary, fundamentally competi-tive, and existing coherently in some real sense apart from and prior to relationship, communion and exchange with other, equally primary individuals (see discussion in Wheeler, 2000, 2008). Thus again the power of story, operating in the background to shape what we perceive, what seems real to us, and then how we language and communicate that to each other.

And yet when we turn to nature, we do not in fact see any genes floating around independently, competing busily with other genes. On the contrary, the only genes we find – i.e., the only "successful" genes which survive and thrive so that we can find them – occur always in symphonic/harmonic operation and cooperation with other genes, in those great orchestras of genetic support for behavior we call "organisms" (including some borderline cases, like viruses, which lack some of the properties of complete organisms until they find a way to a cooperative relationship with another organism). Nor are genes particularly stable in their operation: besides the effects of radiation and other chemical accidents, what we find in development is that "a gene" is constantly being switched on and off by other genes and proteins, under the regulation of environmental effects (ie, of the organism as a whole, in its own larger dynamic/relational context). Again, the pattern is a symphony of complex relationships, nested into a wider dynamic system of relational contexts, which operate most effectively when they are in tune. A gene which separates itself from this cooperation, leading for example to uncontrolled self-propagation without stable dynamic relationship in a working whole, is a cancer gene, and very likely to be "selected out" of the music of life.

Despite long-standing and manifest objections of this kind, this narrative, the "selfish gene" story and its narrative partner, paradigmatic individualism, remain the dominant story of human nature in our culture, at least those parts of the culture which look for their origins tale to the supposedly "objective" data of science. When you consider that this is the version of evolution that is most aggressively and conspicuously on offer, then we shouldn't be surprised, really, if the story of evolution itself actually commands the full allegiance of only a minority of people in North America. It's not just that this story of our origins and nature lacks any spiritual grounding or dimension (let alone the comforting presence and hand of a guiding deity or principle of spiritual evolution). More than that, *it lacks experiential validity.* In my "real life" I love my friends, care for my children, seek satisfaction through meaningful contribution to larger wholes of shared enterprise, invest in my/our shared community, even may give my life for my brothers and sisters in battle or other emergencies. And I expect that most other people, given half a chance, will do about the same, in their own ways, for their own loved ones and larger causes. Such relational commitments and experiences are inseparable from individual welfare and health, whether measured subjectively or in terms of a near avalanche of confirming data today about longevity, immune response, stress reduction, cognitive power, emotional stability, and all that we know and are learning about the bio- and neuro-chemical underpinnings of health and well-being. Again, it's an odd narrative of "science" that insists on *an individualistic origins story*, to produce a creature so defined in actual fact by relational response.

Within that relational context, to be sure, I certainly do compete for resources, try to advance my own influence or prestige, look out for my safety to some extent (or sacrifice it for others), privilege my children over some others, and so forth – and expect you to do about the same. But I do these self-assertive things out of a background and vital context of social cooperation and synergy, always, whether directly or indirectly (even the most narcissistic tyrant depends completely on commanding others to cooperate, with him/her and each other – and that command itself is a relationally negotiated act)! That cooperation may partly break down, as in war or exploitative domination (though war, including "class warfare," depends entirely on enhanced cooperation within the "ingroup," ie, "our side"). But then we recognize that collapse itself as a dysfunctional breakdown of family or "normal society," which we recurrently try to right, with more or less success. Again, competition for individual (or genetic) gain, in the human species, is only understood *in a context of* social complexity and cooperation, social belonging, and meaningful commitment to identification groups. If this point is repeated here, that is because its opposite is still the default of our societal assumptions and discourse in these transitional times.

All this is the formative power of narrative in every domain of thought, even those areas considered to be "objective" and free of bias. Data can never be univocal, as fundamentalists both religious and scientific claim they are: they are not "given," with meaning already embedded and available: they have to be bounded off perceptually, selected, deselected, constructed, and interpreted – meaning embedded in a meaningful context in dynamic interaction with metanarrative or paradigm. Those metanarratives preexist particular data, and may persist long after contradictory data are at hand.

We'll turn below to a wealth of that contradictory data, which today challenges and revises our inherited story of isolated individuals and "selfish" genes. What we find instead is an emergent new human story coming out of an array of sciences over the past twenty years that gives us an entirely new picture of human origins, human nature, and perhaps human destiny. In this new story human beings are constructed and driven by relationality and evolving relational capacity to be who we are, and to perceive and experience as we do. It turns out that we are relational beings first and foremost, and that this fundamental principle is not just a tenet of philosophy or clinical wisdom, but is also supported by contemporary science.

Our vaunted individuality – also key to our nature and survival as adaptively flexible problem-solvers – is then an *outgrowth of our relational nature*, not the other way around. A high degree of individuality is essential for our species adaptation, in ways that will be discussed below. But that individuality is always derivative, always dependent on context. Likewise for competition: we have deep capacities for competition (as individuals, as groups, and in a certain sense even as vehicles of genes) – but that competition is always in a context of cooperation and relational dynamics. As cultural evolutionary author Robert Wright (2000) has written, competition and even war itself in humans depend on cooperation, and generally tend to result in larger and larger "zones of cooperation" at a social level.

Again, this emergent story is hardly unfamiliar or strange to us. Not only is the "feel" of it much closer to the way we live and experience our lives, as individuals born in families, as parts of multiple social networks, as professionals working with people, as citizens of a shared world, and for many of us, as the agents or vehicles of spiritual yearnings and transcendent experiences that inform our sense of deep belonging to a larger whole. Not only all that, but this emergent narrative is already the story of Gestalt therapy theory, and Gestalt psychology before it. Both of these interrelated disciplines have labored in various ways to present this counternarrative for most of the past century now – often struggling because the narrative of relationality is demandingly complex compared to competing stories of a "billiard-ball" world, and goes "against the grain" of a dominant social discourse or paradigm (itself now much under revisionist attack at last after several centuries of mounting dominance in the West).

What is different now, after this long century as an influential "minority voice" in psychology and psychotherapy (and in mid-century Western philosophy), is that scientific research findings – if not yet a revised and updated scientific metanarrative – are now overwhelmingly on our side. Meanwhile, the "minority voices" of Gestalt psychology and Gestalt therapy have been busily transforming their overlapping fields and the fields around them, to such an extent that there really is no psychology or brain/mind science today which is not infused with basic Gestalt *psychology* precepts of holistic functioning, active selection/construction of percept and meaning, the mediation of behavior by those understandings of integrated units (or "schemata") of meaning and story; just as there is little or no significant psychotherapy or other intervention for change which does not make fundamental use Gestalt *therapy's* present-centered perspectives, problem-solving and creativity as models for human functioning, and the primacy of relational process both in the therapy itself and in clients' lives.

16 ... RELATIONAL CHILD, RELATIONAL BRAIN

Now at last the data are at hand for the relational perspective to transform the controlling narrative of our own field of human development and intervention for change, of the sciences in general, and of the culture at large. More than that, the culture is at last ready for this message, in an age of awareness of how individualist ideology in economics and politics has brought us to the brink, at least, of shared environmental and political collapse. In other words, emergent culture as well as science is now on our side, as we work together to bring forward a new story which will support the new agenda we so desperately need in our work with children and their worlds, with political and ecological issues and policy, and with our shared discourse across our divided world culture, on spirit, community, justice and belonging, and our common striving for sustainable and meaningful living.

What follows now will be a brief overview of important findings and arguments coming out of an array of areas of accruing scientific data and model-building that bear directly on our story of who we are, how beings like us arose, what our nature and "natural life" might look like, and how we might move toward shared meaning and action. The point of this review is to ground or "anchor" the relational point of view in its real evolutionary and neurobiological story/context – at least by reference to developments in those fields that bear on this unifying perspective. For the clinician, teacher, or other "hands on" practitioner with children and adults, it can be very clarifying and very empowering to gain a sense that the experience and intuitions we've developed and relied on over the years, oftentimes in direct contradiction to our received "scientific" models, really are grounded in evolutionary and neurobiological models – now that those models themselves have grown complex enough to begin to address the real dynamics of our lives and human experience.

In this discussion we will refer to and draw heavily on Gestalt perspectives and connections, as our most useful model for understanding complexity and process, the psychology and experience of the kinds of beings we understand ourselves to be. Finally, our aim will be to show where the enormously rich new body of multidisciplinary research from a variety of fields is converging today to support a story of human origins, nature, and destiny which is fundamentally a relational tale at its core. This story, and these data, then both validate and also expand/tranform our own legacy of Gestalt ideas and practices, which open up a new vista for a psychological politics in the 21st Century, the new Age of Complexity (Wheeler, 2008).

Part Two – Twelve Areas of Convergent Theory, Model Building, and Data, Which Taken Together, Lead Us To a Fundamentally Relational Understanding of Human Nature, with Implications for Living and Practice

1) Environmental Change and the Evolution of the Brain

Two mysteries which have long loomed over evolutionary studies are first, the origins of life itself, and second, the origins of the human brain. While we are not yet at the point of being able to foster the spontaneous generation of life in a test tube, we're actually not that far away from that old sci-fi fantasy. Scientists are now able to simulate conditions of the first billion years of the earth's existence, and to replicate the self-assembly of complex polymer chains under conditions like those that obtained in that period (Deamer et al., 2002). The second mystery – what drove the explosive growth of the human brain – has been even more resistant to clear modeling, arguably because of our attachment to an old paradigm of individualism.

The question is this: in the period roughly between two-plus MYA (million years ago) and one MYA or so, the brain size of one bipedal branch (or very likely a number of branches, of which one or one hybrid survives) on the ecological fringes of the ancestral range of the genus Pan (chimps and bonobos, in today's classification) began to lurch into rapid evolution of a number of characteristics, including especially brain size. Over the course of the next million or so years, brain size in this evolving line (generally currently categorized as homo ergaster, homo habilis, and homo erectus) roughly tripled in size – while the growth in prefrontal cortex, the synthesizing and complexity-management centers of the brain was roughly fourfold[4]. For a complex organism like apes this is an amazingly rapid rate of growth, unprecedented as far as we know in large animals. Rapid and accelerating change in the same direction is the sign of a strong positive feedback loop: the technical term for a change pattern in which successive stages of change, rather than triggering a limit correction, each tend to promote further conditions which keep supporting further change in the same direction (until some other natural limit is reached – one being in this case the steady expansion of the human brain case, limited by the pelvic enginerring structure of a bipedal animal.

What environmental conditions provoked such an unusual cascading pattern of growth? Brains are complex organs, "expensive" to build developmentally in terms of the amount of both genetic material devoted to their shaping, and the enormous glucose demand of running higher nervous system operations. What was the trigger, and then what was the ongoing payoff, for all this organismic investment (note

---

[4] Jared Diamond, in *The Third Chimpanzee* (1992), argues very persuasively for the reclassification of the genus Homo, of which we are the only contemporary species, as the third species of the genus Pan, which includes chimpanzees and bonobos, with whom we share roughly 99% of our genes. One of the consequences of such a reclassification, Diamond argues, would be the protection and preservation of our closest remaining genetic relations, with whom we are now able to communicate syntactically, and whose experience of "human" emotions of attachment, loss, altruism, even aesthetic pleasure is arguably as deeply felt as our own.

that the payoff has to be uninterrupted, or the cost at least always manageable, for continual change to occur)?

Now we know that in understanding any complex system, linear causative sequences rarely apply. That is, organisms and species represent evolutionary solutions to a set of complex ecological conditions, and must function as an integrated whole, both individually and ecologically. Any change which survives has multiple interactive causes and continuously successful effects. Still, when we are trying to model a sustained, species-defining pattern of change of this magnitude and duration, we look for some understanding of sustained, recurrent "drivers" of so much change in the same direction. What drove the remarkable growth of the human brain, which in turn makes us who and what we are today? What kind of environmental problem did that brain growth enable us to deal with in new and better ways that led to our survival and spread across every kind of environment as a single species? Why are human beings everywhere today, in amazing (and probably unsustainable) numbers, when the same is not true of chimps or bonobos – or any other single species of large, complex organism, each of which is adapted and limited to a particular environment niche? What is our adaptation, that makes us so flexible, in such unique ways? And what about that adaptive pressure drove the sustained redoubling of human brain size and capacity?

A variety of theories has been advanced to address this kind of question. Man the hunter, man the tool-user, man the killer ape, man the omnivore, the meat-eater, the tamer of fire, the warrior, the maker and user of symbolic language. Each of these has been put forward at times as the key demand driving brain growth; each is a story, and each story is essentially an "alpha male" narrative. This last one, symbolic language, may be closer to the mark; but symbolic language almost certainly comes at or after the very end of the brain growth period, while as an explanation tale it itself calls for explanatory modeling, to understand how symbolic language capacity itself arose out of the less syntactical communication capacities of our various relatives (see below). The other prevailing explanations, as we look back now over a century and a half of Darwinian thinking, may seem to us to be driven by cultural assumptions about the role of linear/mechanical causation, male dominance/determinism, individual competition outside any social context, and other features of 19th and 20th Century European society and worldviews, more than by any basic plausibility in the models or the evidence.

Our Pan genus relatives are also intermittent meat-eaters like us, and conduct quite organized hunts, much as early humans must have done; yet their brains have not grown, so far as we can see, over the past six or more million years. The "tool kit" of hominids, at least as far as we can tell from stone, fossil, and ash remains, was likewise largely unchanged over the same approximately million year period that saw the explosive growth of the brain. This seems to make it implausible that meat and the hunt *per se*, or tool use *per se*, can account for much of the radical shift from proto-chimp/bonobo to proto-human.

And as for "male dominance," by studying chimpanzee society as well as other apes, we now have a much more complex understanding of "alpha male" as a complex *social role*, a group stabilizing function built on alliance and social management, not simply an "super-individual" operating independently of the group. Tenure in this role is entirely dependent on the consent and cooperation of the leading females of the troop (as well as alliance with other males), whose support is key to maintaining any given alpha in his position (deWaal, 1982, 2005). In other words, deference (Beta or Gamma yielding to Alpha in a one-on-one) is not the same thing as dominance in a genetic sense (deWaal reports instances in which Beta, through social manipulation, is leaving *more* genetic imprint in the chimp troop than Alpha, the visible leader). Our closest genetic relatives today, the bonobos, who are like us in bipedalism and the social use of sex outside procreative periods, are actually more female- than male-dominated, in terms of dominance/deference patterns (deWaal, 1985, 2005).

In other words, all these things – dominance and leadership including "alpha" roles, expanded use of tools, manipulation of fire for heat and cooking, expansion of dietary range, use of meat in the diet, competition within and across groups and species – all were and are aspects of human capacities, and in the unitary way of evolution (where the full range of behavioral capacities and expression, like the full suite of genes and their activation, has to work as a unified whole and mesh holistically with the social group and the wider environment), all of them must have some dynamic role in species adaptation and change. But none of them plausibly stands out as a major driving factor of the rapid brain growth that took place over the evolutionary period, and made us who we are. They simply didn't pose enough new demands, cognitively, over what the ancestral species was already doing, to account for such sustained and meteoric change.

To find that factor, we need to look at the remaining obvious variable, the one which the cultural blinders of the first century of Darwinian thinking largely prevented us from seeing clearly: namely, *complex social/relational capacities themselves*.[5]

2) The Demands of the Move to Semi-Open Country

Speciation, the evolution of new species and capacities, often takes place, we now understand, more in bursts of change than in a steady random accretion of genetic drift as Darwin imagined (Gould, 2007). That is, genetic drift is always there, but as long as the environment is fairly steady, the complexly integrated adaptation that any organism or species represents will tend to be stable as well, by a "negative feedback loop" in which genetic deviations from the stable integrated

---

[5] But note that Darwin himself, as an ecologically-minded biologist, was very much interested in human sociability and cooperation as species keys; see for example his long-neglected volume *The Expression of the Emotions in Man and Animals*, 1872, which provides the foundations for both affect psychology and Ekman's (1998) physiognomic studies. Kropotkin (1902) also took up the study of cooperation in evolution, but his work was widely dismissed as too communal and too "feminine" in its emphases, for the age of mass warfare which was then building in the West.

pattern are more likely to be corrected by being selected out than they are to be capitalized on. Stability, not "progress," is the way of evolution in periods when the environment itself is stable. For a "positive feedback loop" to set in you need a rapidly changing environment which the new adaptation is markedly better able to handle (that is, runaway change in which certain deviations from the stable norm fit the new conditions better, and/or the conditions themselves continue to change, thus tending to support more change in the same direction). And note here too that evolution doesn't generally "invent" the new form randomly: more likely, in a species which does survive and evolve through the changes, the "better fit" adaptation was already present to some degree in some outlying members of the gene pool, who then start in rapidly to leave more surviving descendants.

The evolutionary environment of the period following our initial divergence from the common Pan ancestor (approximately the last five or six million years) was very much such an age of instability. The new evidence from climatology, relying on ice cores from the polar regions and pollen and sediment analysis from other areas, shows us now that after a long and fairly stable period when tropical forests covered much of southern Africa, periods of cold, dry weather set in. The tropical forest shrank, at times rapidly, placing enormous pressure on the forest apes of the time, which DNA studies show were the common ancestors of humans, chimpanzees, and bonobos. At the rapidly changing fringes of the forest ecosystem these shifts created pressure on those apes who were already fairly bipedal, such as bonobos, to expand their range out into the semi-open savannah – while probably still seeking the safety of trees at night. (More completely arboreal apes like chimpanzees are "knuckle-walkers," quadrupeds and climbers whose hip and shoulder structure is badly stressed by long stretches of overland travel).[6]

---

[6] The instability was actually even more chaotic than the long-term forest shrinkage would indicate. We now know from ice cores, sediment studies, and other data that the forest/savannah environment fluctuated radically for several million years, oscillating between hot/humid and cold/dry in cycles that ranged from a few millennia to a few centuries or

Beyond bipedalism, what was the key capacity that had to be selected for, over and over, to survive in these new and changing conditions? First and most crucially, living in the open, without the safety of trees, demands adaptation to a whole other level of exposure to predators. No longer can the young, for example, be left alone in small subgroups with their foraging mothers, without additional defense. Some males or childless females have to be "detailed" to that role at a given moment, while still others have to forage or scavenge or hunt further afield. For a small, individually defenseless animal already adapted for simpler social foraging, this means enormous new adaptive pressure on more complex sociability – the capacity to organize socially differentiated and flexible roles, already a hallmark of the Pan genus, but now required at ever more demanding levels.

Now again, in the pressure to adapt to changing circumstances, evolution has to work with what already is, for the simple reason that the organism has to be "adaptive," ie survivable, at every stage of a progressive change. There can be no "shutting down of business" for a

---

less. The effect was to put enormous pressure on the whole Pan family, and then repeatedly isolate sub-populations for some generations around widely-scattered water sources – only to remix them once more, re-isolate the various surviving gene pools after the mixing, etc. We could not invent a more "heated-up" or pressured "lab" for rapid evolutionary change, since enormous numbers of separate "experiments" have a chance to develop undisturbed by competing cousin groups for long enough to establish a consistent gene pool, and then that pool of adaptations is remixed into the whole group for long enough to sort out the "best" adaptations and promulgate them widely, before re-isolating.

And note that the competition that ensues in the mixing is largely *between groups* – a Darwinian idea long disparaged and neglected in mainstream research, but now rehabilitated, partly through more complex computer modeling of group effects. Again, the adaptation selected for is going to be, in the main, *complex cooperative capacity* within a larger and larger "home group" – the psychology which remains the dominant marker of human behavior today, and indeed now threatens the globe. Competition, again, is very much there, and especially acute between groups, but still in a context of increasingly complex capacity for cooperation.

period of time to allow for a complete overhaul of design; a social ape cannot overnight develop fangs or a carapace, or the radically different skeletal plan of an open-field herd animal, and speed away from danger (that indeed would be the kind of evolutionary straw-man the writers on "Intelligent Design" like to mock and discredit). In serious evolutionary modeling, either the design works well enough continuously – or that particular kind of organism faces extinction.

Thus the pressure to build on the already considerable social/organizational capacities of all the Pan genus – such as facial recognition and memory, "social score-keeping" to reciprocate favors or aggressive acts where feasible, the corresponding capacity for cheating and deceit (implying some capacity to regulate in relation to others' probable interpretation of one's own motivational state, or someone else's), ready communication to the group of emotional states and other complex messages and so forth (deWaal, 1982). This adds up to a lot of highly developed social capacity. What more does the protohominid subgroup require to support survival in more open country?

Let's review some major survival advantages and demands on the hominid ape, in these early stages of adapting to a more open, mixed-savannah environment. The move to more open country, at least by day, means the opening up of new food sources outside the range of their fellow forest apes – but also requires long treks into that open country to collect that more sparsely distributed food. Again, these treks probably have to be undertaken by a sub-group, who bring food back to the main group. Whereas male and female chimps forage pretty independently (the females accompanied by the juveniles), getting together for occasional sharing of meat, or the hunt itself, these longer ranges (for carrion, probably, for the most part, taking the leavings from larger predators' kills) mean still further differentiation of social role. If a troop is to survive, then at times some males may need to stay behind to join in protecting the young, perhaps for some days, along with the females who are foraging closer to home, yet still in exposed territory.

Wheeler – Who Are We? ... 25

This in turn means considerable pressure on group size. In any social group, larger group size permits more specialization of role and subgroup. But if roles (and individuals) are differentiated in more complex ways, then the complexity of keeping track of them grows exponentially. Chimpanzees live in semi-structured groups which are termed "fission-fusion," meaning that the group typically spends most of its time apart, but can come together in an organized way for defense or hunting, around an alpha male role (supported, as we have noted, by a strong matriarchal contingent). The apparent size limit on the chimpanzee troop seems to be around 40 members – very likely because that's the limit of complexity the chimp brain can handle and keep useful track of. Beyond that, additional members will tend to migrate out to other bands, or the whole band may divide.

This loose structure works for the well-protected, food-rich environment of the tropical forest, to which chimps and bonobos are tightly adapted, and from which they have never strayed. It also makes for an enormous amount of opportunistic mating: DNA studies have shown that a large majority of many troops' offspring may not sired by the alpha male – and a surprising (to us) minority are sired by complete outsiders, and not by any member of the home troop at all! (so much for the presumed ownership and dominance of the gene pool by the alpha male, which was the central tenet of the old evolutionary narrative).

In other words, it now begins to matter not just that *some* males stay behind to protect the troop, while others forage – but also which males can best be trusted to do which. In chimps and bonobos, the evolution of male tolerance of all the offspring of the troop is a genetic consequence of the fact that under that social system dominant, indiscriminately aggressive males who both sired and killed a lot of offspring, would be killing a large number of their own offspring. It doesn't take conscious awareness on the ape's part to mean that such a pattern will tend to fade out of the gene pool, in favor of a more nuanced, more complex, more cooperative kind of aggressivity – one which is tempered by tolerance of all the offspring of the home troop.

(When male chimps raid and conquer a rival troop, they typically do kill all the offspring, which predictably favors their own group's genes by bringing the captured females into estrus). Our species adaptation to this challenge is discussed in section 4 below, on pair-bonding and long childhood. Before that argument, let's take a look at what the increasing group size of the move to more open country means for adaptive pressure on brain size and capacity.

3) The Implications of Group Size for Evolution of Brain Size and Structure

All this makes for a unique and sharply aberrant set of environmental pressures and demands. There simply is no other large mammal living in open country in nature, which is so poorly fitted out physically for defense and predation (even large herd animals like antelope have the defensive adaptation of speed, so that predator cats [or hominids] can only manage to cull the herd of a few weaker or slower members). What is our adaptation, that compensates for our puny physical equipment? We have considerable indirect evidence that as brain size grew over this period, group size increased as well (Dunbar, 1992). But is group size cause, consequence, concomitant -- or all three together (evolution is nothing if not recursive). What is it about pre-frontal cortex size in particular that translates to handling the new complexity demands – and then how does that affect the evolving brain? What tasks, what kind of demands on the evolving organism, placed the greatest pressure on brain capacity?

Let's think about the implications of living in the larger social group that we've been sketching and discussing here. Like chimpanzees, bonobos also live in the wild in groups which seem to "max out" at around forty or so members. That's a large number of individuals and relationships to keep track of, and no doubt requires the considerable brain capacity of our Pan cousins. By contrast, a large and convergent body of data from anthropology, archeology, and all the other disciplines mentioned above, plus contemporary ethnology and social psychology, comes together now to suggest that a modal number for primary spontaneous organization of a human "troop," prehistorically and still today, is in the range of 100 to 200, and hovers around the number 150. That is, in the absence of a tightly overarching political structure, humans seem to need a troop minimum of upwards of 80 or 100 members to thrive under most environmental conditions (especially in open country) – and seem to undergo fission or else a shift to larger political structures after about 200 (and when that happens, the modal number of around 150 tends to be retained as the size of the sub-units). After 150, even large clans begin split or lose track of members – and apparently this was true 100,000 years ago, from the evidence of group camp remains. Moreover, this modal number often recurs today, even in large urban settings, as an average number of people in most people's primary acquaintanceship network, or the subgroupings of larger organizational units (Dunbar, 1992).

Apparently this is some kind of rough and flexible evolutionary "set point" for our species, bequeathed to us by our long formative period of oscillation around some approximate ideal for group survival under the conditions discussed above – ie, from over a million years ago to perhaps as recently as 50,000 years ago (and still today, or quite recently, in some isolated parts of the world). To support the quantum leap in role specialization demanded by the conditions of open savannah country, it seems that upwards of 80 or 100 individuals, at least, are needed as a pool of role candidates to draw from – of which perhaps no more than half at most are adults, and only half of that number not burdened with childbearing and nursing. (Smaller groups have sometimes been found, but generally in more protected environments).

What are the cognitive demands of this rough quadrupling of group "set point" size, under conditions of individuation and role specialization? Remember that social organization, for primates, starts with facial recognition and detailed social "score-keeping." Given the very long dependent childhood and pair-bonded family units that characterize our species, it becomes highly adaptive (both individually and for group cohesion and smooth functioning) to remember many of the interrelationships among these 100-200, in all their subgroupings, cousinships, lifelong connections – and even to be very skilled at perceiving alliances and antipathies that are not necessarily public (such as who is good at what, who's reliable about judgments of others, or even who else my mate may be attracted to, or yours – all of which may become key factors in team assembly and role differentiation).

And then we come to role *specialization*. As we pointed out above, the only chance of survival for an individually weak and defenseless species in open country is going to be teamwork – which means a much greater importance given to developing and remembering differential skill specialties, which give much greater capacity to the team as a whole. In addition to remembering each individual, plus as many of the possible sub-clusters of individuals as I can, with all the undercurrents of advantage-seeking and antipathy that primate individuals exhibit, I also need to have some idea of the skills, personality, and other variables that may fit this or that individual for this or that role. If I have meat, for example, and a given female wants some, it will behoove me to know whether she or her mate is a skillful enough hunter or gatherer to be able to reciprocate this favor (possibly in some entirely different way) – or will I do better by giving it to someone else? And on and on. Again, this is competition for advantage to be sure – but always in a framework of enormous cooperative capacity and collaborative context, with the fundamental adaptation being a co-operative-enough group. The cooperation frames and contextualizes the competition. Without it, in the intensely social necessities of our species, competition is meaningless, random, and not conducive to survival.

Nor is this group-mapping capacity anything like so simple as one-to-one, among individuals. Your (and my) whole networking patterns are implicated. If you give me some particular advantage, say (whether meat, money, some key introduction, or other useful good, depending on the social circumstances), will I or someone else in my own reciprocation network likely be able to give you (or someone else allied with you in some way) some consideration in the future? If so, then that's "something in the bank" – for contingencies as yet unknown, and yet to be negotiated – *provided* that I also make and remember a correct judgment about whether you're a reliable person who repays his/her debts. If not, will mere social advertisement of me as a powerful benefactor be a valuable payoff for me? (Not that every altruistic act has to be "self-interested;" but if strategic altruism is rewarded, then altruism in general becomes rewarding, and individual who experience that will tend to be favored with more surviving offspring: that's the pattern of environmental demand moving to species adaptation that evolution is all about). You can see right away how complex it all gets – and yet these are the social conundrums we (like our Paleolithic forebears) all negotiate every day, managing and manipulating with more or less skill a group of co-workers, clients, extended family members, neighbors or social group co-members, with more or less facility and success, in the service of our various goals and contingencies.

Now the possible pair combinations of a group of 100 number about 5000. All the permutations of 100 (ie, in all possible sizes of subgroupings) are a number which is already astronomical. Recombine each and every such subgroup with each and every other such subgroup (as you may be called on to do in social group interactions – and remember that a given person might be in both groups, under many circumstances), and you soon arrive at a number which is far greater than all the particles in the universe.

Now add in role variations – different pairings or teams for different purposes, so that each individual has a different "meaning" (utility, risk, skills, reliability, etc etc) in each separate social task or situation – and you quickly reach a number that is vastly more than that. (And note that the potential neuron connections in the human brain are likewise vastly more than the total number of particles in the universe). Hunting per se, "simple" dominance/deference, warfare per se, hand-eye coordination for spear-throwing, tool-making and tool use, "mapping" memory for dealing with enormous open territories, and so on – all of these, all the proposed "instincts" and scenarios put forth over the past century and more to account for the emergence of our amazing cerebral organs, and thus our amazing nature and capacities, -- all of it fades in comparison with the sheer cognitive demands of social organization and complexly differentiated social life, in a band of upwards of 100 specialized individual members (again see Dunbar, 1992, for discussion of the fossil and other evidence tying progressive increases in brain and especially frontal cortex with progressive increases in troop size). Yes, we hunt, we compete, we mate, we trust and we cheat, we form alliances and enmities and incur obligations and organize our group's provisioning, shelter, and defense. And to do each of these requires an underlying ability to manage social complexity at a level exponentially beyond that of our next-most complex relatives – and our brain is likewise interconnected at a level exponentially beyond theirs to the same degree.

It is social organization, social demands, the skills and tasks of complex sociability that have driven and demanded the explosive evolution of the hominid and then human brain. This is the positive feedback loop which was set in motion by the encounter of a socially smart, bipedal Pan family subgroup with a rapidly changing environment, which repeatedly threw groups into isolation (where distinct local patterns become sustained experiments, rather than being "washed out" by negative feedback correction of interbreeding with a larger, stable population) – and then back into intergroup competition (and intergroup cooperation: as soon as sub-groups specialize to different areas, the possibility of trade emerges, and with it other kinds of alliance).

Let us turn next to some of the related features of the emergent hominid social/genetic patterns, which result from, underlie, spin off from, contribute to, and otherwise interact dynamically with the explosive brain/mind growth of this period.

4) The Challenge of Prolonged Dependency in Development

A direct consequence of the push out into the more open savannah, with its sparser food supply and longer trekking, is pressure on the hip and pelvic structure to continue developing toward exclusive bipedalism. Long-distance bipedal walking is extremely exceptional as a physical body plan, and unique to humans (and to some degree bonobos) among mammals as a primary means of mobility – calling as it does for a streamlined hip structure that translates the weight of the entire body trunk straight downward. But this limits the width of the birth canal, which in turn places limits on the size of offspring. As our ancestor species grew larger, and cranial capacity in particular was under pressure to expand disproportionately, there was a hard limit on the size of infant head that the modified pelvic structure could give birth to.

The species adaptation, as head size increased, was to give birth to ever more immature infants, with ever-longer dependent childhoods. This places even more demand on social organization and role complexity. In a chimpanzee troop, any infant may well be the offspring of any male. Therefore males who are aggressive toward infants or don't share food (especially meat), become less likely to leave many offspring, and the genetic underpinnings that support those capacities will tend to become less frequent in the group (while any genetic substrate of the opposite behaviors will likely increase). That's how evolution works, and how we understand it: not by simplistic one-to-one reduction of a behavior to "a gene," but rather by probabilistic variance in deep underlying cluster traits, like aggressivity or altruism, that have biochemical/genetic foundations). The larger the group, the more challenging this tension between "whole" and "part" becomes – because in the larger pool of mates and offspring, plainly those males who do find some way to identify and favor offspring who are likely to be theirs, will tend to be "rewarded" (ie, favored) in the gene pool.

There may be other, more communal solutions to this conundrum, but the one our species has adopted is longterm pair-bonding, with a unique degree of paternal investment and involvement in nurturing the dependent offspring over many years. Key to this pair-bonding pattern is concealed estrus, with female availability for mating outside fertile periods – also quite a rare adaptation (and we're particularly interested in these major rare adaptations here, again, to explore their relationship with the hallmark rare adaptation of the species: our uniquely developed capacity for complex social organization). Ancestor females who began to exhibit concealed estrus would be a rewarding breeding pool for males who tended to hang around and respond to more subtle sexual cues – since conception might take place at any time. Such pairs would then be likely to leave more offspring, because of the greater degree of paternal involvement and provisioning. Such males might be less fiercely aggressive overall, and in the open compititive savannah of warm wet periods such a band, or such outliers within a band, might be overrun by more individually aggressive marauders. But – remember the "pressure cooker" effect of recurrent scattering and isolation of populations in cold dry periods, which "protects" outlying "experiments" for a time, giving them opportunity to develop any possible compensating advantages for the outlying traits (this is also known as the "archipelago model," for the way islands can favor this rapid diversification/experimentation among sub-species with different founder effects). Thus again the complex holistic nature of evolutionary process – the male and female reproductive strategies have to mesh together, it all has to serve successful nurturance of offspring, and in an intensely social species all of that has to work at a whole troop level in a given environment.

In the scenario we are sketching and understanding here, our own "backstory," those "compensating advantages" are almost certainly going to have to be in the area of prosocial capacities and "drives." It's easy to imagine that males (and females) who become more choiceful, less kneejerk in their aggressive reactions, will be more able to form complex and lasting personal alliances and other cooperative patterns

– just as they are doing in the bonded pair. Give this kind of capacity some protected time to evolve through the troop, and the result may well be a better-organized troop, more able to prosper, defend territory, and successfully raise more young. This is "group-level" evolution, which is at last coming into its own as signal component of our evolutionary history. While individually perhaps less fierce, as an organized group competing with other hominid subspecies and groups in the next warm wet period, such a tribe or subspecies may be well able to hold their own, as a whole, against competitors who are individually stronger but socially less complexly organized. Again, the hallmark adaptation, which organizes and selects for or against all the others, is capacity for elaboration of sustained relationship and social complexity.

5) Further Implications of Social Problem-Solving Capacity

Now the kind of creature that hominids were rapidly evolving into, under the complex social pressures discussed above, was becoming more and more adapted cognitively to a pattern of flexible, creative problem-solving in social challenges. To negotiate a social world of this degree of complexity, you have to be able to map social groupings and scenarios in some way on a trial or "mental" basis – and hold those trial patterns, while considering others. This is particularly the task and capacity of the frontal cortex, the part of the brain that was growing most explosively over this key evolutionary period. This capacity derives from the fact that the frontal cortex is linked not to the "outside world," but to other brain centers – functional centers related to emotion, memory, face recognition, internal physiological signals, and so on. We see this every day (or night) in dreaming, where signals from memory and other centers are woven into a coherent pattern or narrative even though we are relatively "unhooked" from exterior stimuli, data, and action (we do sometimes get an indirect "bleed-through" of what's "actually happening" at the moment, translated or represented in some way in the dream).

But this capacity for mental modeling then doesn't apply only to social challenges: the more flexibly adaptive we become with social problems and solutions, the more we can apply that same "mapping" or scenario-imaging capacity to other kinds of problems as well. The creature and group that could deal successfully with novel and shifting social challenges could also deal with novel and shifting physical environments, with their changing availability of food, water, territory, temperature, etc., and the emerging seasonal demands for storage, stockpiling, differential planning in different years, and so on. The orders and types of complexity – and the capacity skills we draw on to map those complex variables and make "best guess" predictions on shifting and incomplete data – are the same in both cases.

Thus social complexity capacity was also key to the spread of humans all across the globe – first with the migrations of homo erectus going back roughly a million years, and then the much more recent emigration of our own species, homo sapiens, out of Africa probably only around 60-to-80,000 years or some 2000-3000 or so generations ago. In that brief time our species spread from a small area in southeastern Africa to range over some 40,000,000 square miles of habitable (or crossable) earth surface area. No species had ever done anything remotely like this, at least beyond the level of single- or few-celled organisms. No species – not even our homo ergaster and homo erectus ancestors – had ever covered the extremes of habitat variation that homo sapiens soon spread across in just this small number of generations. It was *scenario mapping* – a brain equipped to deal with variably complex social organization and flexible social planning – that was equipped to handle the complexity of the task.

Now again, it's not that one capacity develops first, and then a related application comes after, in the way of linear thinking: they develop together, at least to some extent, and each supports and promotes the other. The adaptation to variable physical environments added "push" to the developmental pressure on the planning centers of the evolving brain. But the explosion of homo sapiens out of Africa such a brief time ago, essentially in our present form, means that the species ability to organize socially had already reached a level that made the troop able to move, in as sense, as an organism, adapting to the staggering array of different and unprecedented environmental challenges with behavioral/cultural, not genetic change. Very likely the "final" ability that made this new level of flexibility possible was syntactic language – about which more below.

6) The Human Econiche

But note what this then means. We often speak of "the evolutionary environment" (frequently in the reductionist "me-Tarzan/you-Jane" cartoonish fantasies that sometimes pass for "evolutionary psychology" – and usually serve to justify some exploitative social pattern or practice, in the way of much reductionist thinking). When we do, we may picture jungles, sabre-tooth tigers, and other physical or non-human features of the ecological surround – and then talk about how *that* environment ill-suits us for dealing with modern technological life (which it may – but not quite in the way these simplistic versions mean).

But this misses the point. The point drawn by all the new data in evolutionary science is this: the human evolutionary environment, the relevant econiche in which human beings developed, survived, and thrive or perish, *is the world of other human beings*. It is a tribe, an organized social group, that is our relevant and controlling social environment, *then and now*. Along the way to our distinctively human nature and brain, we became "unhooked" in a sense from our immediate physical surround, which can now show a vastly wider range of variation. Not that we don't depend on it ultimately (as today's ecological crises are forcing us to attend to in new ways). But the "input" is now indirect, through the lens of social organization, which is to say culture – just as the cortex itself depends on the "outside world," but communicates with it only indirectly, interpretively, by linking up patterns of input from other parts of the brain. Brain structure mimics social structure, and vice versa. Our brain is an organ for dealing with our social world.

7) Culture, Learning, Trauma, and Therapy

Instinct is that which is programmed genetically: sequences which, if not traumatically interrupted, flow in a whole series in much the same way every time (like regaining balance) – or at least are "prepotent," ready to be learned "automatically" when the relevant stimuli are presented after birth (an example would be the instinctive organization of visual stimuli into seeing – a unified picture organized around contrasts and edges, with a bias toward attending to cohesively moving parts [ie, other organisms], which to be activated by experience during a critical period). Instinct, by definition, can't vary that much from culture to culture (at least in its basic features, which then become embedded in larger sequences and patterns which do themselves vary).

Culture is everything else. The movement of evolution in our species over the past two million years, at least, is toward culture and learning, and away from instinct: as the brain grew, the instinctive sequences (inborn or readily triggered as whole patterns) became fewer and shorter, while the amount of our behavior that is learned post-birth became more and more important. At the same time, progressive neotony – the steady push toward more and more premature birth in humans – supported this "unfinished" state of the neonatal brain (the better to be finished in relational patterning taking place after birth).

This is key to what we've been calling flexible problem-solving in novel conditions, whether socially or in the physical environment. Obviously, as long as environment is consistent, then fixed, inborn or prepotent behavior patterns are more adaptive, being quicker to deploy and requiring much less brain power to run. To compensate for the time lag in making scenario decisions and the glucose and development demands of more brain capacity, the payoff in terms of adaptation/survival has to be considerable. That payoff, basically, is the ability to adapt to rapid and radical environmental change, which

was the driver of our divergence from our Pan cousi
place. The result is a creature which is born unfinishe
degree than any other animal, and is then "finished" no
maturation alone, but through acculturation. And culture is a set of relational patterns, together with the beliefs and meanings (established interpretive templates) that sustain them. Again, the human infant grows through relational interaction.

Learning then is the establishment of new patterns of firing, or "pathways" in the brain. As these patterns are repeated and linked (in the ideal, non-traumatic case) to more and more different centers in the brain – which stabilizes the learning and makes it more flexible in application, -- then the movement of learning is often from delibe-ration to automism: over time we develop *practiced sequences of thought, problem-solving, and behavior:* whole patterns that activate together somewhat *like* instinct patterns, yet are not inborn, and vary from culture to culture and person to person. This movement to longer and more complex chains of more or less automatic response serves adaptability, as past experience becomes the stable base on which new experience is developed. This is what in Gestalt we call "ground" (and note again that sequence chains, or "if-this/then-this" in simple or complex contingent linkages, are the pattern structure). Thus narrative, again, is the structure of experiential ground.

Of course many of these patterns may have been assembled under stressful conditions of trauma, shame, or other emergency. When this happens the patterns tend to be more like "short-circuits," a deeply "engraved" linear linkage that *isn't* well connected with multiple brain centers (because those centers of relationality, body awareness, empathy, higher cortical judgment centers, self-narrative, memory and so forth weren't active at the time of the initial stress or emergency: that's what stress and emergency are, by definition – conditions that overwhelm the full activation of cortical capacity, thus leading to establishing a "short-circuit" or trauma-type reaction pattern). Thus this type of stress learning, which may often be dysfunctional in the future, may tend to be both very intense and extremely resistant to change.

Indeed, patterns that a culture may hold as charged and essential may be presented to the child under conditions that are specially *designed* to be "indelible" in this sense – ie, protected from further revision and resistant to change from future experience. Certain traumatic rites of passage, harsh parental shaming (over "inappropriate" sexual expression, for example), abuse and other trauma – experiences of these kinds are difficult to deconstruct and change (not impossible, but difficult) precisely because, being poorly connected to other centers of feeling and memory and judgment, they are not impacted and modified in an ongoing way throughout life, like patterns formed under more supportive conditions.

This is important for therapy, as much therapy is naturally addressed to those problematic sequences that are resistant to new learning and development, and thus are repetitively dysfunctional. Our gestalt nature is to synthesize or construct these holistic sequences; the degree of support determines the "size" of the whole that is constructed, and its flexible relatedness (or not) to the rest of experiential ground. Thus therapy is a *de*constructive process – and very much dependent on establishing conditions of extra safety and support in order to lessen the activation of the habitual "short-circuit," and permit the embedding of this new pattern in a system of these trauma linkages to more different brain centers.

And since an attuned relationship tends to "touch" and activate connection to all these "higher" and emotional centers of empathy, memory, self-narrative, judgment, etc, this means an attuned relationship is key to therapeutic change. We all know this; the Gestalt model has long been based on it, and has built on behavioral as well as clinical evidence to reassure us we were on the right track. What these new brain models coming out of interpersonal neurobiology do for us now is to tell us how and why this is true, in the process structure of our evolved brain.

Again, relationship was key to establishing those brain patterns in ourselves and our patients – in individual development as in species evolution. And attuned relationship will likewise be key in relaxing those relatively "fixed gestalts," so that a more flexibly integrated new pattern may emerge and become established.

8) Further Implications of Species-Wide "Premature" Birth

Here we come to considerations that give us a good window into the integrative/ recursive nature of evolution. We talked above about the physical pressure, coming from the constraints on the bipedal pelvis, pushing the species toward earlier and earlier birth as brain size increased – with corresponding pressure toward more stable pair-bonding to support the long dependent childhood, concealed estrus to support pair-bonding, complex social organization to support all that, the resultant need for an ever-larger, ever better-organized troop, and thus the push for constantly increasing brain power to manage the growing complexity demands of integrated social functioning.

The result as we have seen was an ever-more premature infant, with a highly plastic brain not yet "wired up" for full functioning. That "wiring" – the incredible complexity of interconnectedness in the human brain – is then supplied by relational experience and patterning, in a context of the underlying template of culture (see discussion in Wheeler, 2005). This is again what enables – and requires – different human cultures to be so radically different from each other, out of the biological base of a single interbreeding human population. It is also what accounts for the way the imprint of a given human culture can be so indelible on its current individual members – and yet so capable of radical shifts over the course of just a very few generations. All this is a complex genetic "strategy," so to speak, for species survival and groups prevailing in the face of radical climate change in a given local environment (which then translates readily into radical translocation from one region, one physical econiche, to another very different one – the very thing that our Pan cousins are so tragically unable to do). Premature birth, in other words, has gone from being a consequence, a burden on the troop, and an adaptive challenge, to being a key dynamic pattern element in an integrated adaptive whole.

9) The Evolution of Syntactic Language

We spoke above of two great mysteries in evolution – the origins of life and the sudden exponential growth of brain size and connectivity. The third enduring mystery of the evolutionary story has been syntactic language. Syntax – the remarkable innovation which enabled our species to communicate to each other the hypothetical scenarios so key to our social and other strategic planning – is an entirely different thing from communication by calls, signs, and signals that is so widespread through the animal kingdom. With signs and signals, the hallmark of the communication is an invariant, one-to-one correspondence between output and meaning. To a macaque monkey, a particular cry means snake; another one means eagle. Each always means what it means, and every time it's presented, by a troop member or on a recording, it triggers exactly the same behavior response (running for the trees versus crouching under them). The same goes for the fantastic dances of the bees, or the pheromone trails left by ants: they communicate meaning in an invariant way. (We continue of course to use signal communication, like "Look out!" or a scream or grunt, even humming or a lullaby).

The hallmark of syntactic communication, by contrast, is the way the import of a given input (a word or series of words) has an entirely different meaning depending on context – both social and linguistic, in relation to the words around it. Take the word "word," which depending on context can mean speech unit, promise, surprise ("my word!"), affirmation (as in current street slang), rumor ("word is,...."), and so on. Or take the word "lie," which can be a noun, a verb, an accusatory expletive, with meanings ranging from sexual to spatial to dog-training to golf – and on and on. The point is, none of this bothers us. We take it for granted, and small children handle it mostly with ease – to the point where much verbal humor depends on the play back and forth of various sense of a given word or phrase, which can throw a whole communication suddenly into a different key, to the delight (or consternation) of the audience.

Signals and calls are highly communicative. But they are almost entirely limited to news and references that are either physically present, or temporally present (like "food" or "large animal," plus a directional gesture). The organized social planning and strategic empowerment of a group that can then also communicate about hypotheticals is simply immeasurably enhanced ("What shall we do if the following happens...." "which way shall we go out tomorrow, and with which group?" etc etc). Indeed, it is probably this capacity which emerged with and defined the formation of our own subgroup of homo sapiens *sapiens*, and led to the eradication of all the other homo groups in the space of less than a hundred thousand years. Or, the emergence of fully syntactic language may be even more recent than that, corresponding perhaps with the migration of all our small group of fully human ancestors out of Africa (and all through Africa) as recently as 60,000 years ago (all perhaps stemming, DNA studies suggest, from a single group as small as 10,000 members at that crucial "bottleneck" time).

This is what syntactic language does for us, and what we do with it. The mystery has always been, how did we make that leap, which seems so qualitative and discontinuous? How did the brain get to be "wirable" for this context-dependent kind of understanding, where the particular setting and whole of a given picture of understanding determine the meaning of the component parts, as much as the other way around? Where does syntax come from, and how does it suddenly get there, full-blown as it were, in the brain?

A relational perspective and understanding of our human evolutionary and developmental history gives us a whole new answer to this long-perplexing enigma. The answer has to be: the process structure of the human brain, socially understood, was *already syntactic*. As always in evolution, the new capacity indeed can't just arise *de novo*: it has to be "built on" and built out of what's already there. The brain that became adapted to mastering syntactic language was a brain already adapted by social conditioning to handle syntactic social thought.

Think about it: a meaningful set of elements which can be combined in a great number of ways (but not any number of ways – the constraints are very much given) – and where the context and purpose of the particular sequence of elements gives you the value or meaning of each element, which would be different in another context. This is definitional of syntax, and syntactic speech. But it is also a direct description of the kind of social/organizational challenge that was already driving the evolution of the brain and the species, and that our brains are "constructed to deal with." Human social life *is* syntactic; the dynamic whole and changing context and purpose determine the variable meaning of the individual parts. The human social brain is our adaptation to cope with just this kind of challenge.

Certainly the exploitation of this capacity for language purposes, the reorganization of neural networking involved in using social processing centers to support social communication with verbal language, represents a major shift and an intriguing puzzle. But it no longer is something we have to see as "coming out of nowhere," emerging fully developed in a discontinuous way (the kind of thing, again, that extreme Creationists like to mock, and "Intelligent Design" theorists, understandably, find unpersuasive). Here once more, the application of relational thinking and relational models to the evolutionary data gives us a whole new insight on one of the most perplexing enigmas of the entire evolutionary story, from the old individualist model.

10) Emotion, Value, and Individuality

So with all this evolution of sociability and relationality, what happens to our individuality? We are not only the most complexly *social* species, but the most complexly *individual and differentiated* as well. In the perspective we are developing here, these things are not dichotomous or zero-sum; they are complementary, interplaying dynamically and mutually in a gestalt "nested" relationship to each other, of figure and ground. The supposed split between individual and social turns out to be another "false dichotomy," like genetics/environment, nature/nurture, learning/creating, perceiving/ interpreting, and the whole familiar list of other seeming dualities, which are actually mutually entailing.

The brain which adapted to handle complex, contextual, and constantly variable social complexity, and then applied that to strategic and abstract problems in the physical" world, as we have said, was necessarily a brain that moved away from instinct, and toward flexible social patterning. To a degree culture takes the place of instinct, in our species, as we have reviewed here: our prenatal development is "completed" by relational experience in a cultural/relational context. But that too can only go so far, if we are to retain the flexibility that enables us to negotiate our social (and physical) worlds.

What is the criterion for judging and reacting to a situation, if it's no longer instinct or rigid cultural fixation (beyond a few basic biases which are the very definition of culture, such as social bonding and mutuality)? The answer is *emotional response*: that synthesizing of sensory data into value (good/bad, desirable/undesirable, toward/away). Human individuality is of course one consequence of our being born so incompletely "wired," and then "finished" in post-natal experience, which is inherently extremely variable. But here again, the "consequence" in an integral, non-linear model turns out to be itself an essential feature of the integrated whole: what's the point, after all, of all this capacity for scenario generation and comparison, if we're not also equipped, by our inherited emotional capacities and our learned, variable/individual emotion-based preferences, to discriminate or choose between or among them?! The fact that the members of the group are individually variable to an extreme degree means that the group as a whole can benefit from multiple "experiments" being run at the same time, in the ideation and behavior of its members. The group as a whole becomes a source of greater creativity and flexibility of response – again, an essential feature of our species adaptation strategy.

Now development of the "emotional brain" (the "mammalian" or middle level of the tripartite brain) is the hallmark of the mammalian order – deriving from the order's characteristic live birth and feeding through lactation, which implies attachment, individual recognition, and in "higher" mammals lifelong family bonds. What happens in primates and then humans is that the emotional centers are connected up with the frontal cortex, decisional and judgment centers, at a whole new level of complexity. This means that emotional/valuation response is linked with memory, scenario planning, and choice at a whole new level as well. But memory and planning again are highly individual, variable depending on individual life history – while preference and valuation are highly *colored* by group patterns and culture, group support and belonging (and shunning or shame), -- and at the same time highly variable, through early and ongoing relational experience.

This means that emotion – rather than being the source of separation or disturbance – is the key link between individual differentiation and group/relational connection. Darwin was ahead of his time (indeed, ahead of his own followers and model) in recognizing that emotional response is first and foremost *group or interpersonal communication*: that's why, he argued, the human face is relatively hairless, for greater expressive power. Our emotional responses – and the enduring preferences and aversions we call "values" – are at one and the same time highly individual depending on experience, and yet arising out of a relational context, and constrained by the past and present dynamics of our groups. Values and beliefs depend on reference groups, those groups (even absent or past) we identify with and draw our support from, at least in our own minds. Where you find an individual "standing up to a group," almost inevitably if you probe you will find that person identifying with another group, from which he/she draws the strength to "stand against." Our individuality, to be robust and flexible, is always grounded somewhere in belonging. (Where it is not, then we find the constriction, hesitation, and often destructive compensations we associate with chronic shame – the experience of non-belonging, long identified if not well-understood as the most toxic of all human emotions (see discussion in Lee & Wheeler, 1996).

Thus understanding emotion from a relational point of view gives us a further perspective on how individuality and relationality are not discontinuous, much less dichotomous or opposed. They completely interpenetrate: it is our relational evolution which both permits and mandates our highly articulated individuality within and across cultures. And it is our relational capacities which support and inform that individuality, all through the individual lifespan.

11) Evolution and Development

This brings us to one more of the perplexing discontinuities in our inherited, individualistically-biased narrative of our own origins and nature: the longstanding conceptual and research break between *evolution*, which references the species, and *development*, which references the individual. That is, rather than showing a model of continuous evolutionary development from ancestral species through to present-day human fetus and then on through to adulthood, our human story seemed to fall in two discontinuous chapters: how the species got up to the moment of an individual's birth, and then how that individual developed from helpless premature birth to "independent" mature adulthood. Neither story seemed to shed much light on the other, and they were long pursued by separate disciplines (biology and psychology) that had little or no serious dialogue between them.

Certainly Freud hoped the day would come when this gap would be bridged – by, as he pictured it, the complete reduction of psychology to biological determinism, in which he saw his own theory of "drives" as the essential first steps. To deal with the troubling conceptual discontinuity between "savage" ancestors ("nature red in tooth and claw," as Tennyson put it) and the long period of helpless, dependent, attachment-directed immaturity of each individual human, he presented infancy and "pre-Oedipal" childhood as a kind of species aberration, the source of the tragic *flaw* in our species nature, leaving us in a state that might be called existential resignation, at best, as our still-savage "primary" nature warred all through life with the scars of our weak individual beginnings, and the strictures of our tightly-organized social lives. To be sure, this was at least an attempt to accommodate to the impact of Darwin's ideas, and if the accommodation was reductionistic and crudely fantastical in some ways, that was not the fault of Darwin's work itself (which was deeply contextual and complex), so much as of the increasingly individualistic and militarized century and more that followed the publication of *Origin of Species* in 1859.

The attempt to bridge this evolutionary/personal development divide was then carried forward, or at least carried on, in the second half of the 20th Century by the movement known as "sociobiology," from E. O. Wilson's book of that title. If anything, much of what was written under this heading, as with its current relabeling as "evolutionary psychololgy" has been likewise reductionistic, simplistic, linear (one gene = one behavior), and if anything *less* richly fertile and imaginative than were Freud's speculations, which at least had opened up the whole world of the family drama in a new way, giving rise to a rich Freud-inflected tradition in art and literature.

Again, the basic problem here, the source of the oversimplifications and reductionistic contradictions of much popular and much "scientific" writing in this area, has been the hapless attempt to impose an individualistic image and paradigm of our human nature, on the story of a creature whose evolution and development alike are *definitionally, essentially, existentially relational.*

In the Gestalt tradition we've struggled from the time of Goodman, at least, to free ourselves from our own contradictions, cultural blind spots, and "false dichotomies" around these issues. Something similar (often very much influenced by Gestalt present-centered relational work, and by Gestalt psychology models of functional holism) has gone on in many other clinical schools of thought, including the neo-psychodynamic – as it has in biology, neurology, infant development, learning theory, evolutionary theory itself, and the applied areas of education, child-rearing, and other forms of training. Today, the wealth of new research and the beginnings at least of new models in evolutionary theory and also in brain/mind research is coming together to support an emergent new picture of human nature and development – who we are and how we got that way, both as a species and individually – that supports the amassing clinical evidence and experience that Gestalt, along with some other current schools such as Contemporary Psychoanalysis, have long labored to articulate and present.

12) The Burgeoning New Field of Interpersonal Neurobiology

This new work in psychology and brain research comes together in the exciting and burgeoning new discipline of Interpersonal Neurobiology, discussed above in section 7 (see Siegel, 1999,). This is the burgeoning research field of how relational experience actually shapes and builds the brain, not only in the premature and hyper-plastic neonatal period, but then with ongoing brain development and plasticity all through life. Neurobiology of course is a long-established field with an impressive research body. What is different today, with the new possibilities for functional magnetic resonance imaging and other scanning technologies, is that brain activity can be observed and mapped, non-invasively, in real time. Thus the recently developing understanding of mirror neurons and their role in the brain's capacity for empathy, imitation of purpose or motivation (a capacity of young children which has long puzzled researchers, as opposed to mere imitation of behavior), and the familiar but also puzzling phenomenon of emotional "contagion," and its obvious utility in synthesizing group state and activity. The result of this explosion of research and modeling is nothing less than a whole new and dynamic mapping of the brain, its development, and its functioning. With this emergent mapping, combined as we are sketching here with the new research in evolutionary studies, we become able to bridge the gap at last between evolution and development, showing much more about how our evolved, genetic potentials for learning and problem-solving capacities actually become activated, integrated, and elaborated into the emergent capacities of the infant brain – and then how those potential capacities are themselves activated and integrated by relational experience into the amazing array of flexible and novel responses exhibited by most human children and adults. (And even how it happens that those potentials become constricted or blocked through severely aversive experience, as discussed above under culture, learning, and trauma). The result is the outlines, plus considerable filling in, of a map of human nature that is integrated and continuous, for the first time, from species origins to contemporary individuals, first infants and then adults. Our human narrative is transformed, with implications not just for therapy and other forms of education and healing, but also for organizations, politics and social policy, and geopolitical issues.

To summarize what was discussed briefly in section 7 above, we begin with Hebb's classic dictum of neurobiology, "what fires together, wires together." The infant brain is born premature, not yet "connected up" and integrated by established instinctual patterns of whole behavioral sequences. In place of that will be learned patterning, which becomes more vigorous and reliable as it is repeated, especially under conditions of considerable need or demand (ie, organismic activation). Under relational conditions of empathic mirroring, responsive attunment, and appropriate handling and support, the patterns the infant establishes will be well integrated into a wide variety of developing brain centers which are activated during the learning by these kinds of conditions. Indeed, since much of the brain is "uncolonized" by connectivity at birth and thus "up for grabs," the very growth and linkage structure of various areas of the brain will be largely determined by how activated those particular centers are in early development. Thus learning (about the world, the self, other people – the conditions of living) that takes place under these relationally supportive conditions will tend to be flexible, well integrated with judgment, memory, and the body, and thus open to ongoing development and creative variability throughout life.

Learning that takes place under less relationally supportive conditions – including hyperstimulation, misattunement, shaming, relational withdrawal and neglect, traumatic events, active abuse, and so on – will likewise tend to be what we have been calling here "short-circuit learning:" more or less isolated from all the centers mentioned above that would "open the learning up" to new ongoing experience, and make it flexibly applicable to novel and creative situations (because of the simultaneous activation, when that kind of situation or trigger arises, of judgment, memory, emotion and empathy, body awareness, self-narrative, and other relational capacity centers). That's how we work. That's how we've evolved, to be (under at least minimally supportive conditions) simultaneously the most individually creative, flexible, and adaptable of all complex species, and also the most embedded in (indeed created by) relational complexity and unique relational capacities, supported by a unique brain that was itself evolved to deal with complex relational challenge.

The picture itself at last becomes integrated and whole. *Our nature is to be completed by nurture,* which is grounded in (not linearly determined by) our evolved genetic nature. Our individuality is a unique expression of our relational nature, which is what enables us to be so fantastically creative and variably differentiated, both in evolution and in development. Our narrative has been transformed – and with it our possible destiny, and the politics that supports that possible positive future.

Conclusions – The Challenge Today and Tomorrow

The politics and specific social policies, locally and globally, that follow from these considerations are radical by today's standards (yet for the most part relatively inexpensive and demonstrably effective). This will be the material for another paper or series of papers. For here, we will close these reflections with these thoughts:

Our nature as a uniquely evolved species of the Pan lineage is this fantastic development and elaboration of our capacity to function as a complexly organized tribe or troop. Suddenly, in the course of just the last 5000 or so years, this capacity has platformed the amalgamation and organization of larger and larger social units, now amounting to millions or hundreds of millions of individuals more or less identified into "nations," and acting as more or less coordinated wholes.

But three deeply problematic things stand out about this social development into mega-units. First, there is the inherent instablility of groups which are no longer face-to-face. Nations tend to fracture, shift, often violently, exacerbating the frictions between them with frictions within them, and all of this at a level of technological power that now threatens our species itself. The nature of the nation state as a cultural form, history tells us, is war. It remains to be seen whether, how, and to what extent today's and tomorrow's social web connectivity may constitute a mitigating cultural adaptation, to the instability of these evolutionarily overlarge, non-face-to-face groups, which have so far depended on hypertrophied out-group hostility, to create a viable level of in-group cohesiveness in these unprecedented size groupings.

Second, there is no natural limit to these expansive and exploitative tendencies, which served our unified troops in the evolutionary period, but again, threaten our very existence today. All this is obvious and constantly if ineffectually commented on. The third implication grows out of all these relational considerations and perspectives here, and is less obvious: as a species, we are founded on *belonging*. Exploitation and oppression *within* a group is always possible, but there are natural constraints on those destructive capacities by the dynamics of identification and belonging. It is those dynamics and those complex, inborn relational capacities that made our survival, evolution, and then individual development through long dependent childhood possible in the first place. This is our basic relational nature, which it has been the aim of this paper to lay out in a new, integrated narrative from species descent through individual growth and individuation.

Now as has often been remarked by social philosophers, every culture has its own moral codes, and some kind of protection for its members, its own kind of ethic. Moralities differ from culture to culture, to some extent; but the fact of them does not differ, and those cultures that prosper resemble each other in their moral codes more than they differ. Murder may be a fact of human life, but it is always negatively sanctioned, always problematic – *within* the identified group.

Outside the group boundary has generally been another matter. Murder that occurs across group boundaries, outside the context of belonging, often isn't murder at all, but war. Morally stressful, yet clearly the subject of effortful justification (generally it's presented as being for the sake of the identified group of belonging: ie, "us.")

Everything in our narrative indicates that we cannot change this. Exhortations to peace and justice so often remain just that – exhorttations – unless the context has changed, and the moral argu-ment now rests on a felt basis of belonging. This experience of belonging has to be the key to our social evolution toward a world more often characterized by justice and peace. These things are possible, as the entire history of the species and world culture demonstrate – *when they take place within a context of felt belonging and identification.* Our efforts for political justice and change will continue to fail, unless and until they are grounded in programs for promoting experiences of belonging, across the world spectrum of cultural and regional differences.

To paraphrase popular author-turned-social-activist Deepak Chopra, the success of all our crucial social action initiatives in the world today depends on a change of consciousness. That change has to be in the direction of a sense of belonging and identification with the whole of humanity, not our local cultural group -- and beyond that, of course the whole of life, the living, breathing organism that is our small planet itself.

This all seems obvious when we say it, but it isn't at all the direction of much social action and policy, even that part which is directed toward peace and justice. We have much to contribute, as Gestaltists, as psychologists and practitioners, and as citizens of our groups and the world, to how the skills of contact, relationship, and dialogue (three takes on the same process) may be developed and applied to "grow" this wider sense of identification and belonging. All our political (and clinical/educational) efforts have to be grounded in this awareness – just as all our creativity, all our individual and joint efforts, are grounded in our capacity for relationship, identification, and belonging themselves.

References

Darwin, C. (1873). *The Expression of the Emotions in Man and Animals.* London: John Murray.

Dawkins, R. (1976). *The Selfish Gene.* New York: Oxford University Press.

Deamer, D., Dworkin, J., Sandford. S., Bernstein M., & Allamandola L. (2002). The First Cell Membranes. *Astrobiology.* 2, 371-381.

deWaal, F. (1982). *Chimpanzee Politics.* London: Jonathan Cape.

deWaal, F. (2005). *Our Inner Ape.* New York: Riverhead Books.(

Diamond, J. (1992). *The Third Chimpanzee.* New York: Harper Collins.

Dunbar, R. (1992). Neocortex Size as a Constraint on Group Size in Primates. *Journal of Human Evolution, 20,* 469-493.

Ekman, P. & Rosenberg, E. (1998). *What the Face Reveals.* NewYork: Oxford University Press.

Gould, S. (2007). *Punctuated Equilibrium.* Cambridge MA: Harvard University Press.

Kropotkin, P. (1902/2005). *Mutual Aid: A Factor in Evolution.* Boston: Peter Sargent.

Lee, R. & Wheeler, G. (Eds). (1996). *The Voice of Shame: Silence and Connection in Psychotherapy.* San Francisco: Jossey-Bass.

Perls, F. (1947). *Ego, Hunger and Aggression.* London: Allen & Unwin, Ltd.

Siegel, D. (1999). *The Developing Mind.* San Francisco: Harper.

Wheeler, G. (2000). *Beyond Individualism.* Hillsdale NJ: The Analytic Press/GestaltPress.

Wheeler, G. (2008). The Age of Complexity: Paul Goodman in the 21st Century. *Gestalt Review, 12*(3),. 206-228,

Wright, R. (2000). *Non-Zero.* New York: Pantheon Books

Editors' Note:
Neurobiology gives an underpinning which supports, and from which we can add further detail to, our Gestalt ideas and understanding of relational development. This brings a greater clarity to the role of the key relational modulators of the affects of shame and of belonging. As Robert Lee shows, the relational management of strong affect, both positive and negative, is a resilient and normalizing process, and yet one subject to the vagaries of failures of relationship, fractures in the supportive web in which normal development occurs. He puts the experience of developmental trauma and its consequences in the context of the relational field, and surveys the rapidly growing literature which unites the microscopic, at the level of the amazing and electrifying wiring project that goes on so radically in the growing infant brain, with the nuanced and, hopefully, attuned dance between the baby and his/her caregiver. He shows that infants and young children who are exposed to an enduring experience of deficient connection and support develop patterns that define ground-shame, and that there is then an inevitable process of impairment of development of the relational brain, mind and self. The implications for healing processes that are relational are then obvious and powerful.

2

Shame & Belonging in Childhood:

The Interaction Between Relationship and Neurobiological Development in the Early Years of Life[1]

Robert G. Lee

Gestalt field theory heralds the importance of attuned relationship in childhood development. This idea and the correlates that stem from it emanate from Gestalt's long held tenets of how we are interconnected and how intersubjective, co-constructed experience is the basis of self/other development.

---

[1] The author wishes to thank Lee Geltman for his help in editing this manuscript.

This idea is now being reinforced by current brain research, findings of which parallel, support and inform Gestalt theory. For example, note the similarity to the Gestalt idea above to what Siegel (1999) says in the introduction of his book, *The Developing Mind*: "The mind emerges from the activity of the brain, whose structure and function are directly shaped by interpersonal experience." (p. 1) With regard to the developing infant, Siegel states:

> Though experience shapes the activity of the brain and the strength of neuronal connections throughout life, experience early in life may be especially crucial in organizing the way the basic structures of the brain develop. (p. 13)

In this article I review the neurological literature around brain formation in the first two years of life. Not only does this information have much to offer in appreciating and refining Gestalt concepts, it also generates further possibilities when viewed through the Gestalt lens.

To a large extent I have used the extensive information gathered by Alan Schore as a source of neurological research. Because the technical aspect of this topic can detract from what I am attempting to do here, I have endeavored to use the least technical language possible. However, for those who are interested I have included some of the underpinning neurological information in footnotes.

Through out this article we will be looking at the factors that shape a child's developing sense of shame and belonging. Thus as a foundation for this exploration, let's review what shame means from a Gestalt field theory perspective. (Lee, 1995)

What a Shame!

The phenomenon of shame encompasses much more than our common cultural sense of having done something wrong, thus being shameful, or of being flawed in some manner. At its core, shame is about pulling back (Tomkins, 1963). It is our way to attempt to protect our selves or others when we perceive that we won't be received (Lee, 1995; Lee & Wheeler, 1996). This larger meaning is contained in a common usage of the word "shame" in our everyday conversation, although without our awareness. For example, our common reply to being told that 2-year old Jenny lost her favorite "blankie," or that 6-year old Mark's ice cream fell on the ground, or more profoundly that 13-year old Maria's mother just died, or to any incidence of hardship or loss for anyone of any age for that matter, is "What a shame!" This usage of "shame" isn't just a coincidental colloquialism. It makes sense, as on a compassionate level we understand that the yearnings in these examples couldn't get met, and so the children involved had to disengage from mobilizing on their yearnings in these situations. Thus they were primed for the experience of shame to pull them back.

Shame is our body's natural way of retroflecting when we are off-balance without sufficient support, when we have a desire/want/yearning to connect in some way with someone/something, and we sense that our desired connection may not be possible. As such the potential for shame is woven into every instance of contact. The experience of shame, in this manner, helps us identify the places where we sense connection is not possible so that we can move to and find the places where we can connect.

Shame's family of affects, which help us pull back when we sense that a longed for connection is not possible, include shyness, embarrassment, chagrin, ignominy, shame, humiliation, even "feeling lousy" (Kaufman, 1989; Lewis, 1971; Retzinger, 1987). Ironically, we experience shame as information about our self (as being inadequate, worthless, unlovable, inappropriate, too much, too little, and so on), when in reality it is information about the field around us (others being preoccupied, disapproving, disinterested, uninformed, not knowing how to respond, absent, or the like).

As stated, this form of temporal shame we need as we move through life; we will often experience it as disappointment, shyness, or embarrassment. Among other things, the experience of shame in this manner represents a respect for other's boundaries (again we may experience it as information as about ourselves). We might see this in others or our selves as a sense of humility. Note that behavior that lacks respect is considered to be "shameless."

There is another way that shame can act to attempt to protect us or others that we care about. If the experience of lack of reception is too severe (as in abuse, neglect, or significant loss) or it is consistent enough over time, then shame will link with the experience that we have of not being received such that every time we have a yearning to be in the world in that manner, shame will automatically be activated to pull us back from mobilizing in the direction of that yearning. There no longer has to be some sensed possibility of unavailability of connection in the environment at the moment. Instead the emergence of our yearning is the trigger for shame. This in effect represents a hardened belief, a fixed gestalt, that our yearning wouldn't have a chance of reception under any circumstances. This form of shame I refer to as *ground shame*. (Kaufman, 1989), who introduced this concept, labeled this form of shame "internalized shame." I prefer to use "ground shame," as our ground is our sense of our relational field.)

In terms of Gestalt theory, ground shame is what Perls called "introjects." (See Lee, 1995) And of course, what we project is the unassimilated shame bind, and at the core of Perl's retroflection is also an element of ground shame. Thus the development of ground shame takes one out of a relational sense of the world and deposits the person in an individualistic paradigm in which they are disconnected, alone, and the subject of blame or disregard. Instead of the excitement and mobilizing possibilities coincident with yearning the person is left with a sense of hopelessness and deflation.

With this summary of shame from a Gestalt field theory perspective, let's move to the other side of this polarity to the development of belonging in the first year of life.

Emotional/Neurobiological Development In the First Year of Life

The last two decades have yielded an explosion of information on emotional/neurobiological development in the first year of human life. Research now shows us that a primary psychoneurological developmental task during this period is enabling the infant's brain to experience and tolerate increasing amounts of elation/arousal, in conjuncttion with intersubjective experience with an attuned caregiver. The importance of relationship in this process is paramount. As Schore (1998) states in summarizing the neurobiological and related research in the field:

> Over the course of this year, the primary caregiver-infant relationship co-constructs an increasingly complex dynamic system of mutual reciprocal influences that mediates the formation of an attachment bond within the dyad. This interactive mechanism regulates the infant's psychobiological states, thereby allowing the child to tolerate more intense and longer lasting levels of heightened, yet modulated, arousal. This ontogenetic achievement, central to human development, enables the infant to experience very high levels of the positive affects of interest-excitement and enjoyment-joy by the end of the first year (p.58).

This is an example of how the learnings coming from neurobiologycal research so parallel and support Gestalt field theory's constructionist, intersubjective sense of this human interaction. (See Frank, 2001, and Wheeler & McConville, 2003, on child development.) Schore continues, saying that this process is highlighted by caregiver-infant mutual gazing, coordinated with auditory vocalizations, tactile touching and body gestures. Stern (Stern et al., 2003) describes how interacttive mirror neuron and adaptive oscillator circuits are also important in this process. Caregiver and infant become an energy resonant system with the caregiver reflecting, and in essence holding and amplifying, the crescendos and descrescendos of the infant's psychobiological, internal state. (Schore, 1998; Stern, 1990)

Trevarthen (1993) describes, from his research on mother-infant interactions, this process as an interactive mechanism by which older brains engage with mental states of awareness, emotion, and interest in younger brains. He concludes that infant neurological growth literally requires brain-brain interaction occurring in the context of an intimate (positive) relationship between caregiver and infant.

As this implies, it is now thought that the attachment relationship is essentially a regulator of arousal (van der Kolk & Fisler, 1994). It is further believed that the regulatory process is the precursor of psychological attachment and its associated emotions (Hofer, 1994). All of which underscores that psychobiological attunement is the mechanism that mediates attachment bond formation. Again, this highlights the Gestalt principles of the primacy of co-constructed, intersubjective contact and the importance of the field and support in development. (Frank, 2001, and Wheeler & McConville, 2003)

From a neurobiological perspective, as outlined by Schore (1998), the mother's (caregiver's) gaze influences the neural substrates for emotion by directly regulating the levels of important neurotransmitters (catecholamines, dopamine and noradrenaline) some of which are involved in arousal/elation and others of which act as regulators of neural development.[2]

---

[2] Amplified levels of interest-excitement in the mother's face also initiate/support three other effects in the infant's brain – (1) elevated levels of corticotropin-releasing factor (CRF), a neuropeptide produced in paraventricular hypothalamic centers that activates the energy-mobilizing sympathetic division of the autonomic nervous system (ANS), (2) increases in plasma concentrations of noradrenaline, there-by intensifying levels of (sympathetic-dominant) arousal, seen in heightened infant activity levels, and (3) increased levels of endogenous opiates (endorphins) that biochemically mediate the pleasurable qualities of social interactions, social affect,

Schore states that the developing control center of this neurological structuring in the infant's brain is located in the right orbitofrontal cortex, an area of the prefrontal cortex hidden behind the orbit of the right eye. This area, which is learning to monitor increased levels of elation/arousal in accordance with intersubjective experience with the caregiver, undergoes immense neural growth during this period. (See Schore, 1998, for details of pathways projected to various limbic areas of the brain.)

By the end of the first year, as the infant begins to toddle, the orbitofrontal cortex is sufficiently developed for the infant to be able to access internal working models that include more varied and complex expectations of being matched by and being able to match another, as well as increased ability to participate in the state and experience of the other. These increases in the child's innate ability to appraise self and other in order to meet in a mutually supported, intersubjective state of arousal with the caregiver provides the toddler with the beginning cognitive-emotional foundation necessary for the next step in neurological development. (Schore, 1998; Stern et al., 2003; Trevarthen, 1993)

Shame in a Minor Key: The Normalization of Disappointment

In the second year of life, a task opposite from supporting arousal becomes figural. The toddler can now explore the world considerably more independently than during the first year of life. However, with this extended ability of the infant comes the parental task of providing secure enough limits for the infant's safe exploration. This dictates an alteration in caregiver-infant interactions and presents a challenge in negotiating this changed landscape in an attuned manner. Schore (1998) estimates that at 10 months 90% of caregiver behavior is

---

and attachment. The latter occurs via activation of the ventral tegmental dopamine system. (Schore, 1998)

concerned with affection, play, and caregiving; whereas by the time infants reach 13 months, caregivers are expressing a prohibition on the average of every 9 minutes.

Remember that through the first year the infant comes to expect that new experiences of interest or joy will be met with a basically holding/approving gaze by the caregiver. However, in the second year there are now many more times when the caregiver, because of safety or other considerations, does not find it in keeping with this new goal to fully support the child's behavior and doesn't enter into the co-regulated state of arousal that the infant expects, instead instituting some perceived needed limit. From the infant's perspective, in accordance with what we discussed earlier, we might say, "What a shame!" And in fact, this interruption in the infant's desired arousal supporting connection triggers the experience of shame, even though an attuned caregiver will wisely deliver the inhibition in a caring manner. As Schore (1998) states:

> The ensuing break in an anticipated visual-affective communication triggers a sudden shock-induced deflation of positive affect, and the infant is thus propelled into a state which he or she cannot yet autoregulate. Shame represents this rapid state transition from a preexisting positive state to a negative state (p. 65).

This, of course, facilitates the child's pulling back from mobilizing on his/her yearning, through the involuntary experience of a painful state of distress, characterized by "a sudden decrement in mounting pleasure, a rapid inhibition of excitement, and cardiac deceleration"[3] (Schore, p. 66).

Schore states that the experience of shame is mediated by the production of corticosteroids[4] that start the process of "pulling in." He

---

[3] Cardiac deceleration is achieved by means of vagal impulses in the medulla.

[4] Corticosteroids are a class of steroid hormones that are known to be secreted by the adrenal cortex in response to serious injury or stress and

mentions two such corticosteroids – cortisol and corticosterone.[5] Others report that even short-lived increaseed levels of corticosteriods induce inhibition and withdrawal (Stansbury & Gunnar, 1994). Schore sees this interpersonal-dependent experience of shame in the infant as shifting from a state of heightened arousal into a low-keyed inhibitory state of conservation-withdrawal that occurs in helpless and hopeless situations.[6]

How long the child remains in this stress state is an important factor (Schore, 1998, p. 66).

The last quote from Schore is of particular significance. If the child is left too long in this corticosteriod bath of shame the literature then turns to describing trauma. Of course, attuned parents intuitively understand this and do not allow this to happen. Instead the attuned

---

that tend to shift the body from carbohydrate to fat metabolism, to regulate blood pressure, and to affect immune response and regulate inflamation (Coleman, 2001).

[5] A number of other researchers have reported finding a connection between forms of shame and increased levels of cortico-steroids (cortisol in particular) — for example see :Dickerson & Gable, 2004; Dickerson, Gruenewald, & Kemeny, 2004;Lewis & Ramsey, 2002; and Tops et al., 2006. At the same time the relationship between shame and corticosteroids, as well as the damage that coricosteriods may do, appears to be complex and involvie the role of receptors as well (de Kloet et al., 1999; de Kloet et al., 2005; Stansbury & Gunnar, 1992).

[6] The onset of the interactively triggered shame state thus represents a sudden shift from energy-mobilizing sympathetic to energy-conserving parasympathetic dominant ANS activity, a rapid transition from a hyperaroused to a hypoaroused state, and a sudden switch from ergotropic (sympathetically driven) to trophotropic (parasympathetically driven) arousal.... In such a psychobiological state transition, sympathetically powered elation, heightened arousal, and elevated activity level instantly evaporate (Schore, 1998).

caregiver will quickly and compasssionately reestablish a mutual bond that serves to regulate and *metabolize* the shame that has been triggered in setting a limit. From a Gestalt field perspective the infant is taken from an experience of belonging (having an interest or experience of joy and wanting to share it) to an experience of not belonging (his/her yearning not being met by the caregiver) and finally to a repair experience of belonging (reestablishment of the arousal bond). In the process the orbitofrontal cortex is further organized:

> The sudden triggering of shame reflects an alteration of the infant's psychobiological state and the onset of a stress reaction, manifested in elevated levels of corticosteriods in the infant's brain. [which initiates the painful inhibition state]... But during critical periods of cortical maturation these neurohormones do more than just transiently perturb states – in fact, they directly influence brain growth.... Developmental shame experiences thus induce a neurobiological reorganization of evolving brain circuitries (Schore, 1998, p. 68).

Thus through experiences of shame and repair in the second year, the infant starts to develop an important ability to regulate his/her arousal when not met by significant others. The site of control of this learning is again the orbitofrontal cortex.[7]

The importance of this experience-dependent maturation of the orbitofrontal cortex must be underscored. From a Gestalt field

---

[7] "This organization includes the fine-tuning of descending projections from the prefrontal cortex to subcortical structures that are known to mature during infancy. Of particular importance is the growth of prefrontal axons back down to subcortical targets on nor-adrenergic neurons in the nucleus of the solitary tract of the brain stem caudal reticular formation and the vagal complex in the medulla ... and in parasympathetic autonomic areas of the hypothalamus .... By this process the organization of the lateral tegmental forebrain-midbrain limbic circuit that brakes arousal and activates the onset of an inhibitory state is completed" (Schore, 1998, p.69).

perspective and from my clinical experience, what this represents is the *normalization of disappointment* – or said more concisely – the start of *the inclusion of disappointment as a tool of belonging*. Through this shame and repair dyadic process, lesser forms/experiences of shame such as disappointment become integrated into the experience of belonging. Thus disappointment becomes a tool that is available throughout life to be used as a part of learning. That is, if this process is carried out in an attuned manner, with a minimum of disconnection and timely repair, the child comes to understand/believe that when he/she is not met with an arousal amplifying/regulating gaze it does not mean that he/she does not belong, instead it means that the caregiver will return to engage soon.

Is what is being described here a significant part of the psychobiological underpinning of the development of basic trust? It certainly is a crucial element in being able to negotiate life in general – to experience one's self as being loved and having value, to be able to stay in tune with other's experience in the field, to have access to connective resources, and to be inclusively creative in problem solving. If not sufficiently attained, this deficit leads to an unbalancing and to isolating and over-aggressive creative adjustments that in time find their way to therapy or sources of social control.

Without the development of this type of brain circuitry, disappointment becomes a trigger for and conduit to deeper experiences of shame. This is the experience of not belonging and of "this is not my world," which carries with it a sense of worthlessness, all of which is the body's way of protectively pulling back when the environment severely enough or consistently enough does not offer a route for meaningful inclusive connection. (In discussing misattunement here and later, I do not wish to blame parents. This is an area in which parents need a great deal of support, especially if they have not been lucky enough to have received this kind of attunement in their own lives.)

As a side note, these research findings, of the need for reconnective repair after the experience of shame in limit setting, speak volumes against the common practice of disciplining a child of any age by using isolating techniques such as timeouts in a closed room, after misbehavior. Advocates of such techniques might say that what is intended is to provide the child an opportunity to think about what he/she did and to reorganize in another fashion. Certainly, such techniques provide a time for parents or other caregivers to organize, giving them support. But what children need is more relationship, not isolation, at such times. That is why institutes that serve older children and adolescents and that operate from a relational basis have the child pick a buddy that must be within arm's length of the child during times of discipline (See Kanner & Lee, 2004). The trick is to find a method of disciplining that restores relationship and at the same time supports the whole field.

To return to the course of development with an attuned caregiver in early development, Schore suggests that, with the experience-dependent neural growth in the first and second year of life, the orbitofrontal cortex becomes the control center for social interaction.[8] From a Gestalt field perspective, this suggests that the orbitofrontal cortex is a central part of the system that monitors shame and belonging in the field.

Shame in a Major Key
The Development of Ground Shame

As mentioned earlier, if the child is left too long in the experience of shame then the literature turns to talking about the experience of trauma. There is significant indication that the experience of trauma also leads to the development of ground shame. Kaufman (1989) has long talked about how experiences of trauma are major sources of ground shame. (Again, Kaufman uses the label "internalized shame.") So it is not surprising that what Schore identifies as the mediator of the experience of shame, namely the release of cortio-steroids, has long been associated with the development of trauma.

In addition, ground shame has been strongly correlated with the majority of DSM IV, Axis I diagnoses (Cook, 1994). So, similarly, it is not surprising that increased levels of corticosteroids (in particular, cortisol) have been associated with many of these same diagnoses.

To list a few of the adverse findings linked with increased levels of corticosteroids:

- A single dose of corticosteroids during early development delays the maturation of auditory-, visual-, and somatosensory- potentials. (Trad, 1989)

- Exposure of the developing brain to corticosteroids affects myelination (the process of protectively covering neurons), neural morphology (premature pruning of cells during critical, early development), neurogenesis (the formation of new neurons), and synaptogensis (the formation of synaptic connections between neurons) (Schore, 1997; Teicher et al., 2002).

- Cortisol inhibits immune and inflammatory processes (Teicher ei al., 2002).

- Increased levels of croticsteriods have been associated with PTSD symptomatology (Schore, 1997).

- Increased levels of cortisol have been associated with both childhood and adult major depression and dysthymia as well as with the experience of worthlessness, helplessness, and with suicide (Trad, 1989).

- Children who lost a parent in the September 11, 2001 terrorist attack were subsequently found to have increased levels of cortisol in association with significantly increased incidence of psychiatric disorders involving anxiety and PTSD (Pfeffer et al., 2007).

- Cortisol non-surpression has been associated with anorexia nervosa, bulimia and opiate addiction (Trad, 1989).

Consider a recent study involving mothers and infants (Morelius et al., 2007). The mothers in this study were selected because of attunement difficulties and correspondingly the infants had developed attachment problems. (To repeat our compassionate response to such situations— What a shame!) It has been known that maternal (caregiver) inattention increases corticosteroid levels (Teicher et al., 2002), which as covered above is the initiator of the experience of shame. Morelius' group found that cortisol levels increased in both mothers and infants during diaper changes. From our theory above, the need for both mother and child to pull away from their yearnings to connect with each other, through the experience of shame, under such circumstances is understandable. Treatment with these mothers improved their sensitivity to their infant's signals, and cortisol levels in both mothers and infants during diaper changes decreased to normal levels for dyads in which the infant was under 3 months of age. However, the cortisol levels did not decrease in infants older than 3 months. Morelius et al. conclude:

> According to the results of the present study, an early intervention is of great importance. Thus we need to continue with early support and to help mothers at psychosocial risk to improve the mother-infant relationship in order to protect the infants from developing long-term health consequences. (p. 137)

I believe that among the long-term health consequences mentioned above is the development of ground shame, which represents the hardened belief that it is not possible for a given yearning to connect to be responded to.

The Need to Diagnose from a Field Perspective

The above example of maladapted mothers and infants highlights the need to diagnose from a field perspective — to understand the human field context in which given symptoms and behavior present. As a further exploration of this concept, consider the dilemma of the child who is unlucky enough to have parents who do not have the ability or support to attend in an attuned manner. The fall into shame for the child, without the needed repair that comes from the reestablishment of an attuned connection, is inevitable. This is an experience that is extremely unpalatable. If possible, the child must then devise a way, most likely without awareness, to avoid similar experiences of shame in the future. From this perspective the creative adjustments that later appear in therapy could be seen in many cases as attempts to avoid this horrendous experience of shame, which in the past have not been followed by an experience of repair.

Along this line, Teicher et al. (2002) point out that the brain is designed to be sculpted and molded by experience. Thus they suggest that alterations in brain structure, seen in early experiences of exposure to corticosteroids, are what we would term in Gestalt as organismic creative adjustments which are fashioned in the service of survival:

> ...we hypothesize that... postnatal neglect or maltreatment provokes a cascade of stress responses [the release of corticosteroids] that organize the brain to develop along a specific pathway selected to facilitate reproductive success and survival in a world of deprivation and strife. This pathway, however, is costly because it is associated with the increased risk of developing serious medical and psychiatric disorders and is unnecessary and maladaptive in a more benign environment (p. 17).

As this implies, the child's creative adjustment must fit with the environmental conditions present in the family. What are the possibilities? Perhaps a child learns to avoid this unsupported bath of corticosteroids associated with the experience of shame by not attending. If we just look at the symptoms, we might diagnose this child as having Attention Deficit Disorder. Or perhaps the child discovers that if he/she activates their energy through rapid movement he/she can, at least partially; avoid the experience of unsupported shame. In this case, if we solely notice the behavior we may diagnose the child with Attention Deficit Hyperactivity Disorder.

Aggression is a frequent strategy used in attempting to avoid shame. This is not surprising from a Gestalt point of view, as Perls thought restoring a person's ability to aggress was the primary path to undoing neurosis. While this strategy is at times useful, he did not see hidden shame (Lee, 1995). The shame-rage cycle as a means of attempting to avoid shame was long ago pointed out and studied by Retzinger (1987). From a neuro-hormonal point of view, several researchers have found that cortisol increases are not correlated with hostility, physical aggression, or delinquent behavior (Popma et al., 2007).

In a recent study concerning interparental conflict and child maladjustment, Davies et al. (2007) found that a child's diminished cortisol reactivity predicted parental reports of the child showing externalizing symptoms and exhibiting problematic behavior. Interestingly, the researchers were able to determine through their research design that it was the diminishment of cortisol levels that enabled this aggressive creative adaptation in the face of ongoing parental conflict.

In my view, the children in these last several examples have acquired ground shame, which controls their underlying yearning to connect, and they have learned to mask and cope with this condition through aggression. (See Kanner & Lee, 2004, for a description of working with adolescents in a relational manner.)

All of this points to the importance of understanding the family context in which the child's symptoms and behavior arise. What does a child's symptoms and behavior say about the underlying needs for support in the family in general? Answering this question means embracing the humanity of the family, and the family's connections in the larger world, in an appreciative manner.

Wrapping Up

Starting in childhood and continuing throughout life, the experience of shame is always an attempt to protect (both ourselves and others) —

automatically initiating our pulling back when we perceive that we won't be received and we don't have sufficient support. In mild forms (e.g., shyness, embarrassment, and disappointment) it assists us to identify the places where we don't believe connection is possible under the current conditions so that we can change our approach, support the needs in the field, or notice and move to the places where we can connect. Neurobiological research gives us a further understanding of how gentle limit setting followed by reestablishment of an arousal bond, early in life, normalizes this process (normalizes disappointment) as a part of belonging and as a tool for learning and living.

Neurobiological research also confirms that if infants are, consistently or more severely, left too long in the experience of shame, and don't experience a reparative connection of belonging, then trauma and ground shame result.

All of this points to the need to appreciatively understand the field context, in which symptoms present, when we diagnose. Following the signs of shame appreciatively in an individual can open doors to healing and belonging in the larger field that might not otherwise even be noticed.

References

Coleman, A. M. (2001). *A Dictionary of Psychology.* Oxford University Press: On Line

Cook, D. R. (1994). *Internalized Shame Scale: Professional Manual.* Menomonie, WI: Channel Press. (Available from author: E 5886 803rd Ave., Menomonie, WI 54751)

Davies, P. R., Sturge-Apple, M. L., Cicchetti, D., & Cummings, E. M. (2007). The Role of Child Adrenocortical Functioning in Pathways Between Interparental Conflict and Child Maladjustment. *Developmental Psychology 43*(4), 918-930.

De Kloet, E. R., Joels, M., & Holsboer, F. (2005). Stress and the Brain: From Adaptation to Disease. *Nature Reviews Neuroscience 6,* 463-475.

De Kloet, E. R., Oitzl, M. S., & Joels, M. (1999). Stress and Cognition: Are Coricosteriods Good or Bad Guys? *Trends in Neursciences 22*(10), 422-426.

Dickerson, S. S., Gruenewald, T. L., & Kerneny, M. E. (2004). When Social Self is Threatened: Shame, Physiology, and Health. *Journal of Personality 72*(6), 1191-1216.

Dickerson, S. S. & Gable, S. L. (2004). Emotional and Physiological Effects of Avoidance Motives and Goals Following an Acute Physiological Stressor. Poster presented at the annual meeting of the Society for Personality and Social Psychology, Austin, TX.

Frank, R. (2001). *Body of Awareness: A Somatic & Developmental Approach to Psychotherapy.* Hillsdale, NJ: The Analytic Press/GestaltPress.

Gruenewald, T. L., Kemeny, M. E., & Aziz, N. (2006). Subjective Social Status Moderates Cortisol Responses to Social Threat. *Brain, Behavior, and Immunity 20*(4), 410-419.

Hofer, M. A. (1994). Hidden Regulators in Attachment, Separation, and Loss. *Monographs of the Society for Research in Child Development* 59, 192-207.

Kanner, C. & Lee, R. G. (2004). The Relational Ethic in the Treatment of Adolescents. In R. G. Lee (Ed.), *The Values of Connection: A Relational Approach to Ethics* (pp. 113-134). Hillsdale, NJ: The Analytic Press/GestaltPress.

Kaufman, G. (1989). *The Psychology of Shame.* New York: Springer Publishing Co.

Lee, R. G. (1995). Gestalt and Shame: The Foundation for a Clearer Understanding of Field Dynamics. *The British Gestalt Journal 4*(1), 14-22.

Lee, R. G., & Wheeler, G. (Eds.). (1996). *The Voice of Shame: Silence and Connection in Psychotherapy.* San Francisco: Jossey-Bass.

Lewis, H. B. (1971). *Shame and Guilt in Neurosis.* New York: International Universities Press.

Lewis, M. & Ramsay, D. (2002). Cortisol Response to Embarrassment and Shame. *Child Development 73*(4), 1034-1045.

Morelius, E., Nelson, N., & Gustafsson, P. A. (2007). Salivary Cortisol Response in Mother-Infant Dyads at High Psychosocial Risk. *Child: Care, Health and Development 33*(2), 128-136.

Pfeffer, C. R.; Altemus, M.; Heo, M.; & Jianq, H. (2007). Salivary Cortisol and Psychopathology in Children Bereaved by the September 11, 2001 Terror Attacks. *Neural Mechanisms and Treatment* 61(8), 957-965.

Popma, A., Vermeiren, R., Geluk, C. A. M. L., Rinne, R., van den Brink, W., Knol, D. L., Jansen, L. M. C., Van Engeland, H., & Doreleijers, A. H., (2007). Cortisol Moderates the Relationship Between Testosterone and Aggression in Delinquent Male Adolescents. *Biological Psychiatry* 61(3), 405-411.

Retzinger, S. M. (1987). Resentment and Laughter: Video Studies of the Shame-Rage Spiral. In H. B. Lewis (Ed.), *The Role of Shame in Symptom Formation* (pp. 151-181). Hillsdale, NJ: Lawrence Erlbaum Associates, Publishers.

Siegel, D. J. (1999). *The Developing Mind: How Relationships and the Brain Interact to Shape Who We Are*. New York: The Guilford Press.

Schore, A. N. (1997). Early Organization of the Nonlinear Right Brain and Development of a Predisposition to Psychiatric Disorders. *Development and Psychopathology* 9, 595-631.

Schore, A. N. (1998). Early Shame Experiences and Infant Brain Development. In P. Gilbert & B. Andrews (Eds.), *Shame: Interpersonal Behavior, Psychopathology, and Culture* (pp. 57-77). New York: Oxford Press University.

Stansbury, K. & Gunnar, M. R. (1992). Adrenocortical Activity and Emotion Regulation. *Monographs of the Society for Research in Child Development* 59, 108-134.

Stern, D. N. (1990). Joy and Satisfaction in Infancy. In R. A. Glick & S. Bone (Eds.), *Pleasure Beyond the Pleasure Principle* (pp. 13-25). New Haven: Yale University Press.

Stern, D. N. & the Boston Change Process Study Group (2003). On the Other Side of the Moon: The Import of Implicit Knowledge for Gestalt Therapy. In M. Spagnuolo Lobb & N. Amendth-Lyons (Eds.), *Creative License: The Are of Gestalt Therapy*. New York: Springer Wien.

Teicher, M. H., Andersen, S. L., Polcari, A., Anderson, C. M., & Navalta, C. P. (2002). Developmental Neurobiology of Childhood Stress and Trauma, *Psychiatric Clinics of North America* 25(2), 1-32.

Tomkins, S. S. (1963). *Affect, Imagery, and Consciousness: The Negative Affects*, (Vol. 2). New York: Springer and Company.

Tops, M., Boksem, M. A. S., Wester, A E., Lorist, M. M., & Meijman, T. F. (2006). Task Engagement and Relationships Between the Error-Related Negativity, Agreebleness, Behavioral Shame Proneness and Cortisol. *Psychoneuroendocrinology* 31(7), 847-858.

Trad, P. V. (1989). The *Preschool Child: Assessment, Diagnosis, and Treatment*. New York: John Wiley & Sons.

Trevarthen, C. (1993). The Self Born in Intersubjectivity: The Psychology of an Infant Communicating. In U. Neisser (Ed.), *The Perceived Self: Ecological and Interpersonal Sources of Self-Knowledge* (pp. 121-173). New York: Cambridge University Press.

Wheeler, G. & McConville, M. (2003). *Heart of Development, Volume I: Children.* Hillsdale, NJ: The Analytic Press/GestaltPress.

van der Kolk, B. A., & Fisler, R. E. (1994). Childhood Abuse and Neglect and Loss of Self-Regulation. *Bulletin of the Menniger Clinic* 58, 145-168.

Editors' Note:
Once in a while you may know the experience of being in the presence of a great teacher, somebody who fluently and clearly, and with great presence, tells you the nitty-gritty about something important and cutting edge. Thus it was with Dan Siegel at the Esalen conference in 2007. The audience was gripped and enthralled way past their bed times as he laid out new thinking about the issues of relational neurodevelopment, the concept of the mind, and the power of mindfulness. From his classic, *The Developing Mind*, published in 1999, through *The Mindful Brain* (2007), which he introduced hot off the press at the conference, and since in *Mindsight* (2010), and *The Mindful Therapist* (2010) he has pushed the frontiers of neuroscience as it applies to relationship, child development, to therapy and to a well-lived life. His most recent books are one for parents (written with Tina Bryson) called *The Whole-Brain Child (2012)*, and a professional text called *The Pocket Guide to Interpersonal Neurobiology: An Integrative Handbook of the Mind (2012)*. Those who were at the conference knew how fortunate they were to have Dan present, and in this chapter, which is a verbatim (and slightly edited) record of that presentation, you, the reader can be in the audience.

3

Attachment and Mindfulness:

Relational Paths of the Developing Brain

Daniel Siegel

Dan: What I'm going to do in our time together tonight is talk to you about the human mind, and about what we know about how the mind develops, in particular about three big areas. Hopefully by the end of our talk we'll be able to get a feeling for how these areas may come together. These three areas have to do with something called "attachment." *{Dan speaks to someone in the front row.}*

Dan: And how old is your daughter?

Audience Member: Two.

Dan: Two. She's two. And what's her first name?

Audience Member: Sophia.

Dan: Sophia. So, we're going to talk a little bit about Sophia, and about how her relationship with her folks shapes the nature of her mind. And that's called "attachment." Sophia will be my co-teacher tonight. *{Audience Laughter}*

And then I'll talk to you a little bit about the notion of mindful awareness, and how there may be, in fact, an overlap between secure attachment and mindfulness that hasn't really been explored in the literature yet though I hope I am making a useful contribution in my book *The Mindful Brain* (Siegel, 2007). The book makes a proposal, that you can understand mindful awareness in a certain kind of way by insight from parent-child relationships. I will relate that to findings in the brain that are just emerging. So those are the three domains we'll be looking at, and if we can get that integrated in some way and show practical applications, then I think we'll have a good evening.

Let's start with attachment. First, a little context about how I became acquainted with this subject: When I went through medical school, I specialized in pediatrics because I was very interested in how kids develop. I wanted to know things like "How does the way Sophia interact with her mom right now shape the way her mind develops over time?" But for any of you who have ever studied pediatrics, you know you actually don't focus much on how children's minds develop. So, I switched to another field – Psychiatry, which literally means the discipline that takes care of (the "iatry" part) the psyche. I thought it would be pretty cool to learn about the mind in psychiatry.

What is the definition of "psyche?" Does anyone know?

Audience Members: Soul.

Dan: It's the soul, and in Webster's Dictionary, it's also defined as the spirit, the intellect, and the mind. And, in particular, Webster's defines the mind as this subjectively perceived entity that's based ultimately upon physical properties, but it has properties of its own, independent of those physical properties. It governs the organism and its total interaction with the environment. So, the mind is a pretty cool thing to try to study. However, I found in my psychiatry training that we didn't talk about the mind much. We talked about disorder and diagnoses and evaluations and medications and treatment approaches, but there wasn't much talk about the mind. So, I decided to go into child psychiatry, and I learned a bit more about normal development. Then I became a research person. I started studying normal kids and their families, and how the interactions between the child and parent shape the development of the kids.

Now, if I said to you "What's the best predictor of how a child will turn out?" What does science tell us about the answer to that question? What is actually the best predictor for a child to develop emotional intelligence, social intelligence, equilibrium, to have a sense of good connection to themselves and others, and to be able to meet their intellectual potential? Does anyone know what the answer to that is?

Audience Member: Attunement.

Dan: Well, yes. If you're going to observe the child-parent interaction, it would be exactly that. It would be attunement. But it turns out that researchers don't know exactly how to look carefully at certain kinds of attunement, so the best predictor is actually something that blew my mind when I first heard about it. It's how the parent has made sense of his or her life. Again, how the parent has made sense of his or her life, not what happened to that parent.

The best predictor was something called "the coherence of the narrative," which basically means, in English: in your life story, can you make sense of what happened to you as a child? And those parents who did make sense of what happened to them? The kids would be great, even if the parents had horrible things happen to them. The research shows that if you've had a terrible childhood, but if you've made sense of your life, your children will do great. They will thrive. I was amazed at that finding. This was back in the mid-80s when this came out. So, when I did my research, I wanted to know everything I could about why was it is that a parent making sense actually made so much sense? Right? And certainly as a therapist, which I do for a living, that's what we do all the time in psychotherapy. We have people make sense of their lives, and here was a totally independent field of science, attachment research, that said it isn't what happened to you that will determine what you do, it's how you make sense of what happened to you. And that's also great news because a lot of people feel like attachment is about fate. If you were maltreated as a child, you will maltreat your child. Not true if you make sense of your life.

Now, if you don't make sense of your life, it *is* true: you will likely pass on, generation after generation, the same stuff you were exposed to. So, it's really a call to arms to have us encourage people to do self-reflection. Personal transformation is a form of prevention. Personal transformation is the idea that you actually look inward at your own mental experience and transform it. I was really fascinated with that. We're talking back in 1989-1990, just to give you a context. And what happened in 1990? Does anyone know what happened in the field of science in the 1990s? What were the 1990s called?

Audience Member: Decade of the brain.

Dan: The decade of the brain. Exactly. So, I became a training director in child psychiatry, and the decade of the brain happened. I found myself dealing with a lot of people who had been abused. The field of trauma was in a very interesting place because no one could figure out a lot of what was going on. In the late 80s, an amazing discovery came out in brain science – how memory is processed in the brain. I became very interested in that.

Integrating that into my study of this narrative business, I wanted to know what the biology of autobiographical stories was. How did we use the brain to make sense of our lives? Let's say I'm a person who had a terrible childhood and I haven't made sense of my life and we know that I will not treat my children well. But if I do something like have a great relationship with a spouse or go into psychotherapy, and now that I've made sense of my life, I will not do these terrible things to my kids, and in fact, I will appear in my narrative as a very different person.

What does the making sense process do inside the brain? Because it was the beginning of the decade of the brain and because we had these studies of memory that were just coming out in the late 80s, I was just like a kid in a candy store. Basically, what happened in science was we developed certain kinds of scans that we didn't have in the early 80s, where you can peer underneath the skull and look at what the living, normal brain was doing.

It was an amazing time back in 1990-91 to start figuring this stuff out. Because I was doing all of this stuff on trauma, there was a proposal I made back in '90 about the role of an area in the brain called the hippocampus.

How many of you know the difference between implicit and explicit memory? Let me give you kind of a sense of how this brain science was so relevant, and then you'll see how it relates to this business of attachment.

In the brain, you have these two layers of processing of memories that help us elucidate the nature of post-traumatic stress disorder in ways we couldn't do before. What is one of the general features of trauma when you have it as post-traumatic stress disorder? What do you know, just generically about what happens if someone has PTSD?

Audience Member: Flashbacks.

Dan: They have flashbacks, right. And what is a flashback?

Audience Member: It's a memory.

Dan: Good. It's a memory. And if I were having a flashback right now. Actually, I'll tell you this true story: I had a horse accident one time where I was dragged by a horse and broke my arm. Many years later I'm giving a lecture in Baltimore, I'm done with the lecture and go to my hotel room. I'm relaxing, having a nice dinner, watching a movie on the television, totally relaxed. And I'm watching the movie Seabiscuit. So, I'm sitting there with my feet up, just totally chilling out and watching Seabiscuit. Now there's a part in the movie where the saddle goes to the belly, which is what happened to me. I'm looking at this and suddenly my body is going like this and I'm tightening up. *{Dan contorts his body as if he is trying to right his seat position on a horse.}*

Now, I know I'm watching the movie, but my body is experiencing something which we could call memory but it doesn't feel like I'm remembering anything. I just feel like I'm falling off a horse right now. I know I'm sitting in a hotel room, but I feel like I'm falling off a horse. And that would be an example of a flashback – it's a form of memory, but it feels like the thing is happening now.

Nothing we knew before the decade of the brain, would explain how that happens. But it turns out that Larry Squire, a fellow at UC San Diego and Dan Schacter of Arizona, pulled together studies that could help us understand that there were two kinds of memories. One is called implicit memory. The other is called explicit memory. And here's the deal: when you have an experience, like when I was riding on this horse, everything comes into processing centers in the brain – perceptual processing, emotional processing, bodily processing as well as processing of your behavioral responses. At least those four kinds: emotional, perceptual, bodily, and behavioral.

You also have something called mental models, which is where you generalize things. So, let's say Sophia has a sense of her mom being this care giving person because that's the experience she is having, and she generalizes it. So, she creates a general mental model that that's her relationship with her mom.

Mental models are a form of this implicit memory. And then we have a sixth thing which is called priming, where you get yourself ready. So as I'm watching this movie, my implicit priming sees that this guy is starting to lean over on the horse, so my whole system readies itself to fall off the horse.

So, here what you see is that the brain is at its first layer of memory, a process that is constantly happening. And there are two things about implicit memory you need to know about that are different from what anyone could ever describe before.

Number One: you do not need to pay any attention to encode things into implicit memory. Very, very important. In trauma sometimes, people are able to do something called disassociate. I can think about these beautiful beams in the ceiling or trees in a forest while my body is being assaulted. So, I'm not paying attention to what these intruders are doing to my body, I'm imagining this forest full of beautiful trees. I'm paying attention to trees in my imagination, and everything that is happening to my body I won't remember in this other kind of memory: explicit. You don't need to pay attention to get things into implicit memory. That's number one.

The second thing that's really important is when you retrieve an implicit memory, it doesn't feel like it's coming from the past — a really amazing finding.

Now, under normal conditions, you automatically pull together the important parts of these puzzle pieces of implicit memory in an area of the brain called the hippocampus. Now we're talking about the second kind of memory — explicit memory, which works through attention. It pulls these pieces of implicit memory together into two forms of memory. One is factual memory, otherwise known as semantic. This includes all the facts we have about life. And the second thing is it pulls them together in something called episodic memory. Like, I'm remembering when I fell off the horse. So, explicit memory is episodic, and factual memory.

This capacity starts around 18 months of age. So Sophia now is encoding explicit memory. When she was 12 months of age, she wouldn't have been able to do that because the hippocampus (a certain part of it called the dentate gyrus) isn't developed enough. So, at 12 months, she could only encode implicit memory. But by 18 months of age, the hippocampus is developed well enough.

The bottom line with explicit memory is you do involve attention, number one. The second thing has to do with your experience when you remember it. What's it like to remember what you had for breakfast? Think about it. Now, do you know you're remembering something? Yeah. That's an explicit memory. If you retrieve something from your memory storage, and it feels like you're retrieving something, that's an explicit memory.

Aduience Member: Are you talking about this like being a narrative sort of structure?

Dan: Not yet. What happens next – thank you – is when the child gets to be about three years of age, the prefrontal cortex, this part behind the forehead, develops enough to start functioning in a sophisticated capacity to tell the story of your life.

This raises an important question because it's all about answering this issue of what's the difference between this person "not understanding" and this person "understanding." Why are they different? How are their brains different? And what you can say is that what autobiographical memory seems to do is pull on explicit representation. Explicit memory, but it's influenced in the themes of your story by those implicit experiences. So you can find, for example, novelists who don't have much early explicit memory (because they had terrible trauma); literally all the fiction that they write is driven by what they can't remember. Explicitly. Similarly, we say "Oh, I think I'll write about this. I think I'll do this. I'll paint the picture this way. I'll sing the song like this." And it's all driven by implicit recollection.

Okay. When children get to be between three and five, they start narrating a lot. And what you notice about them is that a different part of the brain is very much involved in something that's called "mental time travel," a really cool idea by Endel Tulving, one of the fathers of modern memory studies (e.g. Tulving & Craik, 2000). And what Endel said was that it's this prefrontal area that assembles all these explicit maps together and selects them, sorts through them, and sequences them so that you can tell the story. That's kind of the crash course in the neurobiology and developmental memory.

Now, returning to attachment. Why would it be that a person who has somehow driven all these representations into this processing where we say they've made sense, why would they be more attuned to their child? Why would that have anything whatsoever to do with attunement? Wouldn't you think it would have more to do with how you were treated as a child? *{Dan points to an audience member with a question.}*

Dan: Yeah?

Audience Member: Maybe because that subconscious mechanism, that implicit memory isn't driving the bus anymore?

Dan: Okay. Great. Beautiful. So maybe you have greater presence because when you've made sense, you've actually done something with those previously non-integrated implicit memories that used to drive the bus of your behavior. That's beautiful. And that's actually a wonderful way of describing maybe what happened. We don't know for sure. But what I was trying to do, when the decade of the brain came around, was try to explore with about 40 scientists for about 5 years, these kinds of questions such as: How does the mental experience of making sense of your life relate to what happens in the brain? And we're going to come back to this question about why it affects parents at home, but first let's focus on another intriguing question.

What is the relationship between the mind and the brain? And why do we even care about that? First, when people usually think of the brain they think of an isolated thing in the head. We have one mouth, two nostrils, two eyes, and one brain. But really we have a nervous system, and whenever you hear me use the word "brain," I always mean this nervous system that's an integrated part of the entire body. Right? Even though we say "brain," you can look at it as part of the whole body.

The next question is, if the brain is the physical stuff in the body, what's the mind? How many of you have heard scientists say something like "the mind is just the activity of the brain?" Have you ever heard anybody say that? You think that's true? It's an interesting issue because a lot of brain scientists will have you believe that the mind is sort of the passive product of the activity of the brain.

That's actually, from the decade of the brain, one of the biggest fights that have gone on. You'll see people in the field, who we might call "brain supremacists," who will say things like "Genes determine connections in the brain and then that's all that shapes the mind because the mind is just the activity of the brain." This leads to conclusions like what I once heard one of these folks say in a presentation: "it doesn't really matter whether you're nice to your kids or not. It's irrelevant. I guess what I would do is just have some interesting books around the house so they got some interesting ideas. Yeah, that's what I'd do." He actually said that.

So, the first thing to say is, "absolutely not." In fact, the brain is determined in its connections by genes, but then experience absolutely, one hundred percent shapes the ongoing development of the connections in the brain. And the reason we're interested in connections in the brain is because it's the connections that determine, in part, how the mind emerges. Or, the best way to say it is probably how "the mind rides along the neural firing patterns."

But the other reason, besides genetics, is to be very cautious about the words we use because here's what we've discovered in the last few years: the mind, which we'll define in a moment, can change the brain. The mind can absolutely change the brain.

In fact, I work at a place called the Center for Culture, Brain, and Development at UCLA where we have anthropology people, and psychology folks, and brain-mapping people, and psychiatry and education folks. And we believe deeply that culture is the way, through the flow of energy and information, you can define the mind. Culture is the way, in fact, that we harness the brain to allow the mind to create itself. And for the last 40,000 years of human evolution, it has not been genetic evolution of the brain that's shaped human culture. It's been something called cultural evolution, which is basically the passage of memes or ideas that shape how the brain functions.

So, if we have a child who was born 40,000 years ago and got frozen. And we brought her in her ice block. And then we had a baby that was born today and brought her here. And we defrosted the frozen baby here, and she was fine. And we had our baby from the present here, and she was fine. And we raised them together. They would be at equal potential to use iPods. *{Audience laughter.}*

They are at equal potential because nothing seems to have changed much in the structure of the brain, in terms of its level of development at birth. But our experiences within the culture massively change. You'd know that if you have kids around and see what they can do and you have no idea how to do that. *{Audience laughter.}*

The brain and its connections are constantly being shaped by experience. So, let me do a crash course in something called neural plasticity while we're talking about the brain. There's a wonderful book that came out a few weeks ago by Sharon Begley that was hosted by a wonderful organization called the Mind and Life organization, the head of which is the Dalai Lama and Adam Engle is the CEO. And what they did was they had these meetings with scientists who go to Dharamsala and meet with the Dalai Lama and they talk about how meditation can alter the brain. And what she did was write a book called, *"Train Your Mind, Change Your Brain."* (Begley, 2007)

And it's a wonderful review of neural plasticity. What's neural plasticity? Neural plasticity is the way experience shapes the structure of the brain. And so if you want the most current view – literally, it came out last month – it would be her book.

It's a fun story to read. It's just written like a novel. It's really exciting. It's like an adventure story. And here's the take-home message about it: there is no question in science that experience shapes the connections in the brain. It's an absolute fact. And the interesting thing is that one of the most powerful features that influences how experience affects the brain is something called attention. Attention.

Wait, let me give you just a little example. You can train animals to pay attention to certain things because they know something good will happen if they do. If you expose an animal to sounds versus lights, rewarding some anaimals to pay attention to sound and some to pay attention to light – you know, the same amount of stimuli bombarding the animal in either situation, if the animal is paying more attention to the sound, the part of the brain that processes the sound will be larger than the animal that was paying more attention to the light, with the reverse being true also. So you can show that attention does that.

We were able to show something else in our mindful awareness research center pilot project. We gave people, who had been assessed as having attentional challenges training in mindfulness meditation. We found huge improvements in this population in just 8 weeks.

Mindfulness training, which we'll get into in a moment, is all about what you do with your mind. And you may know Sara Lazar in Boston – in Harvard. She was able to show that mindfulness meditators have certain areas of the brain that are thicker, that's proportional to the amount of time they've been meditating. (Lazar, 2005) We'll get back into that later. What is mindfulness meditation? We're going to talk about that, but ultimately, it's a way of focusing your attention.

These are examples of neural plasticity. So, we know that the "brain supremists," who we talked about earlier, are absolutely wrong. Parents help shape children's minds for sure, most likely their brains.

Let's return to this issue of "the person who hasn't made sense of, and the person who has made sense of their childhood experience." When someone comes to you who has been traumatized like me, let's say, with the horse accident, and I tell you that every time I go by a picture of a horse, I start getting a panic attack. What are you going to do to help me?

Audience Member: Drugs

Dan: Drugs? *{Audience laughter.}* Alright, let's go for it. Drugs. Because you have stock in the drug company.

Audience Member: We're not talking about those kinds of drugs. *{Audience laughter.}*

Audience Member: Exposure therapy.

Dan: Exposure therapy. Ok, what do you do in exposure therapy?

Audience Member: Show you a lot of horses.

Dan: They show me a lot of horses. Ok, so I get more and more panicky. *{Audience laughter.}*

Audience Member: Be there for you to experience that?

Dan: Ok, be there for me to experience it. And what would that do?

Audience Member: Re-traumatize you.

Dan: It could re-traumatize me. It could be re-traumatizing. Maybe just avoid the subject altogether. Just say, "Please avoid pictures of horses." *{Audience laughter.}*

Audience Member: It could help you make a connection.

Dan: There are lots of different approaches. If we took Peter Levine's wonderful somatic experience approach, you would say that I would stay with a bodily feeling? In my awareness, and here's the important point to tie these things together as we slowly build a picture – in my awareness, I'm going to allow myself to feel this pain in my arm.

Let me give you an example of a case in which that was the issue. This 26-year old woman is a business student and she gets offered this great job and she's terrified to take it. She's afraid she's going to fall flat on her face if she takes the job. She just doesn't want to take it, but it's a great opportunity. She's about to graduate, a new company, etc. Wonderful opportunity, but she's just afraid, and she's panicking. With these ideas in mind, I say, "Tell me what comes to mind about you taking this job?" She says, "Well, I'm afraid to fall flat on my face because if I try, there's all these details and blah blah." There's something about the way she uses the phrase, "I'm going to fall flat on my face," that just resonates in my body, as a therapist. You probably know there's a whole set of circuits we have that allow us to resonate with each other. As a therapist, it's very important to use your body as the instrument of connection with the people you work with.

So I say, "You know, there's something about you saying 'fall flat on your face.' Can you say more about that?" She goes, "Well I don't know what more I can say." I say, "Well, just say what comes to your mind." Now, I'm trying to create a spaciousness of her awareness that goes away from the automatic – "Oh, I'm going to fall flat on my face" [panic], to an openness of the mind where now, within our relationship, she may be able to tolerate seeing what that means. So, she sits there and she goes, "I don't know why this comes to my mind, but I just can't ride a bicycle." I say, "That's irrelevant. Go onto something else."

She replies,"No." *{Audience laughter.}* I say, "Go with that." It's kind of simple, but it's really important. Because within the space of her looking at me and seeing what's happening in my body, I'm basically giving her a signal like, "Whatever is going to come up, you and I can handle it. You may not be able to handle it by yourself, but together we're going to handle it." So, I say, "Go with that." She says, "Well, it's weird. I don't know what – OW!" *{Dan grimaces and holds his left arm.}* She goes like this. And I'm thinking, "OK." She says, "What's that?" And what do I say? "Go with that." Because what I want to do is give her this spaciousness of a receptive mind where the prior implicit recollection, instead of being automatically warded off, can be tolerated. So, she goes with that and gets this big pain up her arm and her jaw starts tightening up. I think, "Oh, I wish I had a camera." Because no one believes this when you're describing it in words. She's having this big episode and says, "Oh man, what is this?" I said, "Just go with it, you don't know what that is. You're going to be ok, just go with it." How do I know she's going to be okay? Because she IS okay! She's not dead. Right? There's nothing she can feel that will kill her. You know what I mean? That's what people think. Well, she might have been killed, but if she was killed, she wouldn't have been in the office, would she? So, I can tell her that she's going to be okay because it's true. The idea is – and Peter Levine has described this beautifully, you see it's just generally true with mindfulness – the idea is can you actually accept things as they are instead of having your brain tell you how they should be, which, of course, is "shoulding on yourself." And you don't want to do that because when you "should on yourself," it actually clamps down on trauma, totally. You know the story of the dog bite? You're walking along and a dog bites you on your hand. What is your natural impulse to do? Pull your hand away, right? And what does the dog do? *{Audience murmuring.}*

Dan: He clamps down deeper. So then what happens?

Audience Member: Rip.

Dan: Right. He pulls the flesh off your bones. Bad. Hard to heal. So, everyone's impulse to trauma is to pull away like the dog. And it scars our psyche.

The trauma was bad enough, but what's even worse than the trauma is the way we adapt to it and resist dealing with it. So, what do you do instead of pulling away?

Audience Member: Push in.

Dan: Push in. Because if you push in a quarter of an inch, your finger is going to go down the dog's gullet and what is it going to do? He's going to gag, and you lift away and you have a few puncture marks that are easily healed. It's the exact same thing with trauma. We have to put attention's focus right down the throat of trauma, make it gag and let go of our souls. *{Audience murmurs in approval.}*

Seriously. That's the idea. So, this woman who was grabbing her arm in pain; I wanted to give her a mindful awareness that wasn't an automatic pulling away from the trauma. That's the idea. Within mindfulness, what you see is that you get a transformation of suffering. And the same thing is true in the treatment of trauma. When you can bring full receptivity and acceptance – and I'm an acronym addict, so if I give too many acronyms, just tell me to stop.

But the acronym I love is COAL, which stands for Curiosity, Openness, Acceptance, and Love. And when you bring a COAL stance of your mind to whatever is going on in your memory system, it is healed. It is just amazing because the brain has a natural drive to heal itself. Our job as friends or lovers is just to try to liberate the brain's innate tendency to heal. It has a natural drive to do that. The problem is things get in the way. In order to make healing happen, we have to get the junk out of the way to allow it to happen. There's a wonderful saying, "I don't create the figures. I just liberate them from the stone." Is that Michelangelo? *{Audience confirms.}*

Thank you. The idea is that the sculptor knows that the figure is in there and their job is not to create it, but to liberate it by getting the other junk out of the way. The same thing is true with therapists. We don't create healing. If we had to create healing, we'd be just exhausted. Our job is actually to let go into the natural healing process and just let ourselves be a part of the pulling away of the junk that's in the way.

Anyway, to get to this idea of implicit and explicit memory, there's a natural drive to do something about letting implicit elements move finally into what you can call an "integrated state."

Now, here's the weird thing that happens. There are these different attachment groupings, and I want to tell you about one of them that represents about twenty percent of the U.S. population. If you say to someone in this population, "Tell me what your childhood was like. What was your relationship like with your parents? What happened with them?" you will get a narrative that goes like this: "Well, I don't really remember my childhood too much, but it was your average kind of childhood and I would say it was normal. In terms of my relationships with my parents, well, they were neat. My father was extremely organized and my mother was the president of the PTA. And that's what my childhood was like." *{Slight laughter from the audience.}*

Twenty percent of the U.S. population. When you're a researcher, like I used to be, and you research this, you're not allowed to ask more questions. You have to stick with the paradigm, but I would get these people and have them for long periods of time where I could actually get to know them. And that's really how their minds work. It wasn't just the research interviews. The research had always said, "Maybe that's not the way they are." But that's really the way they are. And here's the strange thing you get in couples' therapy. Say I'm the guy and I have my spouse here and she's crying, I act like I don't even notice she's crying. Or if she looks at me funny with these nonverbal signals, I don't even notice she's looking at me funny. It's called "dismissing."

Now, brain science can help us understand this whole paradigm of this person. If we dove into the brain, how many sides does a brain have? Two. That's an easy one. It's got a left side and a right side, and what's the difference between the left and the right side of the brain? One's on the left, one's on the right. *{Audience laughter.}*

No. Let's go with the "L's" first. Nature did this on purpose for memory's sake. There are four Ls. The first is Linear. Like, this sentence that I'm saying right now? My left hemisphere loves this sentence. It's going in a linear direction. It wouldn't like a painting. There are no paintings up here [on stage], but it wouldn't like a painting. Left is linear, whereas the right is more holistic. What's another "L" for the left?

Audience Member: Logic.

Dan: Logical. And the kind of logic that the left does is called "syllogistic reasoning." What that means is it's always looking for cause-effect relationships. What caused that? Why did that cause that? So, if I tell you that the left is in charge of those "why" questions, and I said to you, "At what age does a child's left hemisphere really start developing a lot?" Three. Two to three years of age is when most kids boogie like crazy with "Why?" And you know that their left hemisphere has finally arrived. It turns out the right hemisphere develops first, and instead of having syllogistic reasoning, it specializes in visual-spatial processing, just seeing things as they are. It doesn't really care about why things are the way they are. So, logic, linear...

Audience Member: If there's trauma early on, at two or three, does that impact the linear development?

Dan: Sure. There are some really important studies on trauma in the brain, and one of the things it affects is the corpus callosum, which connects the two hemispheres. It doesn't grow as well. For severe abuse, it doesn't grow as well. There are different areas of the brain that are probably integrative, that some studies suggest, don't grow as well either. The cerebellum and certain fibers that come from the prefrontal brain downward don't seem to grow as well. Those are all integrative fibers that don't seem to do as well with trauma. So, what's a third "L"?

Audience Member: Language.

Dan: Language. Good. Linguistic language. Words. And instead of the words of the left, what does the right have going for it? Non-verbal communication. If we want to teach this to other people, this is the way we do it. Watch me right here. You do eye contact, facial expression, tone of voice, posture, gestures, timing, and intensity of response. You can teach people to be more attuned. Very important. Instead of language the right brain has the non-verbal stuff.

And then the fourth "L," which I never knew about until a left hemisphere patient of mine told me about it. He said, "Dan, you left one off your list." I said, "What is that?" He said, "Literal. We are very literal." I said, "Ah, okay. That's a great one." Literal, Linguistic, Logical, and Linear.

Now, the right has got some amazing things going for it. First of all, it develops in the first two or three years of life, and it's not only developing in a huge way, but it's dominant in its activity. So, Sophia is a big right hemisphere kid. If you have a parent who doesn't know how to communicate with right hemisphere signals, that kid is going to be left-brained. It's a very important issue when we're parents to remember how to communicate with our right hemispheres. Here are the things the right hemisphere does: stress regulation, primarily in the right. Integrated map of the whole body is only in the right hemisphere. Primary spontaneous emotion is primarily in the right hemisphere.

Here's the thing that blew my mind, I couldn't believe it, it's such an amazing reality: right hemisphere autobiographical representations are non-verbal.

Here's the really amazing finding: 40,000 years ago, we started to make paintings in caves as a people. As far as we could tell, we're the only species that could tell stories. What is a story in modern times, not just a cave painting? If you had to define a story, what is a story? We were talking about this autobiographical story that makes sense or doesn't make sense.

Audience Member: Memory.

Dan: Story is memory.

Audience Member: A beginning, a middle, and an end.

Dan: A beginning, a middle, and an end. Some people say it's a linear telling of a sequence of events that has two components to it. One is the landscape of what is called action, and the other is the landscape of consciousness or mental events. The mental experience. There's the stuff you can see as behaviors and the stuff of the mind. If I said to you that a linear telling of a sequence of events that includes the behaviors and the mental life of a people in it, how do you tell a story? What part of your brain is driven to tell a story?

Audience Member: The left part wants to makes sense.

Dan: The left hemisphere wants to make sense in a linear way. Exactly. And a guy named Michael Gazzaniga who is down in Santa Barbara will tell you that, in fact, the left hemisphere has what is called a narrator. The left hemisphere has the drive to tell a story. If you're going to tell an autobiographical story, how do you do it? Where do you get the autobiographical goods? Where are they? The right hemisphere. But you're telling the story with the left, so what do you have to do?

Audience: Integrate.

Dan: Integrate. Bravo. So, there is one of the take-home messages. When you've integrated the left and right hemisphere, you've made sense of your life.

Audience member (referencing a revelation): That's funny. It feels like an "Ohhh!"

Dan: That's right. It feels like an "Ohhh!" And, in fact, integration can be seen as pulling out implicit memory, integrating it through the hippocampus with your explicit memory. That is a form of integration. Narratives that make sense integrate all sorts of things. One of the ways that I can't remember things about my childhood is that I've grown up over here in the left hemisphere and I really don't have much of my right that I have access to. When you actually understand these folks from that perspective, you can do something I call, "SNAG the brain." Snagging the brain is Stimulate (S), Neuronal (N), Activation (A), and Growth. If you have this in your mind, which is this interpersonal neurobiological approach to psychotherapy; if you have a person like that with you, you do the adult attachment interview, you assess where they're at, you understand that they've grown up with this as a survival mechanism being primarily left-brained. I have a guy in his 90s who came to me with that kind of narrative, and I'm telling you after six months his wife came to me and thought that I had given him a brain transplant. That's what she said. Sixty five years of marriage, she goes, "What did you do to my husband? He is...great!" *{Audience laughter.}*

And actually, for you massage therapists, he had never let her give him a massage. After being in therapy for six months, she was touching his shoulders and he goes, "Hey, that feels kinda good. Do a little more of that." And she gives him a full massage. She had always wanted to give him one, but he always said, "No, I don't need a massage." He was Mr. Autonomy. The point is that neural plasticity happens throughout the lifespan, and I can tell you having worked with someone in his 90s that if you know how to snag the brain, you can actually help people by focusing their attention in particular ways to stimulate that neuronal activation. Here's the secret: when neurons are firing, they can rewire. That's the whole idea. It's not about what happens to us. It's about how we use the mind to actually focus the attention in a way that can transform the brain. That's the idea.

The take-home message about attachment is, secure attachment is how a parent's own brain has become integrated in such a fashion that they're able to promote integration in their child's brain. Now you don't have to read "The Developing Mind." *{Audience laughter.}*

The second thing is: How is it possible to develop this kind of making-sense process, like with the person to whom their childhood didn't make sense – again, this person's brain is not all integrated? One route is relationship. For example, let's say you have had a tough childhood, and you have developed insecure adult attachment. You marry someone who is secure; within five years and without therapy, you will become fine. But if you marry someone who is insecure, which is more likely, you won't.

The other route is what you do with your mind. It's like with psychotherapy; I can move over here and become a person who has made sense because I have integrated my brain. Remember, because the brain is an embodied process.

Now, I want to get on to mindfulness. Is it okay if I go on? Is it all right? *{The audience agrees with a collective "yes."}*

Let's talk about mindful awareness. We have the idea of secure attachment as a form of neural integration throughout the entire nervous system. I want to now go into mindful awareness.

Okay, so let me just tell you a quick little story. When I was running this group of scientists, we had many different sciences represented: anthropology, computer science, neurobiology, genetics, psychology and others. All sorts of different fields, and no one had any common agreement about what the mind is. I couldn't find anything in literature that would actually work, because everyone either didn't define it or had different ways of approaching it. Here is the definition that I ultimately gave to them that everyone agreed upon, and which I have been using for the 15 years since, even though I still think of it as a working definition.

The mind can be defined as: an embodied and relational process that regulates the flow of energy and information. And that's it. The mind can be defined – the human mind – as an embodied and relational process that regulates the flow of energy and information.

Audience Member: Is this your definition for any organism?

Dan: No. Information is a process. I'll say this, does a tree have information?

Audience Member: Yes.

Dan: We can argue back and forth but the answer is it does not.... unless someone's carved a letter into it. *{Audience laughter.}* Information is something that symbolizes something other than itself. It stands for something other than itself. That's the actual definition of information.

So, when we talk about information flow, we mean something that symbolizes something other than itself. So, a tree is just a tree. A tree has lots of stuff in it – leaves and roots and all of that stuff – but it's not information. We create information by having the word "tree," for example. Or, our brain has firing patterns where you can remember what a tree looks like. The neural firing patterns are not a tree. It's information about a tree. Anyway, we could spend a long time on this.

The important issues are first, that it's *embodied* so it's not just in the brain. The mind is in the entire body. This is extremely important. You see, "brain supremacists" will just say, "the mind is just the activity of the brain." It doesn't make any sense. It's ridiculous. It's in the entire body. But it's not just the body. Because what's happening right now between me and you? What's happening? There's a flow of energy and information among us. We can't limit the mind to just a body. The mind is a process that happens among people. The mind is a regulated flow of energy and information.

Secondly, it's *regulatory*. Something that's regulatory has to monitor something and also influence it. We're talking about a regulatory process. If we say people are having suffering in their mind, they may have trouble regulating their mind in some way. When I published *The Developing Mind* (Siegel, 2001), it was an attempt to challenge the prevailing opinion in psychiatry, which is my field, where the brain was thought of as this product of genetic processes which can be fixed with pills. I really wanted to make a scientific document that said experience shapes the brain. The outcome of that is a mind that presents in different ways. I really wanted some kind of scientific tome that would be unassailable to prove that experience shapes how we develop. So far, the only single negative thing that has been said about that book was one review that said, "Siegel believes that parents matter. And obviously that's false! So, the whole book is based on the idea that attachment is significant!" *{Audience laughter.}*

That was the paragraph about my book. The rest of the review was an attack on the leaders of attachment research. Anyway, after that book came out I wrote a book with Mary Hartzell, my daughter's preschool director, called, *Parenting from the Inside Out*, in order to make those very dense scientific ideas available for parents. It's a book that lets parents make sense of their lives and basically integrate their brains. Everything about that book is supposed to be like a big hug which supports parents in their journey from not making sense to making sense. (Hartzell and Siegel, 2003)

When the book came out, parents would come to us and say, "Dan and Mary, how do you teach your parents how to meditate?" We didn't meditate, so I would go, "What?" And they would go, "Yeah, your book says that each parent should meditate." I said, "Which book says that?" They would bring my book to me, they'd open it up and they'd say, "Right here." They'd put their finger on the word "mindfulness." I'd say, "Yeah. It's important for parents to be mindful." They'd say, "Meditate." We went back and forth on this, and this is so embarrassing for me to say this, they'd say, "It's mindfulness meditation." And I said, "What is that?" *{Audience laughter.}*

I had based everything I was doing up until that point on science. This was written before 2002. There really wasn't much science of mindfulness meditation at that time. They said, "There's this whole field of mindfulness meditation." I said, "Well, let me look it up." So, I started reading the literature that was just coming out – 2003, 2004 – just a twist of fate, I happened to be a keynote address at a meeting where Jon Kabat-Zinn was doing another keynote address. We were put on a panel together. Was anyone there? *{An audience member raises his hand.}*

Yeah, so you were probably there for that. You probably remember there were about 700 people in this room, and I get up there and I go, "Gosh, I don't know a thing about mindfulness meditation, but I've been reading your work and all the science on it." I said, "I am so nervous because here you are – our nation's expert on mindfulness meditation and I don't know squat about this field. But here's my guess from what I've been reading."

In secure attachment, what you find is there are seven functions that emerge from secure attachment. Number one, regulate your body. Be able to have attuned communication, number two. Be able to have balanced emotions, number three. Number four is something I call response flexibility. That is pausing before you act, thinking about the best thing to do. Number five is insight, which Endel Tulving calls self-knowing awareness. Number six is empathy. Being able to put yourself in the position of someone else. Number seven is modulating fear. Those seven have independently been shown to be the outcome measures of secure attachment. When I hang out with my attachment colleagues, I'll for fun say, "Hey guys. Here are these seven functions. What do you think of them?" They go, "That's what we've proven in what happens when a parent is attuned to a child. Those are the seven outcome measures for secure attachment. What's the big deal?" I said, "I got these seven purely from going with brain research when a patient of mine had a car accident and the steering wheel hit her forehead and she destroyed this part of her brain. These are seven of the nine things that she lost." They'd go, "My God. What are the other two?" I said, "The other two are being in touch with intuition, and morality." Those just weren't studied in attachment research.

When I was looking at the totally independent field of mindfulness research, sure enough, those are the nine outcomes that have been found for mindfulness meditation. So, I'm on this podium with Jon Kabat-Zinn. I said, "I know this sounds weird, but I think that interpersonal attunement, which is the basis of secure attachment, is what stimulates the growth of the middle aspects of the prefrontal cortex. My gathering just from reading, because I've never done it before, is that mindfulness meditation is a form of INTRA-personal attunement. You have an internal attunement with yourself. That kind of attunement stimulates the growth of the exact same circuits in the brain and you get the nine measures." And so Jon got up and he said, "Not only yes, that those are the nine outcomes we've found, but it's also the process of being mindful. It's not just the outcome."

Mindfulness meditation is truly a way of developing the trait of resilience that comes from internal attunement. In our busy lives we're busy attending to the external world, we're never really attending to ourselves in a loving way with curiosity, openness, acceptance and love; what you do with your best friend. We don't do that with ourselves. So, taking the time to develop mindfulness as a trait is really the best gift you can give to yourself.

A month after I presented this to Jon Kabat-Zinn, I was giving a keynote address at my alma mater – at Harvard – and it was really weird because my fifteen year-old son was with me and I went to this place in Massachusetts General Hospital called the Ether Dome. It was twenty-five years to the day that I had decided to drop out of medical school and not be a physician because it was such a horrible experience. It was so inhuman. I was told that because I was interested in stories from my patient's lives, I should go do something else like be a social worker. There's nothing wrong with that, but I was in medical school so it was hard for me to do that. They said, "You know, doctors don't focus on people's stories and things like that," so I dropped out. But here I was, twenty-five years later to the day giving this presentation. My presentation was the role of relationships and stories in the development of the brain. So, I gave this little hypothesis, that mindfulness meditation grows this area of the brain [the middle aspects of the prefrontal cortex]. I finished my talk and this guy comes up to me, leans over to my ear. He said, "Dan, thanks for the talk. I want to let you know something. We just finished the study that proves you're right." *{Audience laughter.}* Sarah Lazar, who is now a colleague of mine, had proven that it's this exact region of the brain that's bigger in mindfulness meditators. (Lazar et al, 2005)

Mindfulness, I believe, is a relational process. People have been trying to study it as a form of attention regulation, which it is, and emotion regulation, which it kind of is too. But ultimately, I think it's a relational process that's actually harnessing the social circuits of the brain. Some people would say, "That's weird. You're alone watching your breathing. What's that about?" Well, you're developing a relationship with yourself. That's attunement. When I was at a mindfulness conference recently I looked at brain scans that other presenters had on their posters. They were looking for attentional mechanisms, attentional mechanisms, attentional mechanisms, and they would show these areas of the brain that are very interrelated with a portion called the mirror neuron system in an area called the superior temporal cortex, and they would ignore it in their findings. I would say, "Do you know that you have a superior temporal activation, they've got one, and they've got one and none of you are actually reporting it in your findings." They go, "We don't know what it does." I said, "It's very much a part of when you tune in to other people. I think your finding these people are tuning into themselves. You're activating this part which I call the resonance circuits. So, there's stuff that hasn't been published yet that you'll see in the book (*The Mindful Brain*) that over and over again shows that mindfulness is actually, in part, a relational process.

I can see that everyone is getting tired, so what I'm going to do is stop for now and we'll take questions. Let me thank you for your mindful attention. *{Audience gives a round of applause.}*

Audience Member: I work with two Asperger's children that I've seen a significant shift in terms of working on an interpersonal level, from not being able to play games with me to wanting to play games with me and making contact. I guess I'm interested in what you're talking about with the prefrontal cortex where that attunement and shifting is possible. With one of them, in doing some movement, and a game he made up, his attention and his ability for contact has significantly shifted. So, I'm wondering: Is that something that will hold over time or not?

Dan: You know it's a wonderful question you're asking, and obviously a huge area. Generally it's the area of social communication. Within that large frame there's something called autism, and there's something that some people think is related and some people think is independent, called Asperger's syndrome. Asperger's is a more highly functional condition, but other people think it's quite different, that there are other parts of the brain at work there. We actually have a school in Los Angeles that's sort of chartered out to bring adolescents with Asperger's syndrome in and try to work with some of these ideas. So, if you're interested in learning about something like that, it's called the New Roads School in Santa Monica.

What's interesting is that kids with Asperger's syndrome, as opposed to kids with autism, can actually follow instructions when you say, "Please look at the eyes," as a task in an experiment about looking at faces showing emotion. They would do it, with support, but avoid doing so when the faces showed a lot of emotion. And when they looked they would have this normal circuitry activation. So it's almost like – versus autistic kids who couldn't respond that way – children with Asperger's could actually engage but there was kind of avoidance of engaging too. It seems that if you could create a sensory world that is safe then they might be able to engage. We need to understand a lot more about that. In mindfulness what you're doing is you're creating, in your nervous system, a state of safety. This activates what you call the self-engagement system. In that self-engaged way, you then have access to all sorts of things like memory and feelings. Your tolerance for all sorts of things that were intolerable changes because you're more receptive. Mindful awareness, in many ways, can be called "receptive awareness."

Audience Member: Thank you for such a lovely relational talk. I think I heard you say that narrative was a very integrative function. I think I heard you say that mindfulness is a very integrative function. So I'm wondering if you could talk about how they relate.

Dan: Yeah. It's really interesting because as you probably know if you study mindfulness, a lot of mindfulness folks don't go anywhere near narrative. I have a teacher of mindfulness who is my patient, and he's spent decades doing this. He has absolutely avoided any movement toward making sense of his memories of a really painful childhood. After many difficult things he's gone through, he's finally come to therapy. In therapy, what we discovered was that in his zen practice, he took this attitude that if it's not in the here and now, he doesn't want to have anything to do with it, which is obviously very convenient! It's like with the dog bite thing – you just avoid it. The issue is: can you actually apply mindfulness to narrative, to an exploration of the past? In *The Mindful Brain*, I attend to that in great detail because I think not only can you, I think you must. To actually become fully in the present, you have to clear out all of the cobwebs from the past. As a novice I had this attitude: "Oh, he who practices mindfulness is great, in this nirvana state." And then teachers would tell me, "You know, people are running from really being in touch with themselves when they go into mindfulness a lot." If you really take it too literally, like "just be here now," you're never going to go there or then, to remember what happened. In receptivity you're really entering this state where you basically go inside your brain. I use this analogy of a "hub of the mind." If you imagine a wheel where you have the rim on the outside, and then you've got the hub in the middle, and then you have spokes that go from the hub to the rim. The idea is that you can widen the hub, which is this receptive awareness, so that any point on the rim is available for your inspection. So, if the rim had all five senses (sight and sound, etc.), you add the sixth sense (which is the body), and you have what I call the seventh sense, which is the mind. And even an eighth sense, which is a sense of relationship to others and the world at large and the larger universe. There are eight senses, at least. Maybe there are more. When the hub is widened in mindful practice what you do is you enter this COAL state (curiosity, openness, acceptance and love) where anything from the rim is invited to come. It's kind of like a stance of "bring it on." Anything that's in there, I'm open to it. It may not be pleasant, but I will accept it and will be curious about it. I'll be open to what it is and I'll be loving to myself. Narrative then is a natural outcome. Mindfulness is not to fight off the brain's tendency to tell a story about life, but to come at it in a very receptive way.

Some patients come into therapy who have very cohesive narratives. They're tightly restrictive and they are in states of incredible rigidity, who are very vulnerable to falling into chaos because they're so tight. They are not receptive in their narrative. They are not in this mindful place.

If integration is found in all these different things we do – narrative, mindfulness, and attachment – is there any science that tells us why integration is a good thing? In searching for an answer to that, I couldn't really find an answer, even though integration is a phrase that was used everywhere. Emotion is integrative, and relationships are integrative. The one science that actually described why integration is a good thing is a science called complexity theory. Here's the fastest overview of complexity theory you've ever heard. Number one, a complex system is open and it's capable of being chaotic. A mind would meet that criteria and so would a brain. Number two, is a self-organizational flow that's built into the inherent qualities of the system which allows the system to move in a weird way that's called moving toward complexity. When a system moves toward complexity it has a number of features, and here's another acronym, FACES. It's *flexible, adaptive, coherent, energized, and stable.* You can say that a system, which is moving toward complexity, is in this FACES flow. It's a wonderful definition for well-being. Guess what complexity theory tells you? The way a system allows itself to move toward complexity, so it has a FACES quality, is integrative. It's integrative. Integration is defined as the linkage of differentiated components. Integration requires two things: linkage and differentiation. It's not the same as becoming homogenous. Homogenized milk is not integrated. A salad might be integrated. You have to have things maintain their integrity and become linked. Now there's a lot of mathematics behind it but the bottom line is when you get into this FACES flow, at the heart of FACES is coherence. Here's another acronym for coherence itself: connected, open, harmonious, engaged, receptive, emergent, "noetic" (noetic – meaning a sense of knowing), compassionate, and empathetic. Coherence describes well-being. In this interpersonal neurobiology, what you have is not only a definition of the mind, but you have the definition of mental well-being. It comes from an integrated system, whether it's a family, a relationship, a mind, a brain, a society. An integrated system is a system that's moving in this FACES flow. Now, how do you tell when a system is not moving toward integration? It turns out there's this incredible statement in complexity theory.

When you allow the differentiated components to be linked you get harmony, which has this vibrant complexity to it. It has a FACES flow. When a system is not integrated, it's either rigid or chaotic. If you take the psychiatric manual of disorders and look randomly, you will find that one way of interpreting every symptom in the diagnostic manual is an example of chaos or rigidity or both. A way of reinterpreting this whole thing through the lens of interpersonal neurobiology is that we can define mental well-being and understand states of unwell-being as being either chaotic or rigid.

When "The Developing Mind" came out and I started lecturing around the world on this subject, I knew there would be different disciplines in the audience like psychology, social work, nursing, occupational therapy, art therapy, dance therapy, music therapy, psychiatry, and psychology.

I thought they would all have different definitions of well-being, so I would ask people. I had this research project of 70,000 subjects from around the world. Only two questions, not a big survey. Question number one: Have any of you had even a single seminar that defined the mind? Question number two: Have you had a single seminar that defined mental health? These are mental health practitioners, just so you know. All disciplines, in all countries. What's the percentage? Two to five percent said yes to both questions. Ninety-five percent or more of us, including me, have never had one lecture defining the mind or mental health. How many of you think that is just flat-out weird? *{Audience laughter.}*

This has been the most shocking reality. I just spoke to a thousand teachers the other day and I decided to ask the teachers that question. It was about the same number. I said to the teachers, "What are you trying to teach?" And they said, "Well, we're teaching people's minds." I said, "Have any of your educational programs told you what a mind is?" No, they haven't. There must be something weird about it because I was at a big, very wonderful conference with the world's leading scientists and Buddhist scholars. I raised my hand and said, "Let's at least define the mind." They said, "No, we probably shouldn't." *{Audience laughter.}*

What is it that makes people so nervous? These are deep thinkers. There's something going on where people, maybe their minds, are hesitant to find themselves or something. It must be me, because I don't have a problem trying to find a consilient view that scientists would agree upon. It's worked before and it's been a useful thing to do. The reason I bring that up in terms of narrative, to get back to your question, is to help us look at the question: "How do we actually live a life moving to well-being?" Then yes, integration is at the heart of narratives that make sense. It's at the heart of mindfulness, which cultivates well-being. All these promote integration. Integration promotes this flow of our system that has all these qualities of well-being: flexible, adaptive, coherent, energized and stable. It can happen not just in an individual being, but in a relationship between two people, a family, a school, a community and, I would offer for you to consider, a society. The more we can promote deep respect for people's differences and allow them to link together, the more we see the emergence of kindness. That's what emerges. There's a science that suggests that we must promote this kind of well-being, that begins with reflection. We must promote reflection as the fourth "R" of basic education throughout the planet. In the old days, people didn't know how to read. Now reading is one of the three "Rs" of basic education; reading, writing, and arithmetic. We should make reflection the fourth R. If we can, I think there's a chance to turn this species around and try to save our planet. *{Audience applauds.}*

Audience Member: In your work in making sense of the narrative, from your perspective, where does expression fit in?

Dan: Yeah. That's a great question. You mean outward expression of what's inside?

Audience Member: Outward expression and also expression in relationship, to another person.

Dan: To another person. There are a couple things that come to mind, and I think I'll get to the point, but if I don't, get connected with me about that. The first is just to say that there are some really interesting dimensions in terms of mindfulness that have been described by Ruth Baer in Kentucky, and I'll just list them. (Baer et al, 2004) They're really fascinating. One is *the capacity to be aware of what you're doing as you're doing it.* So, in a way, what that means is that in your awareness, you're very much connected to the whole process of what's happening. So, right now I'm aware of your nodding. I'm aware of my feet moving forward. It's all present within awareness. I don't know if you can call that an expression, but it's more like a presence.

The second facet of mindfulness is about *being non-judgmental.* There's an interesting way of reinterpreting that which I find helpful for my patients and students when I teach about mindfulness, which is not to use the word "non-judgmental" because the brain is constantly making judgments. So, people are constantly feeling like failures. Instead of using that phrase, which everyone is using, I use the words "don't grasp onto judgments." Because you cannot stop making judgments until you're dead. That just lets people sigh because otherwise you're constantly beating up yourself. You have to have a loving stance toward yourself when you're told, "Be non-judgmental." You go, "Jeez, I don't know how to meditate. I'm constantly making judgments." So, you don't want to create that problem. Non-judgmental really means don't grasp onto your judgments. You say, "I shouldn't have worn these socks today." Then you say, "Well, forget it. I've got these socks on." That would be an example of being non-judgmental. Well it WAS judgmental. I said, "I shouldn't have worn these socks," but I let it go. I would call it not grasping onto judgment. That's the second one.

The third one is the idea of *being non-reactive*. What that really means is if you have a response to something, it's about regaining equilibrium. This isn't really about expression, but it's the idea that as things flow into you, you take them kind of like in Tai Chi where the strength comes from the water, not the stone. This flexibility is what allows you to maintain this equanimity. That's non-reactivity. That's number three. Number four is something that blew everybody away: *To be able to describe and label with words what's going on inside of you*. Now you can see why I'm bringing this up. You're talking about describing bodily sensation. An integrated map of the body is only on the right side, but to use, describe and label words is on the left side, so you're talking about integration right there. This capacity relates to what Vygotsky talked about. Lev Vygotsky was a psychologist during the turn of the last century, and what Vygotsky said was that thought is internalized dialogue. Dewey and others were always talking about how the social is what becomes the personal. This isn't a new idea, but it's an important idea. As we stand on the shoulders of these giants, we can say, "Well, this mindfulness practice of labeling is, in a way, harnessing a social function of expression." Why bother labeling with words? Well, here's the interesting thing. It was found at UCLA in two independent studies. Let me just summarize it for you. You show an image of a face with an intense emotional response to a person in a scanner. The way the brain works is you've got these three layers. You've got the brain stem, you've got the limbic areas where the amygdala is, which responds to faces, and you're got the cortex.

What they found was that when they showed the face, of course the amygdala fired off, but when the person labels, with words, the gender of the person with the face, nothing happens in the limbic areas. If they name the feeling, like disgust or anger or fear, the entire system quiets down. You can show which area actually seems to squirt this stuff called GABA, gamma-aminobutyric acid, the inhibitory peptide. There are these inhibitory fibers descending from the prefrontal region. So, when you name it, you tame it. Words are not the bad guy. Some people say, "Oh, the left hemisphere is bad. The right is good." No. Creativity comes from integration. That was one study. Another study shows that people who do that the best were people with mindfulness traits. They really can squirt that stuff [GABA] down.

Audience Member: Perhaps people are not integrating when they try to explain what's going on rather than naming or describing.

Dan: Yeah, explaining is a whole different thing because then you get into intellectualization. You're getting far from the actual experience. In a way, when we're talking about mindfulness, what you're saying is: Be present with your experience and be so present that you just stay with it. That's a very good point. And so, obviously as a therapist, you go, "Yeah that's what you're always trying to do. Allow people to stay with it and also to speak to it." In my writings, I talk about it being a dual focus of attention, which is basically where one aspect of your mind is with your experience and the other aspect of your mind is attending to some other focus. When you have dual focus, it creates a link so that memory retrieval acts as a memory modifier. It allows these implicit processes to actually be modified. Bob Bjork was my research mentor, and that's his phrase – *memory retrieval is a memory modifier* – if you have this dual focus. If something is retrieved as just a flashback, it's just re-traumatizing.

The fifth one is *self-observation*, which is unrelated to expression, except perhaps that you're expressing something to yourself.

You don't see attunement discussed in the mindfulness literature directly, but in my experience doing it now for a year, I really think there's something about the notion of one entity resonating with another. In relationships, it's attunement. It's literally, "I've got a state. I express my inward state outwardly. Those signals that are coming out are then picked up by the other person who then is going to resonate with me. Meaning that he will be changed by what he picks up from me. Then he's going to send signals back showing me that my mind, my internal state, is inside of him." My energy and information flow, that's in my body, in our relationship, is inside of him. I can recognize that I am in him. His shift then comes back to me. I change in response to his change, and soon we're a resonating system. That's resonance. Attunement has resonance as one feature, but it allows me to maintain my integrity. I don't become the other person. That's that idea of, "I'm now going to be swamped by the other person's internal state and I'm exhausted. I'm depleted. I've lost myself." If I'm a therapist, I'm getting secondary post-traumatic stress disorder. So, we're talking about attunement, not "mirrorment," not pure resonance, not becoming the other. As a therapist, I see people who get so exhausted, they don't have the capacity to have this regulatory system where they maintain "this is me and this is my resonance with the other," which is one part of my experience. Only one part. It's not the totality of me. So, as you can really be mindful, expression becomes a way of joining, not mirroring. That's my response to the issue of expression.

Audience Member: Expression can also be an embodied expression.

Dan: Absolutely. One hundred percent. Totally.

Audience Member: In terms of your nine processes of mindful meditation, those capacities, to me it's about men and boys. Do you think this is just a cultural thing or any hardwired kind of thing?

Dan: Yeah, it's a good question. We were talking about this at breakfast this morning, this issue of male versus female. It's a huge question. There are a few books that have come out recently, some of which have been discredited as being perverted science, others of which have been looked at as being interesting – like a book by Simon Baron-Cohen called *The Essential Difference* (Baron-Cohen, 2003), which is about exactly what you're talking about. So, let me start with a political issue. My concern about saying men are "this way," is that people in our culture expect them to be "this way," and that can have a self-fulfilling prophecy. My personal experience, both being a person and also being a father, is that the last thing I want to do is categorize male-female differences in a way that it makes a person feel badly about being exactly who they are. That's my concern about that. There's a huge difference between the mortality of a male versus female, and learning differences. There are all sorts of differences between the hormones that are running around. So, of course there are lots of differences, and we should be respectful of that. But every child is uniquely different. It is true that more kids who are autistic are boys, and Simon Baron-Cohen would say that's because the male brain is more into mechanisms rather than social functioning, and the extreme male brain, in his view, is what autism is. I find that statement confusing when you really look at his own science because he actually uses as a prime example, a female. He just says, "Well, she has a male brain." What does that mean?

I've got to tell you what I have found as an attachment researcher: In the attachment world there are zero gender differences. Zero. People say, "Oh, you've got to have more men in the dismissive group, the twenty percent who are disconnected, not in touch with their feelings, not in touch with their bodies, and can't remember things. Those must be mostly men." I say, "Wrong." There are absolutely no gender differences in attachment research. I say, "People are people and we all need connection and attunement." We all need to integrate ourselves, but everyone is different. There are six billion different types of people on this planet.

Audience Member: That gives me hope. *{Audience laughter.}*

Audience Member: I've been thinking about mindfulness in the sense that it's kind of necessary but not sufficient and I was wondering what you felt about joy and delight in relationship in terms of neuronal development.

Dan: First of all, yeah, that's a good thing. There's no question. Here's the interesting thing: if you look at the studies of Richie Davidson's work on mindfulness, what he finds is in the brain you have people who do short-term mindfulness meditation and have a movement of electrical acitivity in the left frontal region of the brain. (Davidson, R. et al, 2003) If you look at a paper by Heather Urry, you find a discussion that's really enlightening about what left hemisphere shifts mean. (Urry et al, 2004) You have people who train for eight weeks to have a left hemisphere shift. You have improvements in immune function that are correlated with the degree of left hemisphere shift. So, the more left hemisphere shift, the better the immune function. Then you have people doing meditation for 10,000, 20,000, 30,000 hours and they have the most amazing left shifts you've ever seen. In the old days, the way it was interpreted as the left hemisphere is where you have positive emotions, like joy and delight. And the right is where you have negative emotions like being upset and sad and angry. You say, "Well, I want to have a happier life." Well, that's too simplistic. The Urry article discusses this notion of the difference between hedonic well-being and eudaimonic well-being. Eudaimonic is a Greek term, which means mental equanimity and balance. It's a sense of happiness that comes from meaning and connectivity and mental equilibrium. Hedonic well-being is how much joy and pleasure you get. They actually did an analysis of the difference between hedonic well-being and eudaimonic well-being and found the left shift of mindfulness meditation was not correlated with hedonia, it was correlated with eudaimonia. It's an amazing paper.

Now, the good news about that is that what this research suggests is that our baseline happiness is actually a trainable skill. Incredibly important point. The study of authentic happiness by Martin Seligman says there's kind of like a happiness set point. (Seligman, 2002). Marty has this nice research that shows that people who have a lot in material terms aren't happier.

This week I was doing a radio call-in show and this guy calls in and he says, "My kids want this thing. They want me to buy this thing, this thing, that thing. Buy this. Buy that. And they think what I buy them is going to make them happy." I said, "Yeah, if they won the lottery they wouldn't be happier." The idea is that connection to yourself and others is what breeds well-being and does shift your happiness set point. The idea is you can shift that set point but it's not by what you buy. It's by how you connect, and you can do that through reflection and through interaction. So, when you say mindfulness is not enough by itself, there's no reason to think that someone who was being truly mindful wouldn't have a lot of joy and delight in their life. I agree that if people have troubles and they're just trying to be in the here and now and not think about the past, yeah, they need to actually work on issues to liberate themselves so they can have deep gratitude for life. I totally agree. Those positive emotions are incredibly important. I think those would emerge naturally in mindfulness. I actually think they do. Why? Because I think they come from integrated states. When you get integrated states, you do see this incredible positivity coming out. There is an integrated positivity right here, right now. Thank you.

References

Baer, R., Smith G., & Allen, K. (2004). Assessment of Mindfulness by Self-Report: The Kentucky Inventory of Mindfulness Skills. *Assessment 11,* 191-206.

Baron-Cohen, S. (2003). *The Essential Difference: Men, Women and the Extreme Male Brain.* New York: Penguin/Basic Books.

Begley, S. (2007). *Train Your Mind, Change Your Brain.* New York: Ballantine Books.

Davidson, R. et al. (2003). Alterations in Brain and Immune Function Produced by Mindfulness Meditation. *Psychosomatic Medicine* 65, 564-570.

Hartzell, M. & Siegel, D. (2003). *Parenting from the Inside Out*. New York: Penguin.

Lazar, S. (2005). Mindfulness Research. In: *Mindfulness and Psychotherapy*. C. Germer, R. D. Siegel, & P. Fulton (Eds.), New York: Guildford Press.

Lazar, S. et al. (2005). Meditation Experience is Associated with Increased Cortical Thickness. *NeuroReport 16*, 1893-1897.

Seligman, M. (2002). *Authentic Happiness: Using the New Positive Psychology to Realize Your Potential for Lasting Fulfillment*. New York: Free Press.

Siegel, D. (2001). *The Developing Mind: How Relationships and the Brain Interact to Shape Who We Are*. New York: Guilford Press.

Siegel, D. (2007). *The Mindful Brain: Reflection and Attunement in the Cultivation of Well-Being*. New York: Norton.

Tulving, E. & Craik, F. (Eds.). (2000). *The Oxford Handbook of Memory*. Oxford, UK: Oxford University Press.

Urry, H. et al. (2004). Making a life worth living: Neural correlates of well-being. *Psychological Science 15*, 367-372.

Support

Editors' Note:
Making that vital connection with a traumatized child is often a tricky and fraught process. Mistrust and suspicion are understandable. Anxiety, hesitancy and other manifestations of the possibility of disconnection can be mutual. The environment in which such meetings and moments of contact occur is a powerful factor in the field. Neil Harris takes us into the heart of an organization in which careful attention to context and support of therapists, as well as of clients and significant others, works to enable and enhance the possibilities for relational connection. This study of excellence, through a fuller understanding of the nature and importance of support, is a fruitful learning. Neil folds in concepts from the field of mindfulness, and from Malcolm Parlett's writing on five key abilities for relationship, growth and change, to illuminate just what makes the work of this particular organization with troubled children so effective. Within a field in which opportunities for support of staff and client are grasped and maximized, 'good moments' arise and can be transformative.

4

••••••••••••••••

Something in the Air:

Conditions that Promote Contact when Meeting Young People Who Have Stories of Early Trauma and Loss

Neil Harris

An Introduction, Leading to a Question

The words of an adoptive parent: "When she came to our family she was seven. Now she is fourteen. The last seven years have been so tiring, so difficult. When she first arrived you could see in her face how wary she was, how watchful. She wouldn't leave my side, and at first we would find her sleeping on our bedroom floor in the morning. Then when we got to the point when she could stay in her room the nightmares started and she would wake, and wake us, every night, screaming so loudly it was frightening. Other nights she would raid the fridge, and eat whatever she could find. Things would disappear and we would find them under her mattress and she would deny that she had anything to do with them being there."

"But worst were the rages that she would fly into. Often we just could not tell what might have sparked them off and they could last for hours. She would break her toys, even her favourite ones. She would bite and scratch us if we tried to get close to comfort her or to keep her safe. Other children are always cautious around her and she's really struggled to make friends. It's really upsetting that sometimes you get a glimpse of the loving and lovely child that she is, but that is nearly always hidden. We've gone wherever we can to try and get help, but often it's not there when we really need it. We're worried she's going to really put herself at risk one way or another now she is wanting more independence, but in many ways she is so immature, and really doesn't seem to understand what other people feel, or what they might do. She is just beginning to distinguish between us as family, and strangers, but to start with she was completely indiscriminate in who she went up to to ask for sweets or whatever, and we had to keep an eye on her absolutely all the time. We haven't really been able to enjoy a holiday in seven years. Trying to make sense of it all has been an uphill struggle, and we've only gradually found out how her life was before she came to us. Her parents used drugs heavily, and often she was left to fend for herself. There was a lot of violence in the home, and we know that she saw it, and sometimes she has said how frightened she was, but mostly she hasn't talked about those times. We weren't really given many details before we adopted her, and not much advice on how we could help her."

As I heard this I really felt the exhaustion and concern of this girl's parent, the frustration of not knowing what to do next, and their fear for their daughter's future. There was, literally, a crying need for properly resourced, co-ordinated and informed help. Many readers, I am sure, will be familiar with this kind of situation and response, and we might all try and work with the best possible intent, and with the best current information about the developmental consequences of early abuse and neglect at our fingertips. But I am equally sure that many will also be familiar with the disappointments and frustrations of such work. To quote Dan Hughes (2006, p. 39), an expert in the field who terms his approach Dyadic Developmental Psychotherapy, "We cannot endlessly attempt "family preservation" programs while the children in such programs continue to experience emotional abuse and neglect and remain at risk for physical and sexual abuse. Living for months in circumstances of emotional abuse and neglect is causing significant psychological damage to the minds and hearts of these children. When mental health and social services providers refuse to recognize that reality, we all have little reason to hope that our society will ever take the developmental needs of these children seriously."

So when these children are moved to a placement with an adoptive family, or if they are in long-term foster care it is crucial that they move into a reparative field, a highly complex field that places high demands on all who are part of it. The question I want to address is: What field conditions maximize the chances of successful engagement and intervention with these young people and their families?

Some Background Thinking

There is a huge literature and accompanying industry concerning thoughts on organizations that "work" in terms of service delivery, customer satisfaction, profit – or whatever outcome measure is plucked from the ether against which to measure whatever that word "work" means. More specifically there is a literature considering the effective functioning of organizations that deal with psychiatric and psychological issues (e.g. Main 1957, Bayney 2005). Organisations have also been thought of as if they are themselves a complex organism with mechanisms of homeostasis, and self-regulating dynamics (e.g. Merry and Brown 1987, Bentley 2001). There are papers describing the functioning of residential units, therapeutic milieu, staff groups and the like, informed by group dynamic insights (e.g. Main 1957).

There is a special case – organizations that work with, and intervene with, children who have histories of severe early trauma and very disturbed patterns of behavior in attachment relationships. These issues are being recognized more commonly in the light of the emerging literature on the symptoms, presentation of, and treatment of trauma, and also with more widespread familiarity with the concepts of attachment theory. It may also be the case that children with these histories are in fact becoming more frequent, as a relative breakdown in family structures is a feature of the late 20th century and the early third millennium. There is little literature addressing these issues from the perspective of phenomenology and field theory – one example is that of Kanner and Lee (2004) describing the field conditions that they have worked towards in working with disturbed adolescents.

In my experience, working with severely traumatized, attachment disordered children and their carers can be difficult and challenging. Carers and professionals can often feel overwhelmed by the challenges they face. They can mirror the children in key ways, feeling isolated, anxious, angry and argumentative, and worried about "failure." The possibility of vicarious traumatization is present, especially when the carers and workers do not have the capacity or opportunity to process and reflect on what they hear and experience. (McCann and Pearlman 1990). The theory of issues such as containment, supervision, reflective practice and so on, is well developed, but there are problems putting this into practice that will be familiar to anyone who has worked in a team or unit with this client group. At the worst there is a perpetual sense of impending chaos or disintegration, and high rates of staff sickeness, burn out and resignation. The ways in which these children are primed and damaged by repeated intense experiences of shame are described by Robert Lee elsewhere in this volume.

The thrust of what I want to say is that it may be useful to conceptualise some key issues that support success in such a workplace as intimately related to issues of attachment and neurodevelopment, and the emerging links that these fields have to the capacity for mindfulness.

In order to get my message across I want to describe an experience I had recently in working with an organization that seems to me to be a successful embodiment and expression of good practice, a benchmark in the field. I then want to convey how this organization itself has developed, by sharing my interview with two of the founders of the organization (Family Futures Consortium based in London, England) and to present, in hypothetical form, some possible reasons why the organization seems to work so well.

An Episode, a Meeting

I want to tell you about a meeting I had with a young man recently. He was 17 years old. I was due to meet with him to make a psychiatric assessment. I had been asked to do this by Family Futures, whom I consult to and who work with children with deeply traumatized early histories, especially families who have adopted such children, and also with children in long-term foster care. Often these children have experienced multiple placements, severe neglect, sexual abuse, physical abuse. They may have been exposed in utero to their mother's substance abuse or alcohol abuse. You all know these kinds of children, the ones who have difficulties with their peer group at school, realize this and struggle, and are at risk of becoming depressed. Often this is then enacted through anger leading to further isolation and disconnection from others. Their families report that they have a desperate need to control situations and interactions. They have an acutely heightened sense of justice, fairness, right and wrong but are often only able to see things from their own point of view. Their capacity to empathize is impaired, not only because of a deficit in early modeling of this with care givers, but also, as we now know, because of damage to the developing brain with developmental loss of neuronal connection and neuronal numbers, particularly in the right prefrontal cortical areas, but also in other areas of the limbic system. They are often dysregulated emotionally, with rapid swings into anger and rage, or into fear, dissociation and distress.

I was told that the person I was going to meet might be difficult to engage with. The assessments previously performed had found him to be very impulsive, very fidgety, a person who had difficulty sitting still and talking. He was described as a person who reacted very quickly to any challenge, and there was a high likelihood that he would disengage and walk out of the room in which I would meet him. There was a prediction that he might quickly become angry and I was told that managing his feelings was very difficult for him.

The presenting problem recently had been that he had been in Court facing charges of assault and also theft. He faced a possible custodial sentence. Since that charge he had also been caught on CCTV assaulting a person in the street, holding a knife to their neck. He was drinking very heavily, and lived in squalor on his own.

He is an adopted child. He had been with his parents since the age of four. They were still warmly well-intentioned towards him, despite all the challenges that they had faced, but felt at their wits' end and were wondering how to go on supporting him. All attempts to help him live a more organized and adapted life met with rejection or failure. He was particularly vitriolic in his anger towards his adoptive mother who really did not feel safe when she was on her own with him anymore.

He had been sexually abused in one of his placements prior to adoption and this had been enacted with one or two incidents of abuse towards his younger adoptive sibling.

So who was I going to meet? How was I going to be able to spend time with him? Would I be able to meet with him in a way that would allow any real form of proper assessment? I pondered these questions as I travelled up to London on the train one morning. The first thing I was aware of as I considered the day ahead, was that Family Futures had already moved to take care of me in order that I might make a good assessment. They had told me that they would only book in this one meeting that day and that after that the rest of the day would be filled with consultation slots to members of the team. So I could breathe more easily, girding myself for perhaps the one major challenge of the day. Even that change in the field had taken good connection to achieve. I had been able to feed back to the team manager my sense of exhaustion and of feeling somewhat overwhelmed after meeting two very disturbed youngsters in a day a couple of months previously. I had been invited to a team supervision meeting. I had been listened to carefully, taken seriously, respected and my needs had been taken into account.

So I met with the young man's key worker in the team and we thought about how best to structure the morning. I was going to meet with both him and with his parents. We thought we would do this separately because of the inflamed nature of the relationships between him and his parents, his mother in particular. I wanted to demonstrate to him that, just as I had been taken seriously, so my intent would be to respectfully give him space, have structure, have time boundaries and an appropriate physical setting.

The team works in a converted old Victorian factory building. The ceilings are high, the structure is very solid, the colours are light but neutral. The consulting rooms are, to me, just the right size to meet an individual, perhaps with their parents when the need arises, not cramped and not frighteningly, echoingly, large. The room in which I was to meet him also adjoins the main reception area. People pass outside and can be seen through the windows. There is a sense of privacy and yet connection to the other people in the building.

So whom did I meet? John (that's what I'll call him), met me with hesitant, though definite eye contact and a preparedness to shake my hand. He was dressed in rather dirty, baggy clothes, a peaked cap on his head, carrying his MP3 player, though to my relief the earphones were not in his ears! He came with me to the consulting room and eased himself into the corner of the sofa and I sat on another sofa about four or five feet away from him, similarly relaxing back into the corner of the sofa, against the cushions. I explained that I was going to meet him first and then have a meeting with his parents afterwards. I explained the length of time that we were likely to meet for.

I outlined a little more of the ground conditions under which we would meet, and how we would manage the issue of confidentiality when I spoke with his parents. I clarified with him the purpose of the meeting from his point of view, what he understood he were going to talk about and the sort of professsional that I was. Then we just began to explore what had been happening recently in his life and what his concerns were. Well, an hour and a quarter later, checking the time, I realized that I had overrun the time boundary! I brought the interview to a close myself. During the whole time we had been conversing in a reciprocal, modulated interchange, addressing some very difficult issues in his past and in his present circumstances. We had been able to talk about what he wanted by way of help and the fact that his perceived needs differed from those of some of the concerned adults and professionals around him. We had been able to acknowledge that he had hopes and wishes for the future but that intimate relationships for him were deeply upsetting at times, problematic and distressing, and he was able to say that he recognised that this was also problematic for others.

At no point did he fidget, leap up to roam about, and I had no strong sense myself that I was needing to be very active in helping him modulate affect and arousal.

Given the experience of others who have met him previously, what made this level of engagement and meeting possible?

To my mind the key elements lie in the lived and embodied philosophy, skills and knowledge of the Family Futures team. Entering the building, one encounters an environment which is not only comfortable, but implies possibilities. The building itself speaks of steadiness and endurance but also the possibility of inner transformation. The new space has been considered with care, with deep thought as to the various needs of the people who will come there, and how best to soothe, encourage and, if necessary, challenge them.

I could perhaps best characterize the atmosphere as that of being, as far as is possible in my experience, a shame-free zone. I remember when I first met members of the team, I had made a referral to them myself of a younger boy whose family were having such difficulty in managing their own feelings about his challenges and behaviour and emotions, that he was, in fact, for a while extruded from the family into residential care. The dynamics around this boy and the shame that was hanging heavy in the air, were difficult to tolerate at times. I had begun to dread multi-professional meetings, planning meetings, and so on. There was always an atmosphere of accusation, of a sense of failure held by all in the network. I can see now that the parents had a deep sense of shame themselves that they had been unable to successfully manage, contain and continue to love this child who had been with them as a foster child since the age of six.

When I first met members of the team to present my assessment to them I was anxious. I also was holding on to hope that somebody out there could help instigate change, and in this I know that I was paralleling the family's wishes that somebody out there with the appropriate expertise might help heal the traumatised situation. I remember the sense of being understood at last in my assessment that this child was presenting difficulties as a consequence of the profoundly neglected and traumatised first six years. The relief was huge. I remember saying to them that I felt like crying.

The team had picked up the work with the family, with the wonderful outcome that the family were able to take the child back out of residential care to his home and to have the resources and support and relationship themselves that enabled them to re-establish their love for him, warmth towards him and their commitment to him.

When I had started working with Family Futures myself I quickly felt recognition from them and I think that they felt met by me with my interests, skills and experience. What I see are very high levels of respect between team members; a preparedness to go the extra mile and commit not only to the clients they are seeing but to each other. There is supervision available for them that I know that they trust, respect and utilize well. So there is a network of connection already in existence before any child and their family walk through the doors. Somehow this imbues the space with all the sense of acceptance, understanding and capacity to contain that is necessary. I think the young man that I met somehow sniffed the air as he walked in and lf to be settled by the tone of the place, the tone of the ...ope the tone of myself and the tone of my voice too. He is not an isolated case. There are others whom I could tell a similar story about, but what I want to convey is what is possible when there is recognition that the same issues instilled and activated by early trauma and neglect are activated in assessment and treatment settings. I also hope that I have conveyed some of the necessary steps to acknowledge and work with this so that connection can be sustained just as far as is possible in every nuance of meeting with these young people and their carers.

Going to work with Family Futures fills me with optimism about what is possible with sufficient reflection, planning and commitment. Of course the resource issues are significant but this is inescapable when we are working with highly traumatized and complex youngsters with huge levels of need.

The Ground from Which This Possibility Grew

I was curious about how Family Futures had come into being, the when-and-how of its conception, and about its developmental history. I had the idea that it must have nurtured itself, and been nurtured, in such a way that it had developed fully functioning frontal lobes, well integrated with its limbic system, with a coherent narrative about itself and a capacity to reflect. However, of course it is not made of neurons, but of people. So I arranged to meet with Alan Burnell and Jay Vaughan, who with Christine Gordon are the three co-directors and founder members of Family Futures. Alan was adopted as a child, Jay has an adopted step-child, and Christine is an adoptive parent. To add the final personal ingredient to the field, Alan and Jay are a couple, with the all the potential benefits and pitfalls that this brings to the organization.

First I asked what they thought it took to create an organization that embodies the relational, corrective and reparative as a permeating principle. Alan's immediate reply was a little guarded: "I don't know," he told me. However, some key principles emerged, and the process of our discussion was as a spiral, moving out from their first realization that what was being offered to traumatized, adopted children and their families "didn't work." "We had to do something different."

They intuitively recognized that the therapeutic approach needed to be tightly structured, and intensive enough that, rather than trauma only being re-enacted, an emergent experiment, leading to novel experience that was then integrated in an embodied way, was necessary. To put it another way, the mindful containment of the therapist, the grounded attunement, needed to be directed, goal-orientated and outcome specific. Core values included equality between all involved in the process; inclusivity of carers, child and other professionals; and a philosophy that embraced the social and the psychological. These were counter to a strongly prevailing psychodynamic, individualistic paradigm that defined most therapeutic approaches to severely disordered children at the time when Alan and Jay began to develop their model. To reword it, I would say I was hearing about a field-sensitive approach that sought to create conditions that would support inclusive dialogue, and hence contact, and that through this, experiment with novelty and then integration of new organizations of figure and ground could emerge. That sounds like a description of the development and practice of Gestalt therapy to me.

Another prevailing assumption that they needed to challenge was that telling children about their past was counter-productive, to the point where it seemed anathema. Jay pointed out that it takes courage on the part of the therapist to imagine fully what these children have experienced, in order to be able to attune and empathize, and help their carers to do likewise. Without a proper acknowledgement of the child's experience they cannot be helped, and of course this is a challenge to the individuals in the organization. Jay and Alan were aware of being radical in their approach and had to weather many challenges. It was crucial that a member of the founding team was an adoptive parent who could offer first hand validation of their struggles and successes. Jay remembers moments of doubt and questions such as: Can we do this? Shouldn't we just get other jobs? They found that the emotional connections that they made with parents and with children sustained their passion for the project. They made mistakes. They sometimes "fell out with both sides" with parents viewing them as dismissive, and the Department of Health in the government seeing them as 'beyond the pale'.

The team grew slowly, carefully. "People joined us because what we were doing made sense to them, because they were also passionate, and because we had come to know them." The team grew in a way that had to 'feel right' to all its members. Through this trust is fostered; "there is no room for egos or paranoia, and there has to be a lot of support." The trust is multidirectional. The team members have therapeutic freedom that follows from managerial freedom, and a separation from monolithic bureaucratic structures. So staff do not feel threatened and helpless and this minimizes the conditions for vicarious traumatization. Transparency means that when a new member joins the team they are not likely to encounter, later, the shadow of unspoken politics, or other undercurrents. Compare this to the experience of many children newly in a placement, who say that everybody is nice, and find out the unsaid dynamics and issues later. As Alan put it in measured terms, "There might be an undertow, but 80% of the river is going in the same direction.'"

Words that cropped up in my interview with them were "passion, fascination, freedom, enjoyment, new learning." They relish their nonconformist position, without seeking anarchy or revolution. I asked them, tongue half in cheek, whether they would be able to bear becoming mainstream, to which they responded that they do not know yet what happens at the point where everybody speaks their language. My sense is that a common discourse about trauma, attachment and development of the individual has been rapidly emerging over the last decade, and that new learning is the wave that we can all choose to surf at the moment. And in the way that all parts of an organism integrate to provide maximally aesthetic and effective function, all members of the company integrate and blur roles and function. For example the administration staff are supported and oriented so that they can in-volve themselves in direct ways with the families, ways which are therapeutic themselves. For example, everybody might in one moment be necessary to create safety, for example by stopping a child running out of the building. Calm is a quality which helps bear the brunt of what children bring to treatment. The building is organized with a sense of calm in mind, and calmness is a keynote of the team as a whole.

Within that physical environment, which is a literal manifestation of Family Futures principles, the ground is fertile for the delivery of what Daniel Goleman terms "socially intelligent leadership." He says "Socially intelligent leadership starts with being fully present and getting in synch. Once a leader is engaged, then the full panoply of social intelligence can come into play, from sensing how people feel and why, to interacting smoothly enough to move people into a positive state" (Goleman 2006 p. 280). I think that complex interwoven strands of parallel process can then come into play, with this leadership style radiating out into the field, to team member as therapist, to therapist as leader of a session, to parent as socially intelligent leader within the family, to the child.

Another word that floats in the river and relates to this issue of radiated leadership is "wisdom." The team has a significant number of members in their sixth decade. "We've all been around the block a few times," says Alan. Yet the mixture of a wide range of ages in the treatment team is part of the recipe, part of the family. This is not some kind of mystical chemistry, but comes out of the open adoption of a biological-social perspective which makes intuitive sense, and "ties it all back into the animal kingdom in a way which can be generally understood."

The Challenge of Sustaining Creative Adjustment as a Team

This integrated responsive capacity is central to the abilities that Malcolm Parlett has described (Parlett, 2000). He lists five key capacities that support creative adjustment in the global field.

1. *Responding* – the capacity to be versatile, resourceful and flexible. We have to find ways to stay engaged, not to close down and withdraw. A sense of resignation can develop as a defensive solution to the sense of threat that sometimes is transmitted by the internal and relational experiences of the children we see. This has to be avoided. At the organizational level we need to recognize the possibility of a dissociative style of response – a helpless disengagement, with metabolic slowing and stilling. Curiosity and commitment, with a shared sense of support, vision and realistic goals are key to avoiding this. Staying on the edge of potentially stultifying regulatory systems is also a position that sustains the capacity to respond. The creative adjustment developed by the child in an abusive and neglectful early environment might lead the intervening team to mirror that process. Creative, playful, novel and unique interventions work against that possibility. This is vividly described by Jay Vaughan (Archer and Burnell 2003 p. 164 ff) who also emphasizes that "There is no quick 'cure': it is hard work over a minimum of two years, sometimes much longer" (ibid p. 188).

2. *Interrelating* – the recognition of the vitality that emerges from relationship. The relationships that we as a team can make with the children and parents, carers and professsionals we meet must be mirrored by a rich network of active relationships within the team. Isolation and

disconnection need to be actively addressed. As Main put it in the slightly quaint language of 1950s British academe, "It is important for such patients that those who are involved in their treatment and management be sincere with each other, in disagreement as well as agreement, that each confine himself to his own role, and that each respect and tolerate the other's limitations without resort to omnipotence or blame." That need for transparency, respect and humility is high on the agenda within the Family Futures team, and of course is not always attained. But the principle communicates itself to the families and children, and the fruits of that are ultimately a healing of old trauma, understanding and the growth of loving attachments.

3. *Self-recognizing* – the need to be oriented, and aware of one's position within the field, to have a direction and meaning. Family Futures is on the map, in a complex field of organizational relationships. As Alan and Jay conveyed to me, and as I have experienced at first hand in my work with them, a collective capacity to self-recognize and a continuing commitment to enhanced self-knowing at both the individual and the organizational levels. To self-recognize we must continuously ask ourselves questions: What is our purpose? Are we delivering what we intend? Which of our core principles are we acting from in this moment? What is the impact of this work on us? How are we supporting ourselves and others in this endeavour? These questions and others in the same vein have to be actively brought into the foreground as figures, and not left to become background assumptions. As an organization we have to know who we are in any moment, and of course, this is a constantly changing and evolving process of contact and identity.

4. *Embodying* – the full participation of the body in our creative adjustment. The children coming to Family Futures communicate vividly in somatic ways, often much more powerfully than they do verbally. They carry their histories in patterned embodied ways and within the team we need to have ways to recognize and respond accordingly. That is true at every level, from the attention to the physical in the team through yoga, through health in diet, and in the corresponding recognition of the dietary needs of the children seen, to somatically focused aspects of the therapeutic work. This involves a repertoire of sensitively attuned uses of touch (for example a parent gently touching their child's hand with a feather when touch has previously only been rough and aggressive or generated by a need to keep the angry child safe).

5. *Experimenting* – here with an emphasis on the recognition that every awareness and action has an impact on the changing field and that therefore, every moment has the potential for experiment and discovery and change. Through the attitude of experiment, we stay open to novelty and can continuously question habitual and conservative responses. The whole coming-into-existence of Family Futures has been a major experiment, first in the lives of its founders, and since in the lives of the team. This history can inform every therapeutic meeting and imbue it with the potential for positive change.

And as Family Futures moves into the next moment, this capacity to continue creative adjustment as part of the field is nurtured, developed and sustained by the enacted philosophies of the team members.

Parlett writes: "...we must recognize that *these abilities* are not things which people "have" as sole possessions. The enhancement of these abilities rests as much on the creation of appropriate settings and supportive environments, as it does on work with single individual's experiences" (p. 25). My view is that the individual who has these abilities has, amongst other things, reflective capacity, and the ability to explore and investigate novelty with ways of managing the anxiety that provokes. They have in addition the ability to use relationships in this process, as support or sources of soothing and regulation. And here my vocabulary blurs into that of attachment theory, and of affect regulation (See, for example, Schore 2003). One way of integrating these languages, is to introduce the concept of mindfulness, and to see this as perhaps an overarching description of the abilities that Parlett has introduced.

The Mindful Field

The greatest deficit in the early lives of most of the children who come to Family Futures for help is that of attunement. They have not been "held in mind" by a coherent and mindful carer. Dan Siegel (2007) proposes that "attunement creates coherence in the mind" (p. 193). He specifies that coherence as a collection of qualities. It is connected (i.e. in relation), open, harmonious, engaged (i.e. responding), receptive, emergent (i.e. arising with a sense of freshness and novelty), noetic (i.e. it is embued with a deep sense of authentic knowing), compassionate and empathic.

The key work with these children is to create the conditions in which coherence can develop in their minds. They can then move away from their highly controlling and rigid strategies, to flexibility, without becoming lost in chaos. Siegel puts it this way: "With the three elements in the triangle of well-being – neural integration, a coherent mind and empathic relationships – our lives can move in the direction of a harmonious flow" (p. 208). And in working with these children we are seeking to support neural integration, particularly of the frontal and prefrontal areas of the brain, and the tracts linking these areas to the limbic structures deeper in the brain that modulate and drive affect. I propose that any organization with such goals might consider itself as needing the qualities of mindfulness, that the goal is first and foremost to create a mindful field. In such a field a recursive generation of safety and internal attunement can emerge which "initiates receptive awareness in which executive attention is open to whatever arises in the field of ongoing experience" (Siegel, 2007 p. 132). An essential outcome is the existential freedom to choose, which for me is a key foundation of the Gestalt philosophy, and a foundation stone of resilience.

I spoke with an adoptive parent whose twelve-year-old son had lived in a residential unit for a year because of the challenges of his behavior at home. He returned to the family with the support of the Family Futures team. The parent said that the key ingredients that made this possible were that the team "made us feel that we weren't to blame, that we had nothing to be ashamed of." They had been helped to see that they had been doing their level best, and that it was "alright to struggle." They had "time to think" about what they were doing and how they were feeling. They developed trust in the professionals, and felt liked by them. They gained hugely in confidence, and they are a united family some three and a half years later. The young person himself, asked to give his own view, replied in more age appropriate fashion. "Dunno really!"

References

Archer, C. & Burnell, A. (Eds.). (2003). *Trauma, Attachment and Family Permanence*. London: Jessica Kingsley.

Bayney, R. (2005). Benchmarking in Mental Health: An Introduction for Psychiatrists. *Advances in Psychiatric Treatment 11*, 305–314.

Bentley, T. (2001). The Emerging System: A Gestalt Approach to Organisational Interventions. *British Gestalt Journal 10*, 13–19.

Goleman, D. (2006). Social Intelligence: *The New Science of Human Relations*. New York: Random House.

Hughes, D. (2006). *Building the Bonds of Attachment: Awakening Love in Deeply Troubled Children*. Lanham: Aronson.

Kanner, C. & Lee, R. G. (2004). The Relational Ethic in the Treatment of Adolescents. In R. G. Lee (Ed.), *The Values of Connection: A Relational Approach to Ethics* (pp. 113-134). Hillsdale, NJ: The Analytic Press/GestaltPress.

Main, T.F. (1957). The Ailment. British Journal of Medical *Psychology 30* (3), 129- 145.

Merry, U. & Brown, G. (1987). *The Neurotic Behaviour of Organisations.* Gestalt Institute of Cleveland Press.

McCann, L. & Pearlman, L. (1990). Vicarious Traumatization: A Framework for Understanding the Psychological Effects of Working with Victims. *Journal of Traumatic Stress 3*, 131–149.

Parlett, M. (2000). Creative Adjustment and the Global Field. *British Gestalt Journal 9*(1), 15–27.

Schore, A. (2003). Affect Regulation and the Repair of the Self. New York: Norton.

Siegel, D. (2007). *The Mindful Brain: Reflection and Attunement in the Cultivation of Well-Being.* New York: Norton.

Editors' Note:
Imagine a silent girl who lives in the depths of the forest. One day she makes a trip to town, and so begins the gradual process of her emergence into an expanding world, both outside and inside her home. She finds her voice – as she finds others who want to and are able to hear and connect with it. What she probably does not realize is that there has been a web of support woven about her, with incredible care and thoughtfulness. The web is complex, multi-professional and multi-dimensional. Ami Norén, the head of a Child and Adolescent Mental Health team in Sweden, shows us the depth of commitment and reflection that was necessary to bring this about, and the patience and sensitivity that allowed her young patient to open to opportunities, along with her parents. She allows us to take a trip to Scandinavia and into the community in which Mia lives. This is about clinical practice as an art form and as professional wisdom, and the importance of committed, coordinated, multilevel support.

5

The Tiger Girl:

A Story of Committed, Coordinated, Multilevel Support[1]

Anna-Maria Norén

I think I have a schizophrenic daughter" –

She was on the telephone one morning talking about her six year old, only daughter. The woman continued, telling us that the girl shifted identity constantly – Mickey Mouse, the old man, Pippi Longstocking, the tiger girl, and other identities could turn up during the

---

[1] Author's note: Special thanks to Robert Lee for support, fresh and good ideas, and especially the patience he has shown during our very exciting co-operation on this chapter. Child in society, the existential room, Lewin as an inspiration in Child Psychiatry, the fantastic mixture of inner and outer forces in the child's travel from fetus to adult, all this that has been my passion during my working life has now turned into an article in English. When I think of my work, I always do it in my mother's tongue where the experiences are embodied. To see my intentions and my struggling with words turn into a text, in a new language, has so many implications for me. I feel that it is my text, and I know it wouldn't have been there without Robert's supportive participation and guidance.

day. School was starting and the family's efforts to fulfill the demands on them to bring the girl to class had failed.

We invited them to the clinic, gave them a time to meet with the Erik, the child psychiatrist, and me, head of the clinic, a social worker and Gestalt therapist. When that time arrived and we greeted them in our waiting room, the daughter was silent, hiding behind her father and looking at us only when we had our eyes somewhere far away from her. We can call her Mia.

They were the last visitors for that day. Mia would not respond to our invitation to move to the room which we had planned for the first meeting. So we stayed in the waiting room and tried to engage her and the family there to get an initial idea about what we could do for them. The questions as well as the answers were awkward and tentative.

Mia had never been outside the family's care, never to kindergarten or other groups for children. She had no friends, never played with anyone outside the family, with the exception of sometimes spending a few hours with her cousin when her cousin's family visited on holidays. The grandmother lived next door and she was the only one outside the primary family that had ever heard Mia's voice.

She stood silently, withdrawn, unwilling to sit down, and was impossible to make eye contact with. Not a movement in her body, she kept all of her outdoor cloths on. The mother was the one who talked for the family with a bit of assistance from the father. Slowly we got the start of a picture that would take many years to complete.

It was them and the rest of the world.

Over a period of time, as we managed to avoid looking at or speaking to Mia; she walked up close to her father and stood absolutely motionless as if nothing was happening. But both my colleague and I were sure she was watching and listening – very carefully. In fact, when we attended solely to her parents she came closer and whenever we turned our gaze towards her she stepped backwards.

Eric and I attempted to create a narrative from the child's perspective of how the picture that was being described to us as well as what we saw before us was of a child who was frightened of everything.

Mia was interested.

The mother told a story of her own struggle with isolation – her earlier relationships, the tight bond to her own mother, her longing for her sister who lived far away, the demands she felt from society and the feeling she had that she had to defend her fragile daughter from the environment.

The task of conducting an initial evaluation in the waiting room and gathering sufficient information to arrive at a beginning sense of the interventions that would fit this family was bigger than the resources available in the room. We needed help from others.

It was now dark outside, the family left and Erik and I were left with questions but also with a sense of hope and trust that had emanated from the parents as they departed. We also sat with what we noticed about the dance we had with Mia – conversation and questions with the parents drew Mia closer to where we sat, and the slightest interest in her appearance made her step backwards.

The parents had said this was the first time the family had sat down together with anyone outside of the family to talk about the difficulties they faced in helping their daughter venture out from the security of home. Looking at this first meeting from a helicopter perspective you could also come to the conclusion that Mia was the one bringing her parents to us.

What was it in the field forces that had influenced Mia to develop in this manner? What were her own inner contributions to her difficulties? And most importantly, how could we help this little girl to be interested in contacting the outside world?

We decided that we would go to her world, her environment, to understand how it could be possible to grow up in this well organized Swedish society and be so isolated and so out of contact with the outer world. She must have been invited to check-ups, child controls that every Swedish child is invited to regularly during her childhood – several times the first few years, vaccinations, visits to the child welfare clinic, practitioners visiting the home, later invitations for health controls, developmental tests to see whether she was progressing according to normal expectations for her age. Could health officials tell us something more about her first years of life which could help us learn how we could be useful to this family?

Before they left we had agreed that we would come to the small town where they lived. The family would invite people they thought were important for all of us to get a broader picture about Mia and the life she had lived so far. We also obtained permission from the family to invite people we thought were essential for Mia's future.

The First Network Meeting

Present at the meeting were the family's General Practitioner (who was also head of the Health Care Center in the town), the class teacher, the assisting teacher, the headmaster for the school and Mia's mother, who came by herself without Mia's father. I came together with Erik from the clinic – 35 kilometers away into the forest and many more kilometers away in terms of culture.

We met at the headmaster's office. While we and the family had invited people that we believed would be important in supporting Mia's development, we also knew there was some reason why this girl's and this family's struggles had gone unnoticed until now. Hence, these people might not know how to be interested in or how to attend to what Mia needed, and we would most likely need to be active in focusing the meeting. At the same time we understood these people to be well-meaning, and we did not want to be disrespectful toward them.

In fact, as the meeting unfolded, a picture of emptiness emerged. There were people around the girl, but at a distance. No one was there "with her." Officials had questions, ideas, and interpretations, but with a "wait and see" attitude, low expectations, and a longing for someone else to come in and change the situation. While their stories about the family were factual and informative they didn't have an expectation of engagement. It was clear that people didn't know what to do, had lost their initiative, and were waiting, as Mia waited, for someone to "knock on the door."

In some ways this was all very understandable as we were the only people in the room who were versed in child psychiatry. Still the stark disconnection so prevalent in that first meeting with the family will forever be etched in my memory.

They told us about a teacher who had recently moved from one of the more populated towns in Sweden, who worked at the kindergarten and who had experience in an inpatient child psychiatry clinic. This teacher did not have Mia's family history to relate to, she just saw a child that appeared strange and a family that had been used to that. She had met with Mia and her mother a few times in preparation for kindergarten. All children in Sweden are invited to kindergarten and are expected to have at least the preschool year together with their coming classmates.

Since Mia, although with only a few trials, never managed to attend kindergarten class, this teacher tried to reach out to her at her home, without success. Her approach was to expect and insist on, with patient understanding, behavior that would support the girl's exploration of independent skills. "I will wait for you, Mia, until you cross the door-step and I will be here with you the day you find that possible," was the nonverbal message to the girl.

Although the situation needed further support, at last there was a story of someone who was attempting to engage Mia. She was our woman. We will call her Susan.

The Existential Room

So many people in the family's village had known *about* the child, but who in actuality *knew* her? The emptiness and the silence that surrounded Mia and her family were almost unbearable – so much life that waited to be lived, so many intentions that fell flat without anyone noticing or responding to them, so much longing and love that had never found connection.

We were touched by the history, and astonished and frightened by the multitude and severity of Mia's symptoms. With what we had observed and the initial information that we had collected, from an individualistic perspective, there was already a short list of serious diagnoses for the girl.

The overwhelming question that faced us was whether it was possible for a child psychiatry clinic to "treat" a seriously disturbed child primarily with interventions in the psycho-social field, more or less on a community level. If you offer a better or more nourishing environment – thoroughly investigating the field forces and then intervening on various levels to reduce the impediments to connective growth and reinforce the supportive forces – how much could that help a child like Mia?

Our conclusion was that Mia direly and urgently needed *normal* experiences involving more people in her life – experiences of ordinary "six-year-old girl life."

The culture in which the family lived in many ways was characterized by silence – woodland, small scale industries, one man companies, three-generation families, and hunting and fishing as the main spare time interests. While in some ways this was a culture of isolation, in other ways these were villages and inhabitants who had chosen an alternative life style to the stress and demands in the big cities.

The relational connections around the family had been an important support system for them. At the same time you could also see the family's surrounding connections as conservative and indicative of a living system that could only be limiting for Mia – a background that reduced her life space.

What kind of contact was possible for this girl? Who could attempt to establish a relationship with some mutuality? How could we expand Mia's area of ease in the world? What would motivate Mia to take part in new activities, what could we place around her which would enable her interest to overcome her dread?

We started by asking Susan, the teacher mentioned at the first meeting at the headmaster's office, to be the assisting person for Mia. She agreed; she would be with Mia on a daily basis.

The Society and the Politicians

While it was obvious that Mia was a seriously disturbed child, and there was a great deal more that could be learned from further psychological and psychiatric investigations, what stood out to us most prominently was seeing Mia's big eyes and her movement towards us as long as we did not examine her. We decided to follow the beacon of her eyes as an indication of not only her but also her family's need for contact with the outside world, instead of seeing her many symptoms as something that required immediate investigation and treatment in the clinic. The latter could wait.

She was one of four challenging young patients (under 7 years) we had at that time in this general outlying area. Child psychiatry in that area operated through an outpatient clinic. Institutions for whole day observations and family interactional investigations were located quite far away for these families.

We decided to see what local societal resources might be helpful for the girl and the other three children. If we were to be able to work with these cases, a unified system of support would have to emerge from the ground available in the community in all four cases. To determine whether such a figure could develop we decided to call a conference/seminar of representatives of all the relevant social institutions.

We invited politicians from the school board, the board for social welfare, and the board for health and medical care. Together with these politicians, we also invited the heads of the departments for which the politicians were responsible. Mia as well as the other young patients would be attending school, visiting the health center, and needing support and participation in the rest of what society offers young children and their parents.

Our experience often was that the staff from various disciplines, who came into contact with needing children, understood the importance for co-operation between the disciplines. Teachers, social workers, and others did what they could to support families and fill in missing parts. They saw the children in the children's actual life situations. They saw the children's innocent efforts, their struggles, and the failures – the places where the system was not enough and consequently where people (children and families) didn't make it.

Where was the support both for children and families and for the professional staff that sought to help them?

First Seminar

In the first meeting, with the group of politicians and managers for the different areas mentioned above assembled, we presented case studies.

The impact on the politicians was tremendous.

The whole child was made visible from a variety of perspectives, and boundaries between separate institutions were crossed. Various front line staff that worked closely with children with severe problems in multi-problem families could share how they sometimes had to act on and handle problems that were not intended to be their responsibility.

The picture of the children broadened and deepened. Just as importantly, the picture of the staffs' willingness and often unlimited efforts to include the child in everyday nursery/school life was illuminated.

It was important for us, as well as for all of the other professionals that the politicians agreed that the needs of these children were their responsibility – that the aim of the political echelon was to include all children as far as possible, giving all effort to arrange systems and institutions so children with grave problems could secure the best life possible under the prevailing conditions.

Their understanding that these types of difficulties existed in their area of influence, that "their staff" came in contact with so many children who were excluded from play and fun and from adults that could introduce them to society, was important for the rest of the work.

No decisions regarding structure were made at that time. But for all of us, who regarded ourselves as "child-workers" in the public sector, it was an essential achievement that the politicians on the community level were informed and that they supported us in our struggles to work together in an integrated fashion in addressing the needs of these children and their families. The politicians let us know that they were committed to following the work and that they understood the importance of this type of networking for children with such complex problems. Such an understanding and commitment at the highest level of administration were imperative as we knew that boundary and responsibility questions would arise as the work with these children proceeded, and there would otherwise be many possibilities for splitting and polarizing of forces to occur.

How to Structure the Work?

Competitive demands on the clinic from this and other sources, geographical distance between the family and the clinic, various other perspectives to take into account – what could we offer and what was needed from others? Our aim was to present a plan to last at least one year, with willingness to be there longer if needed. The primary goal of the plan was to help Mia venture out into a society that was willing to be there for her.

Time was of the essence, particularly with the personal assistant attending to Mia on a daily basis. What we had learned from the meeting with the politicians and health care delivery staffs indicated to us that contributions needed to be on several levels and optimally coordinated. However, from the beginning we had no clear picture about how the work should and would continue.

With regard to the home scene, we could see that it was necessary to support the family if we were to have a chance of helping them open their closed system for a more contactful way of relating to the outside world. Sensation, awareness, mobilization, action, contact, meaning making and withdrawal, giving space for a new sensation to turn up[2]. Where along this path of experience could the broken dialogues between Mia and the rest of the world be re-established? What was there to be noticed? What supportive forces were possible, and what disruptive forces could be diminished?

We decided to operate with a multi-axial, wide spread diagnostic process – on one hand cognizant of Mia's own vulnerability and in sync with the way she had made meaning of life in the manner it had been given to her, and on the other hand, taking into account the pressure on the family and the environment to be there for Mia in a way that she could gain from.

With regard to the latter, the common experience of those interacting with Mia was that Mia often withdrew if you could not be on a contact level that she could make use of. How could people show Mia that they wanted to be there for her when they couldn't talk to her without her withdrawing? First and foremost, this requires a great deal of self and other support on the part of anyone attempting to engage Mia.

Regardless of the reasons of why it hadn't been true in the past, we had to reverse the trend and provide an environment for this girl that could be with her in a "good enough manner," as every child deserves.

A Good Enough Field

Our task as clinicians from the child psychiatry clinic was to provide the leadership in creating an overarching structure, using primarily local resources, that would serve as a "good enough environment" to hold this girl.

Towards that end, the various elements of service and influence, as well as the levels within each element, were identified. As stressed earlier, it was important to appreciate that these were interacting fields,

---

[2] Sensation, awareness, mobilization, action, contact, meaning making and withdrawal are elements of the Gestalt Awareness Cycle. For a further description see Melnick & Nevis (1992) and Zinker (1977).

including being interactive between levels within fields. Thus, coordinated communication between and within these fields was imperative.

A top priority was avoiding a common pitfall that could entrap multi-complex families with psychiatric problems as well as the institutions that attempted to serve them. We knew from our clinical experience that, without the support of institutional coordination, such multi-complex families tended to be sent around from institution to institution, gathering new diagnoses while receiving little if any treatment. And, of course, a form of this phenomenon was why the problems in Mia's family had gone unnoticed until she and her family came to the task of her entering kindergarten.

Us as Holders of the Field

We took on the role of the ones who defined and defended the field for Mia. When parents aren't able to hold the field for their children they need help from society. Due to the complexity of needs in this case, more people were invited to be important in the life of the family, and to insure coherence of intent, extra attention was required by us, as the coordinating entity.

Our idea was that contributing elements in the field had to be managed and organised around an agreed upon figure for the whole work. All contracts, all input, all new ideas were passed through us, not because we were the only ones who could understand Mia's situation but because we were the ones who had taken on the mandate to protect the field. From our learning, this was a crucial point. Sustainability reqiuires dialogs around emerging dilemmas, robust relationships and alliances, and an open and flexible atmosphere, all of which best emerges through the watchful eye of a central holder of the field.

In School

Heading our list for creating a supportive environment in general was sufficiently supporting the people who worked with Mia on a daily basis in the school setting. We reached an agreement with the headmaster for us to supervize these people once a month in a group format, in which we could follow their work and supervize their contact process with Mia. In addition, we were available by phone between meetings. These "daily workers" included the class teacher, the assisting teacher, and Mia's personal assistant (Susan). The special teacher, who worked at the school with children with special needs (children with AD/HD, etc.), and who had occasional contact with Mia, sat in these supervision meetings as well.

Susan imaginatively created "communication tools" that could both challenge and comfort Mia in anticipating and facing what lay before her.

Mia made daily advances in feeling comfortable and engaging with what was being offered to her, showing more and more of herself. As she was ready, she attended sport days, took part in activities with other children during recesses, wrote letters to the school staff, and most impressively allowed her mother to leave school, coming to spend the school day without her mother present.

As time progressed, she showed in various ways that she was interested in communication and connection outside of her family. With the support and connective possibilities offered her, she managed to organize herself so she could take part in a range of activities with others.

At Home

The parents of this isolated girl, who due to a variety of reasons were unable to organize around the ordinary parental task of helping their child leave home in age appropriate ways, themselves needed support in order for a "good enough field" to be formed.

We met with the family once a month with the purpose of following Mia's progress and also of seeing how we could assist the parents in understanding Mia's difficulties and inspiring them to creatively support Mia in her steps forward. In particular, our intent was to help all of us to focus on Mia's abilities and to avoid the negatives. A more detailed account of the progress of that endeavour follows this section.

As time went on, after relationships had been established with Mia and her family, we decided that it might be advantageous to use traditional diagnostic tools to get a more precise picture of Mia's and her family's world.

To that end, further investigations in the diagnostic process were made at the clinic, with quite poor results and without learning much more than we had initially learned quite early in the process. On one occasion Mia met with one of our clinical psychologist together with her mother. And on another day we met with the family in our play room in an attempt to get some information about the interplay in the family. These meetings appeared to be by and large stressful for the family, who collectively exhibited many signs of anxiety, consistent with the possibility that they were experiencing feelings of failure.

The General Practitioner

As previously mentioned, we mandated that the health clinic offer Mia's mother a contact on a regularly basis to address headache, back pain and other diffuse illness symptoms. We saw this as an important input to help Mia's mother to replenish her power and to be more present in her changing situation. A general practitioner with good insight into the psychosocial aspects of illness and a pragmatic, compassionate, approach with patients is what most people, let alone parents struggling in difficult situations, need to sort out where pain comes from. And how to address this? We shared ideas about "the good enough field" with the GP and even if our contact times were rare we trusted that we were walking on the same path.

Social Welfare Office

In accordance with the Swedish welfare regulations, an officer was assigned to review the needs Mia might have for "assistance and advice." The LSS law states that developmentally disabled individuals, with particular diagnoses, are entitled to get assistance to be able to, as much as possible, participate in activities deemed part of ordinary societal life. Agreements were made between the school and the social welfare office to contribute what was needed when the staff around Mia managed to arrange for her to take part in activities outside the family. For example, a girl in her late teems was found to assist Mia in getting to riding lessons and other activities outside the family. This was also the agreement that funded the acquisition of Susan, Mia's assisting teacher, who was permitted to follow Mia until she reached grade level performance.

The Politicians

The politicians were invited to the clinic once a year, the purpose of which was largely educational. We presented children's narratives, which in turn illustrated what could be done. We emphasized the importance, for children and teenagers, for society to hold a joint responsibility for their growth. Case vignettes illustrated why overlapping boundaries between various authorities have to be crossed if we want the needs of children to be the primary focus.

The politicians were pleased to get information about the impact of their integrated policy decisions – that they could make a difference in their role of "holding" the larger field. It became apparent that members of the political sector all too infrequently got meaningful feedback as to where their power was useful and needed.

Mandate Givers – Department Heads

Heads of the community institutions were invited to meet with us four times a year. At such meetings, experiences from the work around the children were shared, inter- & intra-institutional responsibility were assessed, plans and ideas for further work were drawn up, and implications for directives for the staff who were involved in the child psychiatry work were discussed. The questions on this level were mostly around how we together could act as a supportive environment for the staff involved in the daily work. Our understanding was that without a stable environment it is almost impossible for staff to take on the type of work undertaken for Mia and her family.

In such work, the possibility of parallel processes, projective identification, misunderstood non-verbal communications, isolating silence, and unsupported discouragement – field forces that could be so destructive if they were not taken care of – were always in the air and needed to be addressed in such a way that splits did not occur among staff.

The Research Team

As a support for us, the holders of the field, we organized a liaison with a research team at the University of Umeå, Sweden, who followed this program (as well as the other similar cases in which we were holders of the field, that we were pursuing at the time), and who measured Mia's progressa regular intervals (De Leeuw, 1996).

Thus we had impartial, reliable feedback as to the effectiveness and validity of our decisions and style of managing this complex, human endeavour.

These were the elements of our construction of a "good enough field" for Mia and her family. I now finish this chapter with a more personal account of what emerged from this field.

A Breakthrough in Language – The Dialogue with Mia Starts

We entered the village and turned up to the house. This was our 7th monthly visit to the family (as usual, to be followed by a school meeting). The building was red and built from wood as were most of the houses in the area. A typical small town Swedish scene, but we knew of the differences from other homes that weren't visible from outside.

Happy to see us, they welcomed us with their usual rural hospitality – spoken pleasantries and as always their coffee table, in their kitchen, bore delicious sandwiches and cake for afterwards. Mia was not present to greet us when we arrived, nor did she take part in the session with her parents. While this was as it had been in previous visits, there was an important difference this time. During earlier visits she had chosen to be at her grandmother's cottage across the road. Today, she was in the house – with the door to her room locked and with only silence emanating from that part of the building.

After comments on the weather and a short "report" on what was new in town, conversation turned to our purpose for the day. We asked, "How has it been since the last time we met?" – "Difficult" was the answer. We continued to explore their sense of Mia's progress. What did they believe was going well and what not so well? Did they feel in sync with the program at school – was the school's pace in line with what they felt Mia could handle? Should we support Mia's father's more demanding attitude towards Mia?

The meeting was, as often had been the case, a balancing act between support and challenge. It was imperative that the parents and the people interfacing with Mia at school be on the same page. The parents, if anything, tended to lag behind the school's pace in offering Mia more contact and space in her life. At the same time, the balance in the family needed to be respected and change explored in accordance with the family's own limits. The meetings were always a shift between psycho-pedagogic explanations and interventions on a more therapeutic and emotional level. Mia's mother once said, "It's so good to see you, I long for you to come, and when you leave I feel shaken for a couple of days. Later I start to look forward to seeing you again."

This statement captures the quality of contact we experienced with Mia's parents. They liked us and deeply appreciated the commitment and concern we had for them and their daughter. Thus, they tolerated our questions and ideas, when at times in spite of our intentions such questions and ideas must have seemed like critical comments on their child-raising abilities. Discussions often arose as to whether Mia should be allowed to withdraw into her room and the familiarity of the toys she had there or whether she should be supported to follow the program that we and the school regarded as quite reasonable.

This particular visit I had to use the bathroom and on the way there I passed Mia's room and heard her from inside. She knocked on the closed door and I stopped and knocked back. I waited a while to see if she would answer, and she did.

As if we knew Morse code we continued for a while until I broke the "conversation" and continued to the bathroom. On my way back to the kitchen through the corridor, passing her room, I saw a small piece of paper emerging from under her door.

"Welcome to the Ghost house," was written on the paper along with some drawings, which were difficult to make out. I took the paper, folded it the way I found it and put it in my pocket. I did not say anything to the parents about the note at that time. However, I struggled a bit with the message.

On our next visit the usual greeting ritual welcomed us, coffee and tasty sandwiches around the coffee table in the kitchen, pieces of cake, and then a follow up from the last month. How was co-operation with school, what new information needed to be shared, were there new challenges that had arisen for them or for Mia? They had talked with the staff at school and were a bit worried that the teachers had too high expectations of their daughter.

Suddenly Mia turned up in the kitchen. It was the first time we had seen her in the home and the second time at all. (The first time had been in the waiting-room in the clinic.)

"You there," she said and pointed at me. "I want to talk to you," and then she quickly walked back into her room. I followed her and stepped into her "sanctuary," a girl's room, full of toys. On the desk lay paper, pencils, and crayons that she had prepared for us. She had a very clear idea about what we should do. "I want you to draw there, and I will draw here. You are a star and I am a cat. We shall make a story."

Afterwards she asked if I could bring paper from the hospital next time, colorful paper that she had seen in the play room at the clinic. We spent further time together as I asked her about the things in her room, and she gave me detailed, thoughtful answers. Surprisingly, for the first time speaking to each other, we had a rich and informative conversation.

The door was closed, and she made clear that she did not want her parents in the kitchen to hear us. Not only was I the first and, for a long time, the only person outside the family who Mia talked to, for some time our special relationship was a stepping stone to a new manner of communicating with her parents.

From Dialog to Family Sessions

With this first meeting in her room another procedure was added to the monthly visit with the family. Henceforth, the first fifteen minutes of the visit were spent in the kitchen together with the parents as before, without Mia, then Mia would collect me and the rest of the time the two of us would spend in her room. We made comic strips, a series of animals playing – the girl and her horse, etc. Mia worked with joy and excitement, creating dialog that went with the pictures. It was possible to connect that dialog to Mia's longing and fear in her life through questions about the similarity with her own situation.

After a few visits spent in this manner, I asked Mia, "What shall we do with our drawings." "Do you think we should go out and share it with Erik and your parents?" For several months that was the procedure. My colleague and I came by car to the family home, spent some time with the parents in the kitchen without Mia, then Mia and I were alone for 30 minutes in her room, and then back to the parents and Erik, sharing what we had decided to share with them.

Mia gradually opened up about her experience of her situation and was also curious and interested in her parents' life. This process accelerated after a particularly touching incident. Following one of the sessions between Mia and me in her room, in which she had created a picture story about an animal that lost her mother, when she came to the kitchen, she sat, to the extent she could, by herself. Vigorously tapping her pencil on the table, she repeated over and over, seemingly to herself, "There's no one there! There's no one there! There's no one there!" Was there meaning in what she was saying or should we just try to get her back into the conversation – we tried both. Suddenly with clarity and deep feeling Mia began to talk about her loneliness and longing for friends and company.

This stirred Mia's mother to share with us her tortuous experiences from Mia's first year of life. Even though she dearly wanted to, she had no sense of how to connect with and comfort her baby, who was frequently upset and crying. Many times she walked to the health clinic in attempts to understand more, and many times she was told that, "It will disappear when Mia gets a little older" – and she waited for that, mostly in a state of isolation. She didn't really feel a connection with her daughter until that happened.

Another alteration in the structure of the monthly visit with the family occurred a few months later. Mia decided she wanted to be with all of us in the kitchen from the start of the visit, welcoming Eric and me, together with her mum and dad when we arrived. The time in her own room between just the two of us more and more turned out to be a preparation for the family sessions. With each visit she came to share more and more of her experiences between the five of us in the kitchen.

In addition, Mia's parents came to talk more about their own untold experience, sharing early memories and family history with us all. Mother's family had, for generations, been well established in the village, and now was reduced to just her and her mother, who lived across the road. Father's beginnings were that of a refugee, fleeing to Sweden with his mother and two sisters, after his father had been killed in fighting for the resistance movement, during World War II. At four years of age, because of economic reasons, he was left in foster care in this area while his mother tried to establish a new life for herself and her daughters. Thoughts and feelings that had been held in silent isolation now were in the open air. Implicit, nonverbal gestures and actions turned to explicit messages between them. The family worked with us toward a new family structure, with a child who more and more took part in life outside the family even if the way still was long and the child needed a lot of support from her assisting teacher.

During the periods that I spent with Mia in her room, Erik had the opportunity to talk to the parents alone about their wishes, longings, difficulties, doubts and also make needed interventions in the parental and couple system. Among other things, he devoted signified time and energy to assuring Mia's father how important he was for Mia's further life.

Mia's parents were supported and advised and challenged in their changing parenting pattern. They had a girl that became more and more active and who was more and more expressing feelings, questions and demands even when Erik and I were present. She went out to play in the school yard during recesses. She started to visit friends alone. She went with an assisting person to the recreation centre. She began to take riding lessons, and step by step she allowed classmates and teachers to hear her voice in school.

The Lucia Ceremony

This story has a heart-warming conclusion. Sixteen months from when Mia and her family first entered our office she was the maiden in front of the Lucia in the traditional annual Lucia ceremony in church at Christmas season. The whole village was there and her parents were so proud of their beautiful, sweet, brave girl.

Mia had earlier said to her mother that she wanted to be the angel, and the teachers encouraged Mia's mother to support Mia, even though at the time they were not sure that Mia would be able to manage this role.

Susan writes, "Together with all the children in school, Mia practiced her role in the play several times. That was impressive in itself, but that she should dare to perform the play in the church, which, as usual on such occasions, was crowded with people, we could not really believe."

Mia not only managed, she gave a perfect performance.

Afterwards, Susan wrote in her diary, "We were many who realized that what we had just witnessed was a wonder, and it was difficult to keep the tears away. It felt as if Mia now was fighting for her new, interconnected life and this morning she had won a big victory."

We, Erik and I, had promised Mia and her family that we would be there with them until they were ready to say goodbye. That turned out not to be for quite a long time. This tight schedule with monthly visits lasted for almost four years. Even after that we were still in contact with the team around Mia, especially when she changed school and new teachers or new arrangements came into her life.

A significant component, in this story, was the continuity with stable frames that supported the all-important relationships surrounding Mia. With the visits in the home the whole contacting process with the family had a "place" where it could exist. Mia longed for us and waited for us. We had family sessions, all five in the kitchen, around the coffee table. New schedules were put up for another semester as needed. Visits to the home and to the school, the same day in the month; we never postponed or changed a meeting. Sometimes only one of us was able to come, but one of us was always there.

Mia knew what she could expect at home, at school, and other places in her life. In addition to those already mentioned, other people were invited into and became very important in her life. For example, someone helped to "look after the house" – to protect the "existential" room. Mia had a safe place for her figural process, she could trust that the environment had sufficient support and would catch her if she fell.

We followed Mia for some years; she came back for a shorter individual contact with me at the child psychiatry clinic in her early teenage years. She wanted to put words on her earlier experiences with us. For me it was also a chance to gather feedback on our earlier interventions in her environment.

When we ended the contact with the family Mia still had a supporting team around her. While she still needed challenges that were appropriate for her skills and her parents needed to be met in their continuing concerns for appropriate support for their daughter, these were now problems more in line with the common developmental concerns of parents in general, that could be sorted out in the school with Mia's parents and Mia herself.

Epilogue

It's now several years since we left Mia. As I mentioned, I had a few follow up sessions with Mia when she was a teenager. I also met with colleagues from the health clinic. Looking back, while there are things you see things that might have been better done in hindsight, what stands out in the work is the tremendous effort and commitment we made and also how important it was, together with the network, to create a united field for Mia as a good enough background for the figural process. It is with gratitude to the family I end this story. The family allowed us to enter and be a part of their life and let us learn so much about how field forces impact on figural formations – the all important, often overlooked or not fully understood contributions to the process of growing up – the role of society as an important field force in the process of becoming an adult.

References

De Leeuw, D. (1996). *Kom in i spökhuset Master Thesis,* Univeristy of Umeå, Sweden.

Melnick, J. & Nevis, S. M. (1992). Diagnosis: The Struggle for a Meaningful Paradigm. In E. C. Nevis (Ed.), *Gestalt Therapy: Perspectives and Applications* (pp. 63-74). Caambridge, MA: GestaltPress.

Zinker, J. (1977). *Creative Process in Gestalt Therapy.* New York: Brunner/Mazel.

Editors' Note:
Support is a multi-dimensional phenomenon. In the following chapter, Bronagh Starrs shares with us how staying in touch with the support in her own life and in particular with the support within her body enables her to be with a deeply troubled adolescent male and his family. In response to the almost overwhelming shock, fear, and shame felt by her client and by his mother, she is able to assess the possibilities of parental support, hold and ground the parents, and reopen the all-important connection between parents and adolescent. She then gives us a rich and thick description of the work she is able to do with this young man, with this vital parental support re-established. In the process, we are introduced to the gifts of her sensitivity to the delicate, gender-oriented realities of this young man's world, and her relational creativity in sensing and restoring the multiple levels of support needed to work effectively with her client and his family.

6

The Adolescent Male:

Shame, Support, and Developmentally Effective Psychotherapy

Bronagh Starrs

Therapy is about making contact; and adolescent therapy requires a specific repertoire of contact skills, often looking and feeling very different from therapy with adult clients. Coupled with the ability to make rich contact with the teenager, it is also essential that the therapist has a solid understanding of adolescent development and of how to support its unfolding in a therapeutic context. Psychotherapeutic work with adolescents must address both the interior and interpersonal dimensions of development if it is to adequately support the adolescent in adopting a more selfdirected and integrated style of engaging in the world. Attending to the figural work of self-exploration, expanding awareness, problem solving, behaviour change etc. as well as assessing family context are key components of the work. It is the relational experience which carries and supports this work: contact with the adolescent, contact with his parents, and contact with self.

Rarely is an adolescent male client willingly referred for therapy – *("I'm talking to no f**king shrink, that's a bunch of bullshit!")*. Mostly a situation with heightened drama has unfolded, with a teenager playing centre stage, who is dragged reluctantly to my office. Adolescent energy is powerful, chaotic and messy and it is easy to get entangled in the confusion – particularly given that we all have our fair share of residual adolescent energy which can be easily activated. The therapist is constantly challenged to honest self-appraisal in order to support the situation with grounded awareness. The following is a description of one of those familiar clinical situations and my therapeutic response:

John was fifteen and actively suicidal: he had attempted to hang himself the previous Saturday night, and this was not his first attempt to take his life. His mother's referral call was a desperate last-ditch attempt to save her son. She cried a lot during the brief telephone conversation. Could I see him as soon as possible?

So much happened for me, as the helping professional, in those initial few minutes speaking with John's mother – thoughts, feelings, body responses, assumptions and judgments made, clinical decisions taken etc. And while the work lasted for a total of 14 sessions, really by the end of the 2nd session, the core of the work had been undertaken. So, what exactly happened for me in this therapeutic encounter?

I consciously do three things during a telephone call like this: (1) I breathe. (2) I remember I have a body and I stay in it. (3) I remember I have support. For me, doing this means the difference between holding and losing my ground as a therapist – for if I lose my ground, we're all on the slippery slope. My initial response is always a body response. It goes something like this: I hear the anxiety in this distraught woman's voice and I match her anxiety intuitively – adrenal glands active, buckling sensation in my knees, not breathing, a scream of agony too loud to ever be heard and understood by another human being stirring in my held breath. BREATH! I'm not breathing. Breathe. Soles of the feet. Breathe. Legs. Breathe. Map of the body. Breathe. Ok. Stand back. We have a situation here, remember what you know. This woman needs support and ground. Give her support and ground.

First major clinical intervention has happened: I have identified and separated my own personal agony from this woman's. My buttons have been pushed for sure. Suicide and I have met before – both personally and professionally. And so my "Therapist-Messiah Complex" quickly kicks in: I *have* to rescue this kid. This live reaction will be my work-in-progress during any subsequent therapeutic contact. It will require heightened self-reflection, support from my personal therapist and, vitally, the support of my clinical supervisor. Mostly it will require me to breathe; remember I have a body and stay in it; and remember I have support.

Right now, this woman is in a panic, this is too much for her and she is overwhelmed. I communicate that I know this must be a nightmare for her so I might say something like, "I can't imagine what this must be like for *you,* his mother." Simple, though effective; my statement informs her that I'm *trying* to imagine it – which means I care, or at least I want to care. It opens the connection sufficiently for her to tell me a little of how she is feeling. At every opportunity I am trying to inject support and calm into the dialogue and I am trying to get this woman to trust that I know what I'm doing. This is literally a matter of life or death for her. It has been my experience, working in a post-conflict era in the north of Ireland, that very often adolescent boys are not brought to me for 'therapy', they are brought with a direct request from parents to keep them alive.

I make my first clinical assessment as soon as I hear John's age. I decide to meet initially with John and his parents, then do some individual work with John. I tell his mother this is what I want to do – she hears this sure direction as some kind of competence. I hear the usual *"I don't think my husband will come".* My response is always the same: *"It's important that he comes."* They nearly always do.

Joint Parent-Adolescent Meeting

My decision to meet with both John and his parents for an initial assessment comes principally from a guess that disembedding is still an ongoing issue. I am mindful that this is an Irish male adolescent in desperate pain: I'm not sure how willing or able he will be to present facts and concerns to me in a reasonably objective manner. This situation which has unfolded is a *"field situation"* and requires a *"field response."* By this I mean that it is not only this fifteen year old who is affected by what is going on – his parents will certainly be finding it difficult to cope with this situation also. It is likely that his parents are feeling very shamed – that they somehow have failed their son. They will all be in need of support initially. Meeting with parents also affords me a direct experience of family contact styles; of how capable these parents are of supporting their son, etc. And I get a sense of how I might be able to influence the adolescent-parent field dynamics. By inviting his parents into the process, there is the potential to harness considerable support for this young teenager – if it works, how much more effective will this be than 50 minutes of therapy with me once a week? I also, of course, am presented with a multilens story of how John has found life so incredibly unbearable. The picture forming has more depth and clarity. I remember Mark McConville's description of working with the adolescent in isolation as *"sheer clinical folly."*[1] I have come to see how this is so.

The adolescent in the first encounter is particularly vulnerable, and frequently enters the session armed and guarded for the criticism that seems certain to come. Remaining interested and centerd, while seeming to need no more from the client than is available at that moment, goes a long way toward establishing a field where contact can develop. I let John know that he is under no duress to engage and I also watch for his cues, inviting him into the dialogue if I spot an opportunity.

---

[1] Personal communication from Mark McConville, May, 2005.

It is likely there is going to be an intense opening to our joint meeting – this can generally be expected when trauma is so alive and evident in the encounter. For me the first ten minutes sometimes feels like *"lancing the boil."* I remember my breath, my body, my support – when I do this I can be a solid support for this family. I make direct, respectful, non-shaming contact with each person. *"I hear you, and I want to support you"* is what I hope they each experience from me. And so much comes from the lancing: John's girlfriend was killed in a tragic accident almost a year ago; he has since been expelled from school and been in trouble with the police for violent, destructive behavior; he is a gifted, passionate footballer who suddenly stopped playing; arguments with his father have recently ended in fist fights; he has been drinking heavily....

I note people's feeling responses to one another during our dialogue and I share this with them, inviting them to respond. This directs the family to make richer contact with each other. It is very evident that these parents care deeply about their son. Part of my work is to try to make that support more explicit and expressive – translate it from the shaming focus on "bad behaviour." So, for example, during the conversation about football, John's father speaks about how proud he is of his son's talent and potential to be a county-level player one day. I could see John's face flinch and he looks angry. I stop his dad and check out with John how he is feeling. Angry indeed, John lets his dad know that the reason he stopped playing football was precisely because he felt he could do no good in his father's eyes. He felt that his father was ashamed of him. When I invite John's father to respond to his son, he begins to sob as he speaks. Through the tears he describes how immensely proud he is of his son, both on and off the pitch, of how much he loves him, of how unfair it is that his son is having to cope with such a difficult loss at this young age, of how useless he feels now because he cannot seem to help his son. John is now also tearful and they begin to speak directly and with love to one another. Something in everyone's experience softens in this moment. John's mother later in the session speaks of how touching it is for her to witness this tender moment between her husband and son; and how she had even been a little jealous of the closeness in their relationship until several years ago when John became a teenager. This becomes a perfect opportunity for John's mother to tell her son how much he meant to her also – another poignant moment in the contact between John and his parents. Towards the end of the session I invite John to return the following week to meet with me individually. I let the family know that an important part of the work will involve John's parents from time to time. They all still believe it requires a miracle, though for now, some hope has stirred.

A Word on Working With Parents

When working with parents I pay attention to several things: 1) how tangled up this adolescent's development and presenting symptom issues in the family, i.e. to what extent is disembedding an ongoing issue? This is evident in all kinds of presenting profiles: teenagers battling with parental control; adolescents blaming parents for issues that they should/could be taking on as their own (like schoolwork), and so on. When there is an experience of trauma, as in John's suicide attempts, I will always involve the parents.

2) Do I think I can influence the family's workings? I rarely meet with a whole family, though I often meet together with an adolescent and parent(s) who are feuding; or alone with a parent whose behavior I want to influence (like the dad I met with last week who regularly gets into mutually insult-spewing, shouting matches with his fifteen year old son). I met with the father alone because (a) I wanted to be fairly direct with him, and I didn't want to risk shaming him in front of other family members; and (b) because their relationship is too volatile to try to do serious work with them in the same room. Often I find that I can influence a relationship more rapidly by meeting, at least ini-tially, with the parties separately.

I also do a lot of pulling marginal fathers into my office for one or two visits. Fathers often feel estranged from and suspicious of the entire therapy process, and for the adolescent, the father's tacit embarrassment and disapproval of therapy can be a huge impediment. I will meet with these fathers once or twice, and attempt to establish some sort of loose "alliance" with them, just so that they will look at their son's involvement with me in a more favorable light. These meetings also enable me, often, to defuse some of the ambient, unspoken *"Am I a bad parent?"* shame that permeates the adolescent's family field. I have learned never to underestimate the significance of the father-son relationship for teenage boys, whether a father is fully involved in or completely dislocated from his son's life.

3) Do I need to experience the cast of characters in the adolescent's life in order to have a deeper appreciation of what he is up against? Just being able to say to an adolescent, *"you're right, your mother's a piece of work"* can be very affirming. And on the other side of the coin, having met a difficult parent gives me credibility if I try to re-frame that parent's behaviour, e.g. *"I don't think that your dad's disappointed in you; he impressed me as a man disappointed in himself.."* etc. And it is often the case that an adolescent's symptomatic behaviour is pointing to painful family issues, e.g., parental addiction, domestic violence, etc. In these instances, it is always deeply telling for the therapist to sit with this adolescent and his parents – experiencing how frozen he is when they are in the room.

Individual Meeting with John

John tells me I'm his third counsellor in less than a year. "The first one made me do stuff even though I didn't want to. She'd say 'do it, it'll help you' but it didn't, it just made me worse. She made me cry all the time. The second one would say something and then there would be an uncomfortable silence for about half an hour, then she'd say something else and there would be another uncomfortable silence for another half an hour and then I'd go home."

This is a scenario often described to me by adolescents: the counsellor is either intensely problem-focused, failing to meet the person behind the issue; or she reveals herself as having participated in a psycho-therapy training heavily oriented towards working with adult clients. Psychotherapeutic intervention with adolescents is a complex and challenging area of work and requires specialized, in-depth training. Certainly in my experience, learning about the dynamics of develop-ment and therapy with this age group has served my adolescent clients much better than relying on intuition, inadequate theoretical ground-ing and no conceptual framework to guide me through the frequently bewildering and directionless experience of therapy with a teenager.

Problem solving, conflict resolution, behavior change etc., although important to address, are not defining themes of therapy with teenagers. The adolescent finds it more natural to describe his or her friends, siblings, parents, music tastes, football interests, school and so on, than to speak in terms of feelings and reflections. This is not avoidance; it is revelation. It is a self-defeating attitude to view the adolescent's outward focus as simply defensive, concealing intrapsych-ic reality – rather than as a window into the adolescent's world.

For me, therapy is about making contact with this adolescent and co-creating a human-to-human meaningful encounter where we are both of worth and we both have dignity and where there is nothing 'wrong' with either of us – contact which isn't shaming. It's about getting interested in who he or she is at the core, liking and appre-ciating that, and communicating that in some way to the adolescent. Once that contact has been established, we can get to work on the "problem" in a way that is supporting and not shaming.

So I get interested in John's world. I keep a glint in one eye: irreverence, humor, my own fiercely rebellious adolescent energy etc. I keep the other eye firmly fixed to this adolescent's developmental journey, contextual field, level of internal and external support. So I make calls on a moment-to-moment basis about where our conversa-tion is going and how much this adolescent can tolerate. He tells me how glad he is to have been expelled, it was a crap school anyway. I get interested in his definition of 'crap'. Actually this is quite a prestigious grammar school and it turns out that John scraped a place in it by the skin of his teeth with a fairly average result. He never felt quite up to the mark, believing that he was the 'stupidest' in his year group. So, rather than be shamed about it, he didn't study – excelling in non-academic subjects like sport and art. We will need to attend to this later in the work. We talk about the initial session – it was the first time he ever saw his dad cry. He didn't think his dad cared; he thinks differently now – just a little differently.

He describes how he can't stop thinking about his girlfriend who died. They were in love, were soul mates, he can't live without her. Teenagers form extraordinarily magnetic, infatuating bonds with one another very quickly – they had been going out for four months. It is a grave mistake to dismiss the adolescent's relationships as 'puppy love'; we must take these connections seriously even though we may have very different ideas. When John tells me that they would regularly spend up to 8 hours on the phone with each other, I get an indication of how this young adolescent felt met in his relationship. Now I begin to appreciate the level of loss he is experiencing. As the first tentative giving of the self is experienced for an adolescent through the formation of a meaningful relationship, there can be a sense of great loss when this is terminated. This is even more poignantly felt when this ending is the result of trauma and tragedy as in John's experience. John describes what his life has been like without his girlfriend – the loneliness, the emptiness, the pressure in his head when he thinks of how she would still be alive if he had not met her after school that day, the relief that comes when he punches something or gets drunk. Two things are apparent to me: he really misses this girl and he's blaming himself for what happened. I offer these to him gently along with my hunch that teenage boys find it easier to translate their hurt into anger. He looks at me. I think I'm getting him. He thinks I'm getting him. We lighten it up after that, preparing to close the session. The irreverence kicks in and we banter about how Tyrone will win this year's All-Ireland yet again. He thinks it's Armagh's turn this time round – I don't fancy his chances!

The Following Sessions

As I said previously, by the end of the second session, the core of the work has been undertaken – a fairly clear picture has emerged of what life is like for John just now and importantly that this family feel met. I know that the quality of work with John would most certainly have been compromised had I chosen not to involve his parents. Later in the work I facilitated some important work between John and his father; I met with the parents alone – educating them about their role in the dynamics of the relationship and coaching them on how to support their son without nagging or shaming him. I also facilitated two more family meetings. Throughout the remaining 8 sessions John and I worked together in one-to-one sessions. John's anger gave way to sadness which he was able to express through our conversations, his tears and some profound art-work, and he found new interest in, and resources for, living. He started playing football again. John and his father started fishing again, which they hadn't done since John was 10 and which they both had missed. I prepared a report for his school (at his parents' request and agreed to by John) which resulted in his being accepted back again. John began to feel surer of himself again.

This adolescent was lost in the world, overwhelmed by the loss of his girlfriend and the confusing task of growing up. His parents had lost faith in their parenting and lived in terror that their son would end his life. My task was to hold my ground and share it with them for a while until they each found theirs once more. The therapist's capacity to stay grounded while tolerating intense anxiety and chaos which spills from the intrapsychic field into the whole family field; while having a solid grasp of adolescent development; while being able to draw up a broad therapeutic plan; while being aware of potential triggers in her personal process; while listening to this mother at the other end of the line describe her son's failed attempt to hang himself the previous weekend depends, for me, on three things:

(1) I breathe;
(2) I remember I have a body, and I stay in it;
(3) I remember I have support.

Editors' Note:
Donald Winnicot famously said that "there is no such thing as a baby," powerfully pointing out that the infant can only be described as existing in the context of relationship. Mark McConville, long himself a major contributor to phenomenological, field-based, adolescent developmental theory and practice, brings further definition to this theme in exploring the relationship between parent and child from a dialogic, developmental perspective. He describes three ways in which that relationship can be organized, and explains how these three modes change in predictable fashion over time, as parent and child grow older together. There are pitfalls along the way, which he vividly illuminates with a case presentation that brings home how good intentions can block development. His writing shows how a therapist's careful listening and a dialogic therapeutic stance can support the parent and child in their transition from a paradigm of "care-taking supervision," through "negotiation-accountability," to the position of "dialogue-consultation" that marks relational maturity.

7

Relational Modes and the Evolving Field of Parent-Child Contact:

A Contribution to a Gestalt Theory of Development

Mark McConville

Introduction

For several years, the Gestalt Institute of Cleveland's Advanced Training Program for Working With Children and Adolescence has worked at developing a field model of development and psychotherapeutic intervention. Our model is based upon Gordon Wheeler's (1990a) contention that "it is... this relatedness at the boundary, this system of contacts, whose development we wish to trace." This premise differentiates the Gestalt model from self-in-isolation models of development (e.g. psychoanalytic, Piagetian, Information Processing), and aligns us more readily with models that stress the role of context and relationship in the developmental process (e.g. Vygotsky, 1962; Stern, 1985). Among our cornerstone principles is the belief that child development, however conceived, takes place within the context of a dynamically evolving relational field. Integral to that field of course is the family and the parent-child relationship.

My intention here is to sketch a model of how the family field, and specifically the parent-child relationship, evolves over time in the service of child development. My belief is that most clinicians who work with children have at the very least an intuitive version of such a model. Most people in fact, whether they have studied child development or not, have intuitions about what sort of parenting behavior supports development and what does not, what is "appropriate" or "inappropriate" for a given child at a given age. In a restaurant recently, I observed a father gently removing a salt shaker from his three year-old's hand, placing it out of reach. To his grumbling, surly fourteen year old, he issued an invitation to join the family conversation. Some time later, he calmly explained to his son that he could choose to wait in the car if he continued to act out his displeasure. Both interactions seemed to me a reasonable fit to the developmental readiness of the child in question.

By the same token, most of us can just as easily cite examples of parenting that seems out of synch with a given child's capacities, where it is evident that too much or too little is being asked of the child. In my office, I've seen parents accede to the controlling demands of nine year-old children. I've also witnessed parents turning inappropriately to a preteen for emotional support. Countless times I've counseled parents who were baffled and hurt by their teenager's testing the limits, and parents of twenty-somethings who were committed to protecting their offspring from suffering even the reasonable consequences of unwise decisions.

In each instance we intuitively grasp something about the fit, or lack of fit, between the child's developmental needs and the relational field organized by the parenting behavior in question. My objective is to articulate some aspects of this intuition within a Gestalt framework, and in so doing to generate a model that will be useful to practitioners who work with parents and their children. The question I am raising then, is how to think and talk about this developing relational field.

The Parent-Child Relationship

As Isadore From was fond of pointing out, contact and relationship are not the same thing. When I encounter another at the contact boundary, the concrete contact episode stands as figure against what Gordon Wheeler (1990b) has called the structured ground of our relationship. Our meeting takes place within the context of our history, our values, and our respective social roles, as well as a certain distribution of power and organization of boundaries within our relationship. When we meet as companions or colleagues, the relational context is quite different from our meeting as supervisor-employee, or as teacher-student. And indeed, if the structured ground of a relationship should change abruptly – for instance, if a colleague is promoted and becomes my supervisor – the ease and grace of our contacting may well be disrupted.

In families, the contact episodes of child and parent occur similarly within a structured ground, a contextual framework that organizes and influences the multiplicity of interactions. There is almost unlimited variety to the ways that this structured relational ground can be organized and expressed. Parent and child can relate as friends, playmates, adversaries, and competitors; they can adopt the complementary roles of teacher and student, mentor and mentee, judge and penitent, provider and recipient.

There can be no question that the quality of concrete contact episodes between parent and child plays an enormously important role in child development. My interest here, however, is to draw attention to the deeper structures of the relational ground that organize and support those contact episodes. My thesis is threefold. First, I contend that contact process of parent and child is organized by the structured ground of their relationship. Second, I believe that the structure of this relational ground necessarily changes over time. And third, I believe this structured relational ground evolves specifically along two related lines: the distribution of *power* to influence child behavior, and *boundaries*.

Let me say a word about each of these terms, by way of definition. By power, I mean the capacity to influence the direction of child behavior and development. This is akin to the question of responsibility for choices and outcomes. If your six year-old informs you that he is leaving the house, you, as parent, own the responsibility for determining whether this is a good idea or not. If your seventeen year-old makes a similar declaration, you have comparatively less leverage for exerting your influence. Power, in relationship, is essentially about the capacity to influence choices and behavioral outcomes. It is the relational analogue of what Perls, Hefferline and Goodman (1951) call the ego function of the self.

By the term boundaries, I am referring to the differentiation of the contact process between individuals. As boundaries evolve within a relationship, the parties come to view themselves mostly according to their own first person experience, and similarly to recognize and confirm the separateness and integrity of the other.

So, in the developmental unfolding of the parent-child relationship, it is this redistribution of power, and transformation of boundary, that is the hallmark of the relationship's evolution. Most of us already know this, whether we have formulated it this way or not. We have an intuitive gauge that tells us when parenting is in synch with the child's developmental status, and when it is not. Remember the father in the restaurant, who so naturally and appropriately addressed the behavior of his three year-old and his fourteen year-old? And the families I described in my office, where parents seemed to take orders from their nine year-olds? What is it, we might ask, that makes it so obvious that the first instances exemplify good form in parenting, whereas the second typifies parenting that has lost its way? The answer has to do with power and boundaries. It seems that most effective parenting, regardless of its particular style of communication or discipline, shares an intuitive wisdom that matches the management of power and boundaries with a child's developmental capabilities and needs.

Modes of Relationship

I am going to describe three very common ways that parents engage their children in the service of influencing behavior, choices, and ultimately, the course of development. Each is utterly commonplace and familiar. What is important is that each presupposes a distinctly different organization of the relationship in terms of boundaries and power. For this reason, I have labeled them *modes of relationship*, to underscore that they differ not only in terms of observable behavior patterns, but in terms of the underlying structures of ground that implicitly organize ongoing interaction. Each mode is potentially available over the entire course of child development, from infancy through emerging adulthood. But by the same token, each mode plays a different role in successive stages of the evolving parent-child relationship.

Mode 1: caretaking-supervision

The relational mode of influence that appears first in the parent-child relationship is caretaking. It is instinctive, necessary for survival, and very much one-sided in terms of the management of power and boundaries. This is not to imply that the infant or young child is a passive participant in the relationship, for this is certainly not the case. The developmentalist Daniel Stern (1985) has shown unequivocally that the interaction of caretaker and infant forms an intricate and delicate dance between partners, a two-way street in which the baby participates as an initiator as well as a recipient. But looking beyond the interaction, we know immediately that the underlying structure of the relationship is complementary rather than symmetrical. Caretaking is a comprehensive posture that the parent assumes, and in that posture he or she accepts unilateral responsibility for the outcomes of development. We may not always know what to do when a challenging situation arises with a young child, but most of us accept without question that we're the ones who bear the responsibility for knowing.

Caretaking-supervision has its own job description. It requires vigilance, decisiveness, good judgment, comfort with being in charge, and clarity about what's negotiable and what is not. At root, it requires a willingness to hold unilateral responsibility relative to the child. It is not open to real discussion whether a child will be allowed to play in the street, or go to school, or physically attack a younger sibling. A parent who is committed to promoting communication skills may well engage a child in conversations about any of these topics, but in the care taking mode that parent knows from the outset where the conversation is heading, and one way or another, how the question is going to be resolved.

Competent caretaking and supervision promote a broad range of developmental accomplishments in children, far too many to catalog here. Suffice it to say that in response to adequate care taking and supervision, children develop a fundamental trust in the world and in their own capabilities. They feel secure knowing the world is held together by a force greater than themselves, and thus are free to express and explore their emergent contact functions. They develop a faith in human connection, and naturally seek out relationships for support and satisfaction. Over time, we see in such children the unmistakable evidence of learning to caretake themselves, and to "supervise" or regulate their own impulses and behavior.

Parenting in the caretaking-supervision mode is not necessarily apparent to the naked eye. It may be expressed under the guise of tender loving care in one situation, and no-nonsense limit setting in another. It is important to understand that caretaking-supervision, as a mode of relationship, is more about posture and intention than style and technique. It is more about being than acting. The parent who is comfortable in this mode is as likely to appear gentle and engaging as they are to appear authoritative and decisive.

All that I have said about caretaking and supervision may seem painfully obvious to anyone who has given even a passing thought to the business of parenting. My point is only to underscore that care taking, in its complementary guises of nurturing support and authoritative supervision, is a distinct relational mode, and that as such it presumes a characteristic underlying organization of power and boundaries in the relationship. As a modality of influence, this strikes us as so coincident with parenting itself, that we notice it only when it is noticeably out of synch with development, as when a younger child is undersupervised, or an older child is excessively protected or controlled. And certainly, for many parents, this dimension of the relationship is the most problematic of all, as the seemingly endless stream of popular books on child discipline surely testifies.

Mode 2: dialogue-consultation

A second mode of influencing children is the sort of ordinary exchange of ideas and views called dialogue and consultation. We can think of dialogue-consultation as the counterpoint of caretaking-supervision, in terms of the underlying relational organization of power and boundaries. It implies that the power to determine outcome lies with the child, and that the parent's role is one of supplying information and perspective, in support of the child's exercise of that power.

As a mode of parental influence, dialogue tacitly acknowledges the child as a valid source of initiative, interest, perspective, and choice. In this mode, a parent may well offer advice or recommendations, but this is offered more in the spirit of consultation than guidance. My adult children ask my input from time to time regarding things going on in their lives, and I am delighted to give it. But it goes without saying that they are free to come to their own conclusions and make their own decisions. I offer my bit when I'm asked (and occasionally when I'm not), but we both take for granted that they are free to do as they see fit.

The cultivation of dialogue in parent-child relationships supports the emergence of initiative and authenticity in children, a capacity that psychologist Carol Gilligan (1982) calls "voice". This development of voice, as Gilligan emphasizes, is a critical dimension of healthy self esteem and confidence. Most of the time in parent-child relationships, this development unfolds so harmonically that we barely notice it. It seems both integral and incidental to the day to day relationship. As with most developmental phenomena, we tend to notice it more readily in its conspicuous absence or excess. As a therapist, I have many times met parents who reduced their role to consultant, skillfully and fully in support of their child's development. But I have also many times met parents unwilling or unable to relinquish their power, just as I have met parents who have done the opposite, reducing their role to consultant when the child truly needed someone else to be in the driver's seat.

One way to think about parent-child relationships is in terms of the interplay of these two modes, caretaking-supervision and consultation-dialogue. When parenting goes well enough, and children seem to be developing more or less as they should, there is a fluid and natural movement between the two. Without needing to stop and think, parents orient themselves in whichever mode seems called for by a given situation. When I sit down with parents and children for an initial clinical consultation, one of the first things I notice is the interplay of these two modes within the relationship. When they occur in balance, and feel appropriate to the topic under discussion and to the child's developmental needs, I often find myself secretly wondering "why are they here?" When supervision and dialogue occur in balance, most child behavior problems are solvable in the natural course of family life. When the opposite occurs, and I encounter a manifest imbalance of these modes, as when a parent is stuck in control mode, or conversely the child inappropriately engages the parent as an equal, I find myself thinking "of course, this is why they're here."

Mode 3: negotiation-accountability

Occupying a middle ground between caretaking-supervision and dialogue-consultation is a third parent-child relational mode: negotiation-accountability. In this mode, we find a distinctly different organization of relational power and boundaries from the first two. In the care taking-supervision mode, we saw a porous relationship boundary where the child's business, according to the very nature of care taking, is very much the parent's business. In the consultation-dialogue relational mode, we discovered an inverse footprint to the relationship. Its boundary is well formed, a genuine meeting place of separate interests, views, and agendas; in short, separate selves. Parents exert influence in this mode largely "by invitation only."

Consider the nature of negotiations between adults, whether formal negotiations over a business transaction, or casual conversations about where to go for dinner. In negotiation, the relationship is organized according to certain assumptions concerning power and boundaries. It is conceded from the beginning that the Other is entitled to his or her own agenda, and that resolution will require some degree of collaboration and compromise. The outcome, in contrast to the unilateral determination in the case of caretaking-supervision, is likely to involve some concession and compromise on both sides. Similarly, when a parent-child relationship is organized within a framework of negotiation, issues of power to influence and relational boundaries -- that is, the sorting out of where the child's business and the parent's business overlap – are precisely what is open to question.

There are a number of important ways that negotiation-accountability impacts upon child development. Most importantly, it teaches children that relationships are necessarily collaborative.[1] Through negotiating and being held accountable, children learn that they must coordinate their own wants and objectives with those of others, and thus that relationships necessarily involve give and take, concessions and compromise, conflict and conflict resolution.

A second byproduct of negotiation is that children learn the incredibly important lesson of accountability. When a child negotiates

---

[1] Harry Stack Sullivan (1953) made an important distinction between cooperation, which appears earlier and involves the coordination of personal agendas, and collaboration, which involves accommodation of differences between more fully formed selves.

for more television time, in exchange for, say, helping out in the kitchen later, he is participating in an important interpersonal transaction. And when he willingly keeps his end of the deal at the appointed time, he is operating developmentally at a more advanced level than his younger sibling, who performs the same chore primarily in accommodation to adult authority and supervision.

Developmental Assessment and Clinical Intervention

There are three important generalizations we can make about the parent-child relational modes I have described here. I will state them first, and then draw out the implications of each in greater detail. The first is that relational modes have a natural tendency to become organized, and as such to provide a structured ground, or framework, for observable contact process. The second is that any family's organization of relational modes can be said to exhibit a greater or lesser degree of "fit" with a given child's developmental status (which is what underlies our spontaneous intuitions concerning "appropriate" and "inappropriate" parent-child interactions, as in the examples cited in my introduction). The third generalization we can make is that the organization of relational modes in family process exhibits a kind of "natural history" -- a succession of predictable reorganizational challenges that is driven by the developmental process itself. Together, these implications provide a useful model for assessing and intervening with client families. Considering each in turn:

1) Organization

When first encountering a client family, I pay careful attention to the expression or conspicuous absence of each relational mode. Are these parents able to comfortably assume the posture of being in charge, that is, of care taking and supervision? Are they capable of horizontalizing the relationship in the form of negotiation? Likewise, are they capable of dumbing down their power and authority and engaging this child dialogically, in the role of a listener and consultant? And, how do these modes interact? Do they shift unpredictably? (I'm thinking here of teenagers who complain about conversations with parents that start with a casual "how was your day?" and end with a lecture on responsibility and planning for the future.) Is this a system where one mode is rigidly entrenched? Is this, for example, a family where *everything* has to be negotiated? Or does this family appear capable of shifting flexibly from one mode to another, as the situation calls for? Essentially, when I first meet with a parent-child system, I ask myself to describe the structured ground of their contact process, and I am interested in grasping the implicit logos, the patterning, of that ground.

In many families, relational modes can be shown to organize themselves into a sort of paradigm, an overarching framework that orchestrates the expression of individual modes. Most often, this takes the form of one mode playing the role of "conductor," or perhaps in a more accurate application of the music metaphor, serving as the "key" in which the other modes are expressed. Thus, for example, in a family with young children we may witness many instances of dialog and negotiation, but generally under the organizing influence of care taking-supervision. Care taking-supervision, in other words, serves as the theme of the relationship taken as a whole, and the other two modes are more or less coordinated within this framework.

2) Fit

As a clinician, what I most want to know is how well this paradigm, this implicit patterning, fits the child's developmental readiness. Given, as I have shown, that each mode presumes a different organization of boundaries and a different distribution of power within the relationship, I undertake to assess how the family's utilization of the various modes fits, or doesn't fit, the child's growth on these dimensions. Does the parent shift from supervision to negotiation in situations when the child appears capable of enacting the self-supervision that negotiation invites? Or does the parent stubbornly persist in the supervisory mode? And if a parent presents such opportunities at what seem to be developmentally appropriate moments, is this child willing and able to take up the supervisory slack? And if not, why not? These are questions of fit, and they are a major component of my assessment process.

3) Development

I think it is safe to say that there exists a natural evolution of the roles played by the respective relational modes in the ongoing developmenttal process of the family field. Care taking-supervision, so utterly critical for the relational milieu of younger children, loses its natural potency over time, waning progressively as the child moves through adolescence and into emerging adulthood. In contrast, dialogue-consultation gradually evolves from its childhood status as an important *component* of the relationship, to become, hopefully, the primary *organizing theme* of the relationship, as the child enters emerging adulthood. And in the gradual process of the transposition of care taking-supervision and dialogue-consultation, negotiation emerges as the organizing theme during adolescence, effectively serving as the bridge for horizontalizing the relationship between parent and child. Negotiation of course is a critical relational mode throughout the child's and family's development, both with young children and with adult children. But in adolescence, there is an underlying developmenttal push for the relationship itself to become a form of protracted negotiation. This is so because adolescence is a time (as I have written elsewhere, McConville 1995) when the child disembeds from the historical relational field of the family, heightening her sense of herself as a source of initiative and influence, and an agent of her own diverging agenda.

Schematically, we might envision the normative developmenttal process of the family relational field as follows:

Figure 1. Normative Developmental Process of the Family Relational Field

CHILDHOOD	ADOLESCENCE	EMERGING ADULTHOOD
Caretaking-Supervision	Caretaking-Supervision	Caretaking
Negotiation-Accountability	**Negotiation-Accountability**	Negotiation-Accountability
Dialogue-Consultation	Dialogue-Consultation	**Dialogue-Consultation**

The premise of this model is that it is not just the individual child who develops, but also the organized relational ground of the family field. In most instances, this development evinces a natural progresssion in which first care taking-supervision, then negotiation-accountability, and finally dialogue-consultation becomes the organizing frame for the multitude of ordinary contact episodes. In effect, the relational ground undergoes several paradigmatic reorganizations over the arc of development. In well-enough functioning families, these transitions occur as a gradual adaptation to the child's emergent capabilities, without a great deal of fanfare. If one were to observe a family with young children, and then again observe this same family as the children reached their teen years, and once again as the children enter their twenties, we would detect the unmistakable signs of this gradually shifting relational paradigm.

In other families however, particularly those that present for clinical assessment, we find struggles that are roughly analogous to those that Thomas Kuhn (1962) describes for paradigm shifts in science. We discover a tangle of forces working both for and against change, children with diagnosable symptoms and problem behaviors, and a family system in crisis. Characteristically, these families experience a great deal of unproductive conflict. At face value, this appears as conflict between parents and their children, but this assessment is insufficient and figure-bound, to borrow Gordon Wheeler's (1990) apt phrase. What is really going on is a conflict between relational paradigms, and typically it is both parents and children who are caught in the throes of an unresolved reorganization of their mutual relational ground. A clinical example will help to show what this looks like concretely in real life.

Clinical example

> When I first met Leslie, she had just turned nineteen and returned home from a failed attempt at beginning college in another city. She was capable enough academically and intellectually, but had become listless and withdrawn over the several months of her college tenure, unable to connect socially and unable to get herself even to attend classes. She had telephoned her parents and announced, "I need to come home."
>
> Leslie and her parents informed me that she had become depressed in her final year of high school, and had seen a counselor for individual therapy and had undergone an unsuccessful trial of antidepressant medication. When September arrived, going off to college offered the hope of a jump starting a new chapter in her life. It wasn't to be.
>
> Indeed, Leslie fulfilled all the diagnostic criteria of Major Depressive Episode (DSM-IV, 2000). She was quiet and receding, socially awkward, "interested in nothing" to borrow her

own words, and unable to summon the motivation for almost any constructive activity. Her plan, she said unconvincingly, was to get a job and move out of the house, but she had difficulty organizing her thoughts and concentrating on the various steps that would move her toward her goal. When asked what she wished was different about herself, she cited her shyness, her passivity, and her lack of assertiveness.

Leslie's parents, who were as well meaning as parents could possibly be, were worried and exasperated. Her developmental stall didn't make any sense to them. "She's very talented," they pointed out, " and people have always liked her in spite of her shyness." But she was no longer the "sweet girl" she had been in high school. At her worst, they said, which was increasingly becoming the norm, she was irresponsible (e.g. over-drawing her checking account), willful, and deceptive. Their interactions at home had become increasingly strained and pained. She was surly, quick to anger (particularly at her mother), and uncommunicative about her seemingly aimless comings and goings. Most of her time at home was spent sequestered in her bedroom.

In particular, tension and conflict had developed around the business of Leslie finding a job. She was intentionally vague about her efforts, resented their queries and suggestions, and accused them of trying to control her. To exacerbate matters, she stayed up to all hours of the night, "doing who knows what," and slept in regularly past noon. "How can she possibly get a job when she stays in bed all day," her mother lamented, and much of their day to day fighting surrounded the matter of when she got herself into, and out of, bed. Leslie, in her individual time with me, complained correspondingly, and with uncharacteristic energy, about her parents intrusion and over-control.

As a contact system, Leslie and her parents exhibited many features of a relationship organized in the modality of care taking-supervision. Boundaries, for example, were porous. A raised eyebrow could send Leslie storming out of the house; a conspicuously absent "good morning" could bring her mother to tears. Her father would leave the newspaper spread on the breakfast table, with viable job postings circled in red marker. Similarly, their collective felt sense of power, in spite of everyone's desire that this not be the case, lay on the parent side of the relational boundary. Everyone wanted this circumstance to change, but all of their best efforts only had the effect of further entrenching the relational paradigm of childhood.

In her individual sessions, Leslie toyed ambivalently with a possible "solution." She had recently reconnected with a former high school boyfriend, a young man several years older than she, and with whom she had had a rather enmeshed and mutually suffocating relationship. She was not especiallly interested in rekindling the relationship, as she had had some difficulty extricating herself from it a year earlier. But the young man was most definitely interested, and urged her to move out of her parents home and into an apartment with him. When conflict at home grew particularly intense, she would threaten her parents to do just that, and on one occasion had packed her bags in preparation. Whenever the conflict subsided, she would confide to me that she knew the move would only amount to jumping from the frying pan to the fire.

Leslie did not move in with her boyfriend, but I mention it because it represents a type of "solution" adopted often by young adults who feel trapped in a care taking relational paradigm with parents. They look for a way to leave home and attenuate their parents' influence, but their solution is geographyical rather than relational. And since this sort of "solution" bypasses the work of truly transforming the relational ground, it typically lands them out in the world feeling more like unsupported children, than viable, self supporting adults.

And all to often, the development of these young people stalls in an oscillating loop between conflicted dependency and make-believe independence.

The work of genuinely horizontalizing a parent-child relationship, that is, bringing it to the state where its organizing principles are dialogue and consultation, lies in learning to truly negotiate. This was the essential task for Leslie and her parents, and was the organizing theme of both my individual and family therapy with them. I knew they needed to experience the transformed paradigm of negotiation-accountability if Leslie was to establish any sense of viability, and vitality, as a psychological self. My proposals were fairly simple, things they had tried haphazardly in the past but without sufficient support. In working with families like Leslie's, it is essential not to locate the "problem" on either side of the relationship, as if one side was responsible for obstructing development while the other was being victimized. In fact, both Leslie and her parents had made efforts to relate in a more evolved fashion, but by the same token both had unwittingly provoked the perseveretion of care taking-supervision behavior. This is exactly the point: both parenting behavior and child development are mediated by a contextualizing, structured, relational field, and it is this field as a whole that must be the subject of our interventions.

I asked Leslie's parents a hypothetical question. "What if this weren't your daughter we're talking about. What if this was your niece, or the daughter of a dear friend, living in your house, with your material support, and with all the same struggles. Someone you love enough to want to help, but someone separate enough to be entitled to her own way of doing things? What would you do differently" I asked? What I was proposing, essentially, was that they consider a different sort of boundary. They wouldn't try to get her out of bed, they conceded, nor closely monitor her job search with such attention and anxiety. On the other hand, they would matter-of-factly establish mutual expectations and obligations for both sides of the relationship.

They would, in other words, approach the relationship more in the spirit of negotiation than supervision. This meant that Leslie's parents were ready to relinquish their inclination to intervene in the *process* of her problem solving, resolving instead to simply *hold her accountable* for her negotiated commitments. This subtle shift of relational mode is ordinarily part of the natural progression in the parent-child relationship, and is critically important in transforming the experience of self for the child, promoting confidence and competence and self-support as felt realities.

Helping Leslie grow into the posture of a negotiator also presented a challenge. Like many young people struggling with independence, Leslie was frightened by the prospects of a more differentiated relationship with her parents. For in families like Leslie's, it is the children every bit as much as the parents who perpetuate the outmoded relational paradigm. Leslie conceded that she often failed to follow through on her plans, and came to see how her behavior often unwittingly solicited her parents' involvement.

From a therapeutic strategy standpoint, it is crucial to support the young person's *initiative* in negotiating expectations and commitments with parents. When negotiated agreements fall apart, it is most often because the adolescent or young adult enters the negotiation process passively, acquiescing to the initiative and agenda setting of adults. I spent several individual sessions helping Leslie identify what she wanted by way of parental support, and challenging her episodic inclination to lapse into childlike powerlessness vis-a-vis her parents.

The contact process of our individual sessions, not surprisingly, mirrored the developmental dilemmas and challenges of Leslie's relationship with her parents. She was inclined to assume a passive posture, looking for me to direct the work. My essential intervention, correspondingly, was to carefully maintain the middle-mode energy of a consultant, never supplying more initiative and power than Leslie herself. This was awkward and unfamiliar for her at first, but she quickly grew into the role of "negotiating" the direction of our sessions together. The result of this work was that Leslie was able to formulate several well conceived proposals, and developed the courage and conviction necessary to present them congruently to her parents.

In joint sessions, the therapeutic task was in coaching this family to have a different kind of conversation, one where interpersonal boundaries felt more "adult" and where both Leslie and her parents could experience her power as part of the contact experience. Leslie's earlier attempts to effect such changes resembled the stubbornness and withdrawal more typical of younger adolescents struggling to alter the care taking-supervision paradigm. In our joint sessions however, she was able to find a voice for her own agenda, and hold up her end of a conversation that truly had the feel of negotiation.

The end result of this work was an agreement that contained a number of boundary and power altering changes: Leslie's parents stopped "helping" her with her job search; they closed the checking account Leslie held jointly with her mother, and had Leslie open one of her own; Leslie agreed to take over her portion of the family auto insurance as soon as she found a job. Her cell phone account was transferred to her name, and she agreed to a modest monthly rent payment. Interestingly, these were all things that had been proposed previously, sometimes by Leslie, sometimes by her parents. But since they didn't know how to separate and stay connected at the same time (which is precisely what negotiation-accountability teaches), these proposals had more the tone of threats and abandonments. My job was to help them experience these alterations precisely as negotiations, that is, as instances of connection within a different arrangement of power and boundary.

Leslie found a job in a local supermarket, and within several months moved into the family home of a co-worker, renting a room from the young woman's parents. This too was handled as a negotiation, with Leslie's parents supporting the move by helping her to buy a car, and Leslie agreeing to join her parents' for meals several evenings a week. I continued seeing Leslie for several months in individual sessions, where we worked to cultivate her ability to know and negotiate for her own agenda, and her confidence in making choices – in short, her experience of personal power.

Not surprisingly, the form of Leslie's contact process with her parents evolved, increasingly feeling to all concerned like dialogue and discussion between adults. And Leslie became comfortable once again with her parents' affection and warmth. When I last saw Leslie, there was nothing that would suggest clinical depression, and she was in the process of submitting applications for admission to several local colleges.

Conclusion

It is a cornerstone of Gestalt theory that child development takes place within the context of a dynamically evolving relational field. Integral to that field of course is the family and the parent-child relationship. This field developmental process can be understood in terms of the acquisition of three discrete relational modes, each of which organizes the relationship of parent and child according to an articulation of interpersonal boundary and distribution of power. Understanding the influence that each mode has on a child's experience of self, and the role that their sequencing plays in the continuity of child development, provides a useful model for assessing and intervening with developmental interruptions.

References

American Psychiatric Association (2000). *Diagnostic and Statistical Manual of Mental Disorders,* Fourth edition, Text Revision. Washington, DC:.American Psychiatric Association.
Gilligan, C. (1982). *In a Different Voice.* Cambridge, MA: Harvard University Press..
Kuhn, T. (1962). *The Structure of Scientific Revolutions.* Chicago, IL: The University of Chicago Press.
McConville, M. (1995). *Adolescence: Psychotherapy And The Emergent Self.* San Francisco, CA: Jossey-Bass.
Perls, H., Hefferline, R., & Goodman, P. (1951). *Gestalt Therapy: Excitement and Growth in the Human Personality.* New York: Dell.
Stern, D. (1985). *The Interpersonal World of the Infant.* New York: Basic Books.
Sullivan, H. S. (1953). *The Interpersonal Theory of Psychiatry.* New York: Norton.
Vygotsky, L. S. (1962). *Thought and Language.* Cambridge, MA: MIT Press.
Wheeler, G. (1990a). Self-in-Contact: a Gestalt Developmental Model. Working Paper III. Unpublished Manuscript.
Wheeler, G. (1990b). *Gestalt Reconsidered.* New York: Gestalt Institute of Cleveland Press.

Applications

Editors' Note:
The history of psychotherapy is replete with descriptions of disembodied minds reaching out to each other, descriptions that are often rich and thick, but also often tenuous and clearly missing the key dimension of the physicality of our embodied lives. In this chapter we are taken into the consulting room of a master Gestalt body process therapist. Denise Tervo works compassionately, nurturing the flickering candle of hope. She embraces the child and her/his parents, dissolving embodied patterns of shame and disconnection. She supports children to rebuild their connection with their full self-hood and with the key caregivers in their lives. Denise compares herself to an aunt who comes to stay in their lives for awhile, radiating warmth, optimism and sureness of the possibility of healing. You will hear, see and feel the process in her three clinical examples, grounded in contemporary knowledge of neurodevelopment and of the profound and enduring effects of trauma on the body and mind of her young clients.

8

Zip Zag Flop and Roll:

Creating an Embodied Field for Healing and Awareness when Working With Children

Denise Tervo

This article describes the process of body-oriented psychotherapy with three children who might be described by people in their lives as "strange," "disconnected," or "a little off," or who have been previously diagnosed as having Asperger's, pervasive developmental disorders, or post-traumatic stress disorders due to early trauma (DSM IV-TR, 2000; Silva, et al., 2000). In my practice of over 23 years, I regularly see such children; often their fears and worries have been swept under the carpet. Alternatively, they have been living with messages that say "live with it," "buck up," or "this will make you stronger." Usually these children have well-meaning families who are overwhelmed, who had poor parenting, or whose family fields are filled with chaos and current life struggles.

The experience of being different and feeling unsupported is excruciatingly painful and difficult for children and adolescents. Many of these children experience frustrations at home, at school, or in their communities as they are teased, ignored, and misunderstood. Their experience of themselves is reflected in their experiences and interaction with others who frequently don't understand their idiosyncrasies or misshaped efforts to connect with themselves or others.

Children carry their histories with them in their stature, walk, talk, breath, and method of making contact with their environment (Tervo, 1997). Contrary to popular belief, they do remember early traumas, deprivations, or insults and may carry these on an embodied, kinesthetic level (Van der Kolk, 2007). Traumatic experiences can accelerate or retard critical developmental transitions (Pynoos, Steinber, & Geonjian, 2007), and traumatized children can become frozen in specific ways in their attempt to respond to a nonresponsive field (Kepner, 1995; Perry et al., 1995).

Children who are suffering from trauma and developmental delay may not have a sense of body awareness. For example, when her finger is bleeding, a traumatized child may look at her finger with surprise that blood is getting on her toy. Her dissociation and constriction of feelings make her the object — not the subject — of experience. When we are estranged from our bodily being and are disconnected or fragmented within ourselves, our contact with the environment may also be fragmented, subject to resistance, and disorganized (Kepner, 1987).

In my work with children who are experiencing this kind of fragmentation, I focus on disowned developmental patterns and physical processes to facilitate greater sensation development and organismic self-regulation (Tervo, 2002).

Before I describe the children and my work with them, I need to explain some key terms and practices that are important to Gestalt body process psychotherapy. The *embodied field* is the intersection of the many ways we influence each other, feel each other, and know each other through our physical sensory experience. We perceive the field through our senses and create it in kind, in response to what we perceive, in our bodies.

The *embodied family field,* a form of embodied field, is an example of how family members, particularly children, carry frequent or intense family interactions within their bodies, as their part in the family field. This includes the embodied patterns and context that are experienced in the moment.

As therapist, my *embodied presence* emerges from my awareness and intention to be in my body, to relate to myself and others, and to be present in the room. I am intentional with my physicality in relation to another, to feeling my body (to being aware of my senses, my breathing, and my movement), and to how I place myself in proximity to the child and family. I intentionally hold an embodied relational field. That is, through my energy, empathy, listening, language, and movement, I respond to the child "body to body" (Kepner, 2003). My role is to develop relationships, create trust and safety, and provide an emotional field that will enhance the child's and the family's sensation, experiences, and awareness.

To this end, I co-create play activities that decrease restriction or enhance large muscle movement and increase bodily sensation, awareness, and contact with the child and with the child's environment. In doing so, I see important shifts in children's ability to increase bodily awareness and fluidity of natural movement, as well as their ability to make relational contact with me and the outer world.

The theoretical assumptions and approach of Gestalt body process psychotherapy (which uses body process work, developmental movements, and the embodied relational field to effect change) have been supported by current neurobiological research findings. Research indicates that mirror neurons in the premotor area of the brain allow people to have an empathic sense of what the other is doing both in actions and intentions (Phillipson, 2006; Siegel, 1999; Schore, 2003). Thus we are wired for affective, relational engagement and connection with others. Daniel Stern (2004) finds that "here and now" experiences help heal "then and there" old central nervous system patterns and neural pathways, confirming body-oriented assumptions about reparative work with fixed Gestalts or frozen developmental processes. Healing and change can occur with new experience in the moment.

These changes can occur when a therapist supports the field of the child and the family as it learns to flex, get re-nourished, and be supported. I co-create a field of acceptance and support for as many family members as possible. Robert Lee (2001) indicates the strong need to decrease shame in the family and attend to everyone's yearning. I intentionally try to diminish shame and blame and to increase awareness and positive shifts in the energy of the family system. Working with the family supports a healthier embodied field in which the child can grow and develop.

When a therapist can co-create an embodied relational field with the child and family, the child is able to shift fixed and blocked Gestalts, re-pattern previous frozen developmental movements, and improve socialization and relational issues. This body-oriented psychotherapy provides a healing and embodied therapeutic field for growth and reparative work with these children. In order for this kind of work to unfold, it is important that the therapist stays curious about what the child is doing and why.

Scenario I: Strawberry Shortcake World: Dissociative States Due to Early Trauma and Childhood Environmental Stress

Sherry is a four-year-old who wandered into my office with her Strawberry Shortcake doll and three other make-believe friends. She took no notice of me or anything in my room as she floated from one doll to the next in a fantasy world.

As her mother told me of the pending divorce in the family, Sherry continued to play on her own, neither interrupting nor showing any interest in the conversation. Sherry is an only child who primarily lives in a world of adults when at home. At preschool, Sherry does well academically, but she keeps to herself and has no interest in interacting in play groups with other children.

Her mom reports that Sherry was adopted at birth and has always been "a little strange and to herself." Sherry's dad is currently in and out of addiction; he struggles to hold onto a job. In addition to the current family tension and dad's addiction, Sherry was molested by her primary babysitter when she was 18 months old. Mom does not know how long the abuse had been going before it was identified. Sherry hardly spoke at that time and was reportedly very quiet and withdrawn. The pediatrician told the family that Sherry would not remember anything and that they should not worry.

Sherry's mother indicated that Sherry was experiencing night terrors and severe anxiety at bedtime when mom left for work. According to both parents, Sherry talked about Strawberry Shortcake and her friends constantly and seemed to have little interest in anything else. Throughout the first session, Sherry ignored all of us and focused only on her doll and her imaginary friends. We did not seem to be part of her world until mom tried to leave the room. At that moment, Sherry seemed to wake up with a jolt. With wide eyes, she took a deep breath, began crying, and clung to her mother's leg.

As I observed and experienced this family in the first session, I was filled with compassion and empathy at how hard everyone seemed to be trying to "keep it together and do the right thing" in spite of their pain, anger and feelings of being overwhelmed. I watched Dad shrink and hang his head as his wife talked about his drinking, his lost jobs, and their current separation. I heard mom's voice crack and saw her eyes fill when she mentioned Sherry's molestation and visits to the pediatrician. As I watched Sherry float around the room, I noticed that she walked primarily on her toes, as if she were willing herself to fly away. The shift in Sherry was dramatic when her mom rose to leave. Sherry energetically came home to herself from her traumatized dissociative state. Her eyes were huge and she looked terrified. Her breathing quickened and she became hypervigilant in a split second. This was a marked contrast to her previous "floating space" in her Strawberry Short-cake world.

Sherry's symptoms of post-traumatic stress disorder were marked. While we didn't know the intensity or frequency of her abuse, the chronicity of her traumatized, dissociative state had significantly impacted her over the last two years. The current family changes had exacerbated her already anxious and traumatized sense of safety in the world.

My work with Sherry spanned a 10-month period. I saw her weekly and was very aware of grading up or down the experimentation with contact based on my experience of her in the moment. For children who have been traumatized (i.e., sexual abuse, violence, severe neglect), the trauma is held on a physiological level. Healing Sherry's trauma would come through supporting her in learning to regulate her contact with herself and with her environment, increased sensation awareness and impulses, and modulating her physiological arousal as she begins to experiment with trust, awareness, and attachment (van der Kolk & Fisler, 1994; Levine, 2007).

Treatment: Embodied Family Field

When working with the family, I needed to create a safe supportive field in which all family members would begin to trust me. With Sherry's mother and father, I began providing parenting interventions, personal support, embodied listening, and direct expression of the unexpressed pain and anger in the system. We talked about normal child development and ways to help integrate Sherry back into the world of children. I strongly encouraged play groups after school and neighborhood child activities. With Dad, I continued to encourage extra time with Sherry and offered support (without blame) for his considering options beyond the bottle.

We discussed trauma related to Sherry's adoption and the sexual abuse that she experienced as a very young child. With both parents, I mirrored and modeled expression of feelings and basic ways of connecting with Sherry and other family members. I continued to use embodied language, gestures, and empathy to support the field (Kepner, 2003).

Treatment: Embodied Field with the Child

Play sessions with Sherry focused on relational issues and being "seen" and still being safe. Initially Sherry ignored me altogether. Mother stayed in the room and served as the safe ground at first. Gradually mom was able to move to the waiting room on the condition that she left her shoes and her watch for Sherry to "guard".

We both "floated" through those initial sessions in a very distant, dissociative way. Sherry's dissociation was a creative adaptation to try to self-regulate and modulate the intensity of her feelings, impulses, and responses to her earlier molestation, when she could not speak or get support from the environment. This had become her frozen response or fixed Gestalt (Kepner, 1995; Tervo, 1997). I did not give her a lot of eye contact or use many words initially, but allowed her to experience me as part of the ground of my room. By slowly creating an environment that was safe and not threatening, she began to sneak a peek and glance my way out of the corner of her eye to see what I was doing as I played with my dolls. I was creating parallel play experiences that were grounded in providing a non-threatening and curious field.

Our relational contact evolved in small increments as trust grew. Sherry began to acknowledge me, to give me eye contact, and even to offer an occasional smile. After our relationship was more solidified, I knew it was time to grade up the experimentation with more sensation development and move into more of the early trauma work.

In early sessions, Sherry did not want me to play or even to watch her act out her stories. She would get mad at me if I disrupted her fantasies. By talking to Strawberry Shortcake rather than directly to Sherry, I began to make initial contact with Sherry through her fantasy world. We started playing many make believe games with Strawberry Shortcake and all of her friends. In these games, Strawberry was usually alone and no one was available to take care of her.

In order to bring part of her molestation history more directly into the field, I began talking to Strawberry Shortcake's cat about a little girl who got hurt by a mean lady and no one helped her. After creating a trusting relational field and establishing myself as someone she could play with and believe, I began taking a more active role directly with Sherry, not just via her doll. Bauer (1996) and others have now indicated that one- to two-year-olds are able to recall memory. Usually the memories are held on a kinesthetic cellular level, and the trauma of Sherry's abuse and initial abandonment (adoption) needed to be experienced in a safe environment.

In dealing with Sherry's initial abandonment at birth and the sexual abuse, I needed to serve as a nurturing and encouraging change agent. Philippson (2006) indicates that when some clients come from severely deprived or abusive backgrounds, the therapist needs to lead the client into more contactful relating, which will support the development of new neural connections. When the therapist serves as a change agent, the client is supported in developing an ability to self-regulate (p. 62). Serving as a supportive change agent was imperative with Sherry since her history of trauma minimized her body awareness, connection with herself and others, and her ability to take risks in her environment.

Following Sherry's behavioral cues, we began playing and creating many early developmental relational games such as hide and seek. Can I find Sherry? Is it safe for her to come out? I would hide Sherry under the large pillows and she would pop out and surprise/scare me over and over again.

Neurodevelopmental therapist, educator and dancer Bonnie Bainbridge Cohen (1993), describes how as children develop, they establish the basic patterns of their movement. Development is not a linear process, but occurs in overlapping waves with each stage containing elements of all of the others. Cohen explores early motor developmental patterns from breathing, navel radiation, mouthing, prespinal, push, and reach and pull patterns. According to Cohen, when uninhibited, each pattern fully develops and automatically transitions into the developmentally necessary succeeding patterns (Cohen, 1993; Aposhyan, 2004).

With this knowledge as part of my therapeutic ground, I continued to provide play experiences and movements that would stimulate and increase Sherry's bodily sensations and awareness. Repetition of the movements helped support her bodily shifts on a physiological level. As she would jump, I was mirroring and encouraging grounding and contact in her whole foot (not just her toes). Her leaping actions increased sensation, development, and awareness in her legs and pelvis. As she stretched her arms to the sky to announce herself, Sherry was also beginning her reaching and connecting movements. There was a marked shift in her affect and energy level and a decrease in the degree of her dissociation during the sessions.

After I experienced Sherry as being able to sense and make contact with herself and her environment more completely, I graded the experimental play movements up once again. Sherry's early issues of molestation and disorganized attachment were further heightened as our creeping and crawling games morphed into reenactments of me saving the baby and the mommy from the wild winds and water or from the sharks. She would insist on playing this game over and over again as body memory was reshifting the previous trauma of no one being there to keep her safe.

Sessions included both of us creeping and crawling on the floor to get Baby Sherry and mommy to safety. Since I do not generally touch children in sessions, we enacted the experience and also had a tiny baby doll and mother doll as part of the game. While we would creep and then crawl to safety, I could carry and hug one while she would take the other. I used a soft soothing and strong voice to anchor the process with Sherry, Little Baby Sherry, and Mommy, despite Sherry's increasingly anxious and worried tone to hurry and get them all to safety.

I would save them both, and we would all creep, crawl, or swim to safety on the island or to the ship. At other times, Sherry would flail on the floor and frantically kick her legs until I could come and save her from drowning and take her back to the ship where her mom was waiting for her. These bodily interventions reenacted the essence of Sherry's trauma experiences on a kinesthetic level. By the repetition of our movement games, we were opening constricted and rigidified parts of Sherry's body (arms, shoulder, pelvis, legs). The reenactment of her trauma within the new safer relational field of therapy supported a paradigm shift in her processing, awareness, and ability to make contact.

Schore's (2003) description of the present moment being able to shift previous experiences on an emotional and physiological level was demonstrated in my work with Sherry and her family. Sherry's family is now less angry and reactive and understands Sherry's style of dissociating when stressed. Her parents have actively encouraged greater socialization and family activities that include other children.

Over time Sherry became less dissociative, walked on her whole foot, not just her toes, and experienced increased genuine contact with the field. Sherry became willing to explore my toy shelves and stopped bringing Strawberry Shortcake with her to her sessions. Mom reported that Sherry seemed happier and more connected with herself and others. Sherry no longer suffered from night terrors and was not as upset when mom left for work each morning. She was more willing to take risks, could feel her body, and know if she was cut or hurt. Sherry had a few friends and went on some playdates! She had moved from the world of fantasy and dissociation into the world of contact and connection with herself and others.

Scenario 2: Polar Bear Knuckleball: Re-patterning Developmental Delays

Six-year-old Ted and his family came to see me for family assistance in dealing with Ted's constant biting of his two younger brothers and chewing on his fingers and shirts. They also wanted support in helping him to get along with other kids. Ted would become very excited, anxious, and impulsive when playing with other children, and he would bite them. He was then crushed if they did not want to play with him, and couldn't understand why he was in "time out" all of the time. Ted's parents were very loving, intelligent professionals who blamed themselves for their child's behavior.

Ted was born prematurely, and there was a family history of anxiety and hyperactivity. Ted's tendency to make funny sounds, drool, and suck or chew on everything was a source of embarrassment for the parents. They had been more understanding when Ted was an only child. But Ted's behavior had gotten worse with the birth of each brother and concern for the younger children's safety overrode curiosity on the etiology of the issue. They just needed help fixing this problem! My bodily experience of Ted's family was one of warmth in my heart and tightness in my arms and back. Ted's parents seemed to have loving intentions that were followed by rigidity and anxiety over the situation. Metaphorically Ted reminded me of Pinocchio, trying to be a real boy. His body seemed disconnected, as was his contact with the other.

My work with Ted took place over the course of seven months. I typically met Ted once a week, followed by a session with the whole family. My work with Ted usually took the form of co-created movement games and use of balls, Matchbox cars, dinosaurs, play dough, and Batakas (soft bats). As Ted was able to increase his sensation and awareness and connect with his own body boundaries and emotions, he was able to express himself more directly and no longer chewed on himself or bit others in frustration.

Treatment: Embodied Family Field

My treatment interventions were focused on supporting the external environmental field as well as Ted's inner subjective experience. With Ted's parents, I provided an emotional container to support their feelings of frustration and concern with Ted's outbursts and his biting. Besides their worries about him chewing on his fingers and shirt collars, they were concerned about the safety of their two younger children: Ted had impulsively bitten both the baby and the toddler when he had not gotten his needs met and he was angry. Ruella Frank's (2001) seminal work emphasizes the interaction between early motor development and psychological development. Frank indicates that reaching with the mouth (the rooting response) is one of the earliest developmental patterns to emerge. Developmental patterns of the mouth, tongue, and jaw expand into other developmental reaching patterns, then integrate into the central nervous system and influence the whole of experience (p 115). Although Ted was chronologically six years old, he had experienced significant developmental delays physiologically, socially, and emotionally.

Due to Ted's lack of body awareness and connection to himself and his environment, it was imperative that I work with the embodied family field to support Ted in repatterning neural pathways and developmenttal blocks. With parental support and interventions, we continued to mirror, model, and actively stimulate alternative body movements to enhance Ted's developmental and relational experiences. By facilitating many of the early motor development patterns described by Bonnie Bambridge Cohen and Ruella Frank, I was able to see Ted increase his contact functions with himself and others.

With Ted's parents, I encouraged playful family experiences that could support greater facial mobility, stimulation, and sensitization. We practiced making silly faces, growling like a lion, chewing gum and spitting it out, and other playful ways to release his tight jaw. I also encouraged family swims – which playfully enhanced full body exercise and movement – along with yelling games and blowing bubbles under the water at the pool and in the tub. Chewing celery or crunchy chips was also encouraged. In Gestalt therapy, we emphasize the discernment of what is me and not me. For children in early developmental stages, discernment begins with differentiation of what we take in orally (i.e., I like bananas; I do not like canned peas) and a child will naturally shut his mouth and spit out what he does not like. I emphasized the importance of the family to continue to kick, roll and throw balls with Ted to support his continued muscle development and improve contact functions.

While working with Ted's parents, I continued to review normal developmental education, parenting, and management skills. The use of consistent boundaries was strongly encouraged and modeled with the parents. Helping reduce the parents' sense of shame that they had an "odd child" not like their friends' sons was a huge part of supporting the family to grieve, reduce shame, and accept all of their son's gifts. Robert Lee (2001) emphasizes the need for the therapist to join the child's parents and create a nurturing experience to help them deal with their own yearnings and abort "shame attacks".

Treatment: Embodied Field with the Child

I spent a great deal of time observing Ted and noticing his ongoing mouth movements, underdeveloped sense of differrentiation, and difficulty with fluidity and flow throughout his body. His arms and legs were frequently in motion, but his body parts appeared disconnected from one another. Relationally, I experienced him the same way. He noticed me and would talk TO me, but in a monotone fashion as if reporting the news to the wall. I did not experience him as being WITH me in the session. We just happened to be in the same place at the same time.

Children with pervasive developmental delay can have a very difficult time responding to external environmental cues in an appropriate manner. They have difficulty with interrelationships and struggle to not push others away, much less try to make connections and or friends. This pattern can be seen when Ted is playing and having fun, becomes hyperaroused, and bites a playmate, but then sobs when the child won't play with him.

With Ted, the experience of his fluidity, integration of self, and his ability to reach or be reached were the key themes of our sessions together.

When working with Ted, I initially mirrored and modeled his behavior. By observing him and trying his movements, I was able to kinesthetically gain greater sensation and gain a richer understanding of ways that he organized himself and his world. We began making soft noises, with him being in charge of the noises and me being a "copy cat". Initially, he totally ignored me. However, as I attended to him and really listened to his words or sounds (monotone as they were), he became curious about my attention to detail. Eventually I had him teach me how to roll my mouth like he did. We began to play with grading up and down the experiment with greater range of expression in sounds and intensity.

Using our relationship and the development of trust in the room, I began to introduce greater expression of anger with different toys (smashing pillows, toy cars, play dough, dinosaurs, Batakas, etc). No matter what type of toy was selected, my attention continued to focus on Ted developing greater flexibility with mouthing and expressing himself and finding ways that Ted could developmentally and psychologically reach and be reached and enhance his sense of self. Oaklander (2002, 2006) reiterates a child's need to enhance his sense of self and make good contact with himself and with others.

As we played on the floor, we crawled all over the room making car sounds and eventually crashing into each other. The car sounds and crashing sounds stimulated his mouth, throat, and diaphragm, and the crawling began to stimulate and increase sensations in his legs, torso, hips, arms, and shoulders. After he increased his fluidity with these sounds and movements, we shifted our weight to our legs, stood up, and became T-Rex dinosaurs. My interest was in having Ted move along developmental levels and experience and feel himself as more powerful and connected to his legs, pelvis, and sense of his ground. Playing as a T-Rex dinosaur helped him increase his vocalization and sense of power with sound rather than his teeth. Soon we were growling through the jungle, standing upright and feeling our power and might. All of this subtle grading up of experimentation with muscle movement enhanced his sensation and knowledge about his self and his contact functions. Frank (2001) reiterates ways in which a client's emerging patterns of movement play a critical role in developing self-awareness for the infant and in maintaining a healthy self throughout life.

In later sessions I added the activity of playing catch with medium-sized squishy balls while we made sounds. As we graded up the experimentation, I began using words, not just sounds of anger. "I'm mad dad is gone all the time... I hate my brother sometimes when he is in my stuff." We gradually began whacking the balls back and forth and making sounds and saying mad words in this game. As we increased the use of expressive play with the Batakas and smashed them together, we again focused on body sensation, contact with self and other.

During our sessions, I consciously introduced developmental patterns of pushing, reaching, and pulling into our play experiences. I found Ted's responsiveness to our movement games staggering. Ted continued to become more aligned physically and emotionally and interconnected with himself and his outer world.

Over time, Ted stopped biting his parents and brothers. The parents were able to model and set better boundaries – e.g., animals bite, people don't – and to tolerate his verbal expression of frustration or anger. His dad began making a concerted effort to play ball and connect with his son when he was home. Ted's mom was able to set better limits and decrease her anxiety over her "problem" child.

Ted's creation of "Polar Bear Knuckleball" became a creative game and illustrative adaptation of his ability to express himself more directly (like a growling and lovable polar bear) and his newfound mastery in being able to make a stand, and also to reach and yield. John Barnes, physical therapist and trainer in myofascial release (2000), discusses the techniques of "unwinding" of muscles and fascia that have been restricted over time. Ted created a complex routine of all Polar Bear Knuckleball players (I was now noticed and included, and we had developmentally moved from parallel play experiences to more collaborative, relational play). Each polar bear had to roll on his back, lift a leg, and zoom the ball under his knee to his partner while making growling sounds. Ted would give me hand signals (as in baseball) on the type of ball to throw.

I was fascinated to observe that once I supported the opening up of Ted's blocked energy and movements – in his ability to express himself (mouth), reach (open up arms and shoulders) and take a stand (better sense of his relationship to ground) – his natural energetic pathways became much more fluid. Naturally Ted began to expand his body movements and "unwind" his whole body – belly, pelvis, and midsections. What a beautiful depiction of organismic self-regulation.

Children's patterns are generally not as fixed or frozen as those of adults due to their chronological age and their continued permeability of their system. By facilitating many of the early motor development patterns described by Cohen and Frank, Ted was able to increase his contact functions with himself and relationally. He was able to increase his self functions (i.e., breathing, grounding, and getting into his legs and pelvis) as well as increase his relational contact (i.e., reaching, pulling, moving forward with his arms). With greater vocalization and use of language, he no longer had to bite to meet his needs.

Scenario 3: Zig Zag Flop and Roll: Asperger's Syndrome, Developmental Delays (Interiority), and Environmental Stress

Head dropped and intent, eight-year-old Jimmy shuffled into my office staring at his Star Wars Gameboy. He did not seem to notice me or attend to the shift in his environment when moving from one room to the next. As he flopped down on the couch next to his dad, Jimmy continued to be preoccupied with his game. He did not respond to either his dad or my comments and remained in his own world of Star Wars. Dad described Jimmy as "a good boy, but kinda different." He didn't have friends and got upset easily. Jimmy's parents were really worried about him.

Contact with Jimmy would come later, only after I had merged with his Star Wars inner world, and he experienced me as a relatively safe person. Jimmy was referred to me because an outside evaluation recommended Gestalt Therapy to assist him with his aggression. Jimmy was diagnosed with Asperger's Syndrome, a pervasive developmental disorder that features severe social interaction impairment, repetitive patterns of behavior, awkward physical movement, and difficulty modulating affect and cues in the environment (DSM-IV-TR, See American Psychological Association, 2000).

Jimmy had a very difficult time with socialization and his temper. He hit and bit his mother and "flipped out" with severe temper tantrums when he did not get his way. Jimmy was in a private school that refused additional services to educate the staff on ways to deal with children diagnosed with Asperger's. When Jimmy was younger, his behavior had not been as difficult to manage. His diagnosis and behavior had been very hard for the family to accept. Jimmy's mother had been in active addiction when Jimmy was born. She began her recovery process when he was five years old. Jimmy's father was retired. His previous job involved extensive travel away from home and he now suffered from severe panic attacks and other health issues. Like a multidimensional puzzle, all of these factors significantly impacted Jimmy and his family and were part of the ground that the family brought into my office.

During the initial session I observed Jimmy and his family and attended to my body sensations and "felt experience" in the moment. My experience of watching Jimmy's intense preoccupation with his Star Wars game was one of disconnection both within my face and eyes and in observing his muscular constriction around his eyes, neck, and shoulders. I did not notice or feel either my legs or experience a sense of his limbs. Metaphorically, Jimmy seemed similar to a constricted and flattened toy top that needed air and expansion.

As I observed and listened to Jimmy's parents and attended to my body sensations in the moment, I was aware of warmth in my heart as well as constriction and tightness through my shoulders, back, and jaw. I noticed Jimmy's mom's tight jaw and neck as she talked about Jimmy regularly biting her and "flipping out" at the grocery store. As Jimmy's dad reported his history of panic attacks, heart problems, and frustrations dealing with Jimmy's private school, I noticed his heavy, labored breathing and collapsed shoulders.

Again, in creating an embodied field, I am sometimes able to feel and bodily register feelings that may be part of the field, but have not been owned or expressed (Kepner, 1987). I began to hold curiosity about the possible unspoken grief, sadness, shame, and frustrations in dealing with their challenging and sweet only child. I experienced the family field that supported Jimmy as filled with care and good intentions, but also underdeveloped with the emotional and developmental supports that this child needed to be able to make contact with himself and the world around him.

I worked with this family over a fourteen-month period. I typically met with Jimmy and his father once a week, Jimmy's mother only came a few times due to her work schedule. My work with Jimmy usually took the form of co-created movement games using the pillows, couch and the floor.

Treatment: Embodied Family Field

I worked with Jimmy's dad to meet his own health needs and understand the powerful impact of his anxiety attacks and somatization in the family system. My time with Jimmy's mom focused on her regrets and shame over her addiction and the possible impact on her son. She expressed her anger that he was not "just normal" and had a hard time experiencing and "seeing him" without a veil of her own anger and regret. Our work together involved my modeling more appropriate responses and ways to interact with Jimmy. I encouraged her to begin to see her son – not just the diagnosis of Asperger's and her sense of personal failure with him. I encouraged additional positive experiences between mother and son. I also encouraged Jimmy's mom to begin to get involved in activities that nourished her as well. We discussed additional psychological and academic testing so that an accurate individual educational plan could be developed for Jimmy. The parents decided to switch schools to accommodate his developmental needs.

By supporting the whole family system (including outside relatives) to "see" Jimmy and appreciate all of his strengths, the family was no longer mired with shame over his diagnosis. Hence the family was able to identify a more supportive school placement and request the additional academic services that he needed. Embodied listening, empathy, and gestures were all used to enhance the embodied field and support acceptance and change (Kepner, 2003).

Treatment: Embodied Field with the Child

Frequently children like Jimmy struggle with recognizing themselves, their disconnected awareness, their contact, and their relationship with others. When asked to draw a self-portrait Jimmy gave his drawing glasses and a beard, just like his dad! Creating a therapeutic embodied field was essential for my work with Jimmy. Similar to the first two children, Jimmy did not have any sense of me or connection with me initially. His sole preoccupation was with his Star Wars Gameboy.

As in early development, we needed to create a trusting relationship before he would be able to experience a sense of self. In my slow merging with his world of Star Wars, Jimmy was willing to be my teacher and educate me on the game, the characters, and the story. Within the context of teacher/student concerning his area of passion, I slowly gained eye contact and minimal connection with the boy behind the game. I focused on greater body sensation and awareness development.

While he was totally ignoring me, I continued to verbalize with embodied, mirroring language when interacting with him. "I see you; tell me about your toy." Our relational interactions moved to Jimmy hiding in the pillows or playing hide and seek in my room. Jimmy loved to hide and listen to me look for him while expressing my sadness that I could not find him under the pile of pillows.

We began squeezing pillows and throwing pillows in a fun and playful way. Jimmy was soon creeping and crawling on the floor, and falling and hiding in the pillows. I continued to "make a fuss" over him, asking him if he was hurt and expressing my joy that I had found him. Although Jimmy was chronologically eight years old, developmentally we were experimenting with fifteen-month to three-year-old developmental patterns and relational issues.

Jimmy's yearning for mirroring and connection further supported the co-creation of our embodied field. Over time, we were able to move from Star Wars as a focus to our own developmental movement pattern game of Zig Zag Flop and Roll. Jimmy created the game, and I enhanced it with awareness of his need for increased body boundary awareness, sensation development, and relational connection.

In sessions, I observe children's movements and ways they make contact with themselves and/or their environment. Using their movements, I try to expand on the movements and increase their breadth and depth. Exaggerating the movement, doing it again, and putting sound to it are all examples of ways to enhance the field with greater sensation and awareness.

I attended to Jimmy's natural movements and supported his body in "unwinding" and opening up. We then created the game of Zig Zag Flop and Roll. This involved quickly running left and right, flopping on the couch, and forcefully rolling off the couch onto the mound of pillows. What was interesting was that Jimmy created the game and I expanded on the movements to enhance sensation development. It was only later, when reading Siegel's book (1999) *The Developing Mind*, that I realized we had created a game that stimulated the prefrontal cortex and supported balancing left and right sides of his body and brain.

For the next several months Jimmy only wanted to play his Zig Zag Flop and Roll game. He created different variations and seemed to be experimenting with his own "unwinding of old trauma patterns" (Barnes, 2000; Levine, 2007). At one time he was sliding upside down off of the couch, as if in a birth canal. I continued to anchor him with my voice of support and encouragement and joy that he was safe.

Another time he wiggled and kicked around and around in a circle and then crept over to me and looked up, completing the spinal movement patterns (Cohen, 1993) and gazing at me, as if an infant.

Our experimental play games were always led by Jimmy and expanded by me to enrich the experiment and expand the boundary of contact. Over time the games shifted to elaborate games of pillow fights and creation of "Gauntlets of Pillows". Once again he created games of zigging and zagging, jumping on his left foot then his right foot, then bending left and right to miss the pillow that I was swinging in a figure eight fashion. This elaborate series of arm and body movements facilitated muscular movement and neural pathways in expanding from their previously flattened or constricted position. His games included reaching, pulling, pushing, falling away, flopping, and rolling over and over again.

Slowly, the games that Jimmy created shifted developmentally once again. He moved to more age-appropriate latency games with balls and pillows. These games had more complex rules and no flops on the couch or mirroring of movements. Relationally we had shifted as well, from initially refusing contact with me, to "sneaking a peek" at me, to me mirroring him, to Jimmy finally gazing and in real contact with me. Our communication and connection continued to evolve from me asking him to play, to Jimmy asking me to watch him, and finally Jimmy making a statement to me: "Are you going to play or what? I am waiting for you!" These subtle shifts are all large relational and developmental markers of his sense of contact and sense of self.

After these intense sessions, the family reported huge shifts in Jimmy's behavior. He had increased his eye contact with others and was no longer biting or hitting his mother. His grades had improved and he was doing his homework without a fight each night. While he would still have periodic temper tantrums, especially when overwhelmed or hyperaroused by the environment, he was able to maintain better self support and direct expression of feelings. Jimmy now verbally argues with his parents, which is more age appropriate for a pre-adolescent nine year old.

Jimmy's socialization and relational skills also developed. He was able to expand his world to include going on Boy Scout outings, having a few friends to play with, and even spending the night at a friend's house.

Jimmy and his family will continue to need to accept and deal with his developmental delays. However with increased contact with himself and his external field, Jimmy expresses more joy in this life and no longer focuses only on the fantasy world of Star Wars.

Summary and Conclusions

The previous case examples and descriptions of co-creation of the embodied relational field are intended to help the reader get a sense of this body-oriented way of working with children and families. Recent neurobiological research confirms what child therapists have already known: the therapeutic alliance and the emotional relationship that is co-created is of utmost importance in supporting change for our clients (both the child and the family).

Research also indicates that present moment experiences can shift neural pathways in previous experiences. Hence, creating an embodied field and utilizing embodied interventions is very therapeutic for many clients.

These research findings, the relational and embodied field concepts, and the physical process interventions employed are relevant for young and old alike, regardless of diagnosis. However, the early developmental patterns and many of the relational attachment interventions (peek a boo, hiding and seeking, early gaze, sensation development, and large muscle movement unwinding and releasing) are all very helpful with the more nonverbal and/or fragmented, traumatized children and families.

When serving as a therapeutic change agent, especially with severe cases of trauma, deprivation, or developmental delay, it is imperative to ensure that children initially have enough relational support. As previously indicated, these children by definition are disconnected from themselves, their bodies, their interrelationships, and from their ability to take risks and make contact.

In the case of Sherry, her dissociative retreat into her fantasy world no longer served as a creative adjustment to her separation from her birth mother and early sexual abuse by her caregiver. As I served as the significant other who saved the baby AND the lost mommy, Sherry was able to get her bearings and finally swim to shore. Sherry now makes contact with her "here and now" mother and plays with real girlfriends rather than imaginary characters.

Ted's journey through early developmental patterns of mouthing, biting, reaching, and Polarbear Knuckleball supported him in increaseing contact with himself and his world.

Jimmy's Zig Zag Flop and Roll unwinding game creatively supported his developmental repatterning through early trauma and neglect. Now, rather than playing alone with a Gameboy, Jimmy goes to a friend's house to spend the night. Rather than biting his mom when he is angry, Jimmy argues like other nine year olds.

The therapist's role is one of "seeing" the child and family and co-creating an embodied field that supports growth. The therapist creates shifts both relationally and on a muscular, cellular level through the use of movement, body awareness, knowledge of dissociation, and repatterning fixed Gestalts on a developmental level. Major shifts can occur for the traumatized child or one who experienced pervasive developmental delays. As the field evolves and the child experiences internal and external changes in contact functioning, major changes in socialization, body awareness, and self support may also occur.

Our existence is embedded in the relational field, and the child is embedded in the family. I assume the best for all family members and I work to develop their trust. I work with the relational field of both the family and the child. As if a distant aunt who comes to visit for a while, I enter both fields and serve as a nurturing support, witness, cheerleader, and change agent. I support both fields to increase their contact and self functions.

May we all Zig Zag Flop and Roll or play Polar Bear Knuckleball with others!

References

American Psychiatric Association (2000). *Diagnostic and Statistical Manual of Mental Disorders.* 4th ed., Text Revision. Washington, DC: American Psychiatric Association. pp. 69-84, 463-468.

Aposhyan, S. (2004). *Body-Mind Psychotherapy: Principles, Techniques and Practical Applications.* New York: Norton.

Barnes, J. (2000). *Healing Ancient Wounds.* Paoli, PA: Rehabilitation Services, Inc.

Bauer, P. (1996). What Do Infants Recall of Their Lives? Memory for Specific Events by One-to-Two Year Olds. *American Psychologist* 51(1), 29-41.

Cohen, B. B. (1993). *Sensing, Feeling, and Action: The Experiential Anatomy of Body-Mind Centering.* Northhampton, MA: Contact Editions.

Frank, R. (2001). *Body of Awareness: A Somatic and Developmental Approach to Psychotherapy.* Hillsdale, NJ: Analytic Press/Gestalt-Press.

Kepner, J. (2003). The Embodied Field. *British Gestalt Journal* 12(1), 6-14.

Kepner, J. (1995). *Healing Tasks: Psychotherapy with Adult Survivors of Childhood Abuse.* San Francisco: Jossey-Bass.

Kepner, J. (1987). *Body Process: A Gestalt Approach to Working with the Body in Psychotherapy.* New York: Gardner Press.

Lee, R. (2001). Shame and Support: Understanding an Adolescent's Family Field. In M. McConville & G. Wheeler (Eds.), *The Heart of Development: Gestalt Approach to Working with Children, Adolescents and Their Worlds.* Vol II: Adolescence (pp. 253-270). Hillsdale, NJ: Analytic Press/Gestalt Press.

Levine, P. A. & Kline, M. (2007). *Trauma Through a Child's Eyes: Awakening the Ordinary Miracle of Healing Infancy Through Adolescence*. Berkeley, Ca: North Atlantic Books.
Oaklander, V. (2006). *Hidden Treasure: A Map to the Child's Inner Self*. London: Karnac.
Oaklander, V. (2002). The Therapeutic Process with Children and Adolescents: A Gestalt Therapy Perspective. In G. Wheeler, & M. McConville (Eds.), *The Heart of Development: Gestalt Approaches to Working with Children, Adolescents and Their Worlds*. Vol. 1: Childhood (pp. 85-112). Hillsdale, NJ: The Analytic Press/GestaltPress.
Perry, B. D., Pollard, R. A., Blakley, T. L., Baker, W. L., Vigilante, D. (1995). Childhood Trauma, the Neurobiology of Adaptation, and "Use-dependent" Development of the Brain: How "States" Become "Traits." *Infant Mental Health Journal 16*(4), 271-191.
Philippson, P. (2006). Field Theory: Mirrors and Reflections. *British Gestalt Journal 15*(2), 59-63.
Pynoos, R. S., Steinberg, A.M., Goenjain, A. (2007). Traumatic Stress in Childhood and Adolescence: Recent Developments and Current Controversies. In B. A. Van der Kolk, A. C. Mc Farlane. L. Weisaeth (Eds.), *Traumatic Stress: The Effects of Overwhelming Experience on Mind, Body and Society* (pp. 331-358). New York: Guilford Press.
Schore, A. N. (2003). *Affect Regulation and the Repair of the Self*. New York: Norton.
Siegel, D. J. (1999). *The Developing Mind: How Relationship and the Brain Interact to Shape Who We Are*. New York: Guilford Press.
Silva, R. R., Alpert, M., Munoz, D. M., Matzner, F., & Dummit, S. (2000). Stress and Vulnerability to Posttraumatic Stress Disorder in Children and Adolescents. *American Journal of Psychiatry 157*, 1229-1235.
Stern, D.N. (2004). *The Present Moment in Psychotherapy and Everyday Life*. New York: Norton.
Tervo, D. (2002). Physical Process Work with Children and Adolescents. In G. Wheeler, & M. McConville (Eds.), *The Heart of Development: Gestalt Approaches to Working with Children, Adolescents and Their Worlds*. Vol. I: Childhood (pp. 113-146). Hillsdale NJ: Analytic Press/GestaltPress.
Tervo, D. (1997). Physical Process Work with Children and Adolescents. *British Gestalt Journal 6*(2), 76-86.
van der Kolk, B. A., Fisler, R. E. (1994). Childhood Abuse and Neglect and Loss of Self-Regulation. *Bulletin of the Menninger Clinic 58*(2), 145-168.

van der Kolk B. A. (2007). The Body Keeps the Score: Approaches to the Psychobiology of Post Traumatic Stress Disorder. In B. A. van der Kolk, A. C. McFarlane, & L. Weisaeth (Eds.), *Traumatic Stress: The Effects of Overwhelming Experience on Mind, Body, and Society.* (pp. 214-241). New York: Guilford Press.

Editors' Note:
For more than ten years, Peter Mortola, Howard Hinton, and Stephen Grant have been leading strength-based counseling groups for boys in both private and school contexts. They have written a curriculum about these groups, entitled *BAM! Boys' Advocacy and Mentoring* (Mortola, et al, 2008), from which this chapter is adapted. In the following pages, they first outline some of the relational and educational challenges that boys face, linking these challenges to problems with contact. They then show the ways in which both social and biological influences shape a boy's particular "contact style." They conclude by describing ways to work with boys that can help boys shake off the limitations of their socialization while at the same time honoring and working with their biological contact tendencies and strengths.

9

A Different Kind of Contact for Boys:

Understanding the Influence of Nature and Nurture on a Boy's Relational Style

*Peter Mortola,
Howard Hinton,
& Stephen Grant*

The Challenges Boys Face

Who hasn't marveled at the natural exuberance of boys? We watch with amazement as they skateboard for countless hours, run with boundless energy, and express unbridled enthusiasm for their latest interest. Young boys are often eager to please their teachers, free with expressions of love, and open with their expressions of tears and sadness. Picture a little boy stricken with grief over Ole Yeller's death in the classic movie. Imagine how a little boy trembles with excitement as he lines up his cars in just the right way or builds a cool Lego contraption. Recall an image of a group of boys as they, in their excitable goofiness, fall over each other like puppies and amuse each other with wacky boy humor.

Most boys, when they are very young, are fully engaged in the world. They are in full contact with their own inner lives and experiences, their feelings, thoughts, and imaginings. They are also in full contact with the environment around them, literally poking it, touching it, and climbing all over it.

But then something happens to many young boys as they grow older. They start to lose their enthusiastic contact with important aspects of both their inner and outer lives: They lose touch with certain emotions, they struggle to participate authentically in relationships with significant others, and many of them begin to lose touch with the meaning and purpose of schooling.

To put it bluntly, boys, on average, struggle in significant ways both academically and relationally. In higher education, women now outnumber men as both enrollees and graduates. According to the National Center for Education Statistics (2005), girls are also outperforming boys in terms of grades not only in college, but also at the elementary, secondary, and high school levels.

Given these statistics, it is perhaps not surprising that only 44% of high school boys as compared to 54% of girls report that they do at least one hour of homework per night and only 55% of boys versus 68% of girls report that they are motivated to do well in school. (Leffert et al., 1997) Boys are also 30% more likely than girls to flunk or drop out of school (National Center for Education Statistics, 2005). As a measure of the ultimate and tragic form of "dropping out," boys also account for 86% of all suicides between the ages of 15 and 24 (Anderson & Smith, 2003).

One place where you will find more boys than girls in schools is in Special Education classrooms (Soifer, 2002). Special Education programs in public schools across the United States have been described as "largely a boys club" with twice as many boys being identified as requiring such services as girls (Vaishnav & Dedman, 2002). It is important to note that this "imbalance" in the special education population grows even greater as the diagnoses become more subjective. For example, boys are only slightly more likely to receive the ob-jectively measured label of "hearing impaired," but they are more than twice as likely to be labeled "learning disabled" and more than three times more likely to receive the highly subjective label of being "emotionally disturbed."

This tendency for boys to be viewed as having more emotional and social problems than girls is also seen in the data collected on behavior rating scales used in schools throughout the country. Using these scales in both elementary and high schools, teachers and parents predominantly identify boys as possessing glaring deficits in social skills such as "cooperation," "empathy," and "study skills." Sadly, boys are also seen as possessing significantly greater problems in the areas of "aggression," "attention problems" and "hyperactivity" (Reynolds & Kamphaus, 1992; Merrell & Popinga, 1994).

The link between boys and the diagnosis of Attention Deficit with Hyperactivity Disorder (ADHD) is one of the clearest examples of how young males are seen as problems in our schools and communities. In the United States, boys are up to three times more likely to be both referred for and diagnosed with ADHD (Barkley, 1998). In some school systems within the United States, up to 20% of boys in the schools' populations are receiving psycho-stimulant medications for ADHD (Castellanos, et al, 2002). Perhaps the most sobering statistics are these: With less than 5% of the world's population, the U.S. now accounts for 85% of the world's consumption of Ritalin and 90% of all children taking Ritalin in the U.S. are boys (Pollack, 1998). The rise of the use of Ritalin within the United States has been exponential over the past two decades. "No country besides America is experiencing such a rise in Ritalin use," states Lawrence Diller, M.D., in *Running on Ritalin* (1999), "It brings into question our cultural standards for behavior, performance and punishment; It highlights the most basic psychological aspects of nature versus nurture" (p. 23).

Clearly, boys are facing some real problems and they are in need of real help. Facing such a myriad of problems both academically and socially, it is perhaps no joke that males have also been found to smile less than females in social situations across the lifespan (LaFrance & Hecht, 2000). With so many problems being attributed to boys, attempting to help them can be overwhelming. Where do we begin to help boys with their struggles? How can we in the counseling and teaching pro-fessions approach boys as anything other than problems? In this next section, we share our insights on these two fundamental questions.

The Necessity of Good Contact

We need to remember that it is at the edge of anything - system or medium, that the most interesting events take place.
        David Holmgren (2007)

We have just outlined how boys, on average, are facing significant challenges in three broad areas: 1) successfully engaging in schools (e.g. problems with academic success, learning disabilities, drop out rates); 2) successfully engaging in interpersonal relationships (e.g. problems with cooperation, empathy, and attention deficit disorder); and, 3) successfully engaging in the regulation of their own emotional lives (e.g. problems with emotional disturbance, aggression, and suicide). A close reading of these three broad problem areas reveals "successful engagement" as the common underlying thread: Many boys are losing touch. We therefore see this basic issue of helping boys make better contact with themselves, with others, and with school systems as our primary goal in our work with boys in BAM! groups. In the following paragaphs, we define and describe this foundational idea of "contact" that grounds our thinking and our approach to working with boys.

The Gestalt notion of contact offers a useful model to understand how some boys become disconnected and provides a theoretical basis for remedying their disconnection.

From a Gestalt perspective, healthy contact takes place at the boundary where the individual meets the world (Perls, et al, 1951; Wheeler, 1991; Mortola, 2006; Oaklander, 1978). Good contact with the world using all aspects of our organism: our senses, our emotions, and our minds. Good contact is necessary for us to engage with the environments that surround us – both natural and social – and to get our needs met.

For example, when Ramon, a boy in one of our groups, lost a valued pet and needed some support, he reached out to us emotionally. He made eye contact with us and he spoke eloquently about his loss and what his dog Rudy had meant to him. He conveyed his loss in a way that allowed us to empathize with him. He used an appropriate tone of voice, congruent facial expressions, and the poignant movement of his hands to show how he used to hold Rudy in his arms when he was a puppy.

By using his body, his emotions, and his thoughts in such a "contactful" way, Ramon strengthened our relationship to him. We felt close to him, we were able to empathize with him, and we were therefore able to respond to him in ways that were helpful. After Ramon had finished speaking, for example, another boy in the group described how he also had cried when his pet bird had died, thus "normalizing" Ramon's feelings of grief. The whole group also attended to Ramon during these minutes and gave him the time and attention he needed to feel supported. In these ways, Ramon was able to leave the group that day feeling a little less alone, a little less sad, and a little more connected.

As Ramon demonstrates, good contact is the ability to be fully engaged with our world. Good contact with the *self*, however, is also a necessary aspect of making good contact. Ramon couldn't have asked for understanding about his own experience of grief if he wasn't first aware of and in good contact with his own feelings of being sad and lonely. Ramon demonstrated good contact with himself through his ready awareness of his own thoughts, feelings, and needs. In this way, Ramon provides us with an excellent example of how good contact is both the ability to be in touch with one's own inner experiences as well as the ability to communicate one's experience in appropriate ways in the world in order to get one's needs met.

Simply put, we know good contact when we see it: contact looks like presence and may reflect a multitude of feelings, it is animated, and it is an honest representation of a person's inner world. Contact is knowing who you are inside and bringing that knowledge to interact with others. It is showing up fully, being present, allowing others in and letting yourself out. Contact is possible when we allow ourselves to be vulnerable, to be "in touch." In contrast, the inability to make good contact looks frozen, insensitive, guarded, stoic, and aloof. Not surpriseingly, these are the very words we use to describe men who have internalized limiting and dysfunctional definitions of masculinity.

So how do boys begin to lose contact with themselves and the world around them? In this next section we address the social influences on boys that limit their ability to maintain good contact as they grow and develop.

The Social Influences: The Impact of Dysfunctional Aspects of Traditional Masculinity on Boys' Relational Styles

As we have noted, boys enter the world full of zest and fully "in contact" with the world and with themselves. Their desires to connect with other people gets expressed in the strong attachments they form with their family members, other caring adults, and their peers. As boys age, relationships with other boys become particularly important. Research findings from the psychological literature show that boys' friendships tend to be stable and characterized by mutual support and companionship shared through active and competitive types of activities (Buhrmester, 1996; Camarena, Sarigiani & Petersen, 1990; McNelles & Connolly, 1999). These friendships are vital to a boy's well-being.

Unfortunately, some boys are exposed to a harsh socialization process that forces them to internalize outdated and dysfunctional notions of masculinity that can impair their ability to make deep emotional connections with others, although males generally are more like than unlike females in their emotions (Wester et al., 2002). However, many boys are taught that emotional openness is a liability. They are subject to challenges such as "boys don't cry," (i.e. men don't show vulnerability) and shaming taunts if they do cry (e.g. "Don't be a girlyman!"). Many boys learn to censor the aspects of themselves that they fear do not meet social expectations for "being a man" (Pollack, 1998).

Although there are certainly variations across cultural, ethnic, and socio-economic groups (Chu & Way, 1999), we believe there are pervasive, dysfunctional aspects of traditional masculinity that influence many boys throughout the United States. These limiting and dysfunctional aspects of traditional masculinity are media-influenced – the muscles of G.I. Joe "play action figures," for example, are thirty times larger now than they were when first sold (Pope, et al., 1999) – and they affect the lives of boys from many different backgrounds, unnecessarily constricting their definition of what a man is supposed to be and how a man is supposed to act.

Boys who internalize these dysfunctional beliefs regarding masculinity become convinced that expressing vulnerability is not cool, and crying about the loss of a pet, for example, is certainly not permitted. Guarding against shame, many boys develop a coat of armor to protect themselves against ridicule and humiliation. The armor boys wear may serve as a defense against what they see as a threatening world, but it also separates them from necessary contact – from their own experience and from the ability to connect authentically with others.

This process of armoring eventually teaches some boys to deny their own experience and results in a loss of contact with their own internal compass, leaving them susceptible to peer pressure and unwise influences. Unable to navigate their own emotional landscapes, these boys are in danger of not only losing touch with how to care for themselves in healthy ways, but also with knowing how to appropriately empathize with others. If Ramon was feeling lonely and sad, for example, but couldn't identify, respect and "own" those feelings, he may have pushed them away as something only "sissies" feel. Lacking access to and ownership of his own feelings, Ramon would not only lose touch with himself, but he would also begin to lose the ability to connect empathetically with others in similar situations.

We have seen the results of these internalized social pressures to conform to an unrealistic, unhealthy and limited standard of what it means to be a man, ripple out in numerous ways in our practice:

> A parent calls to set up an initial counseling appointment and says, "My son used to excel in school. He was in the talented and gifted program. Now he is in middle school and is getting C's and D's. I don't know how to talk to him. He just doesn't seem to care. He seems so unhappy."

> A 14-year-old boy discusses the impact of getting teased when he was younger. He remembers the time when he began to build his tough façade to endure the teasing. He acknowledges how this façade has led him to harden, to be less friendly, and to be more of a loner. He demonstrates some understanding of the dilemma this creates when speaking about switching schools and hoping to make new friends. "I don't know what I am going to do. You can't be too open but you can't be a total dick either," he says.

> A 20 year old discloses that he uses marijuana daily because he feels anxious and scared. He says that he could never reveal his feelings of vulnerability to his friends out of fear of being

humiliated. So he hides his feelings and continues to use marijuana instead of being honest about his experience.

We see many boys at about the age of twelve beginning to censor themselves, imagining they need to be tougher and cooler than they actually are. Following the lead and copying the mannerisms of older boys, these younger ones begin to strive for a cool indifference rather than a warm connectedness. This is why we have focused our efforts on fifth grade boys: To give them a group social experience in which their quickly limiting definition of what it means to be a man can be expanded to include the relational and communicative abilities to make healthy contact with themselves and the world around them.

We have stated that many boys receive clear messages from the culture that limit their abilities to make good contact with themselves and with the world around them. These boys get put in a box that is too small for them and they end up lopping off important aspects of themselves in order to conform and fit to that constricted definition of masculinity.

We think there is another aspect of the way that many boys are socialized that creates problems for them in their development: If boys were books, they are being misread and misinterpreted. Through this misreading and misunderstanding of who boys are by their nature, we are tending to treat and socialize boys in our nurturing in ways that are not helpful to them.

On the whole, for example, boys seem to process emotions differently than girls (Manstead, 1992). Researchers have found that boys tend to get overwhelmed by strong emotions and, when facing potent feelings, may appear to shut down. In one relevant study (Kraemer, 2000), six year-old boys and girls were placed in a room by themselves and played an audiotape of a baby in distress. Upon initial observation it appeared that the girls had a stronger emotional reaction than the boys. Researchers observed the girls being visibly upset and attempting to comfort the crying baby. Boys, on the other hand, displayed a flat affect or even turned off the switch that played the tape.

At first glance, this appears to support a stereotype that boys are unfeeling and callous. However, upon closer examination, the researchers found that internal measures of agitation such as heart rate and sweat response revealed that boys were *more* agitated than girls. It appears that the boys in this study were besieged by a strong emotional reaction and attempted to end their discomfort by shutting down any outward signs of emotions and by turning off the tape.

In addition to boys' demonstrations of apparent apathy, we have found in our own work with boys that they may react with anger or defensiveness when overwhelmed with vulnerable emotions. This may come as no surprise given the effects of being "put in the box," as we described earlier. Wouldn't you react defensively if you were socialized to believe, as many boys are, that you should never feel vulnerable and certainly not appear that way?

Most boys, then, are actually having and processing the normal range of human emotions, but it may not look that way from the outside. Because of this incongruity between what boys are feeling and what they are showing, we may tend to take boys' demonstrations of apathy or anger at face value and fail to look deeper. Assuming that boys aren't vulnerable, and that they don't need us, we may allow ourselves to be pushed away by what appears to be boys' indifference. What we fail to see is that boys' demonstrations of anger and apathy are often a defense against emotions that overwhelm them.

When we view boys' indifference as evidence that they are tough, strong, unemotional and don't need contact with others, we fail them and contribute to their disconnection, their lack of contact. We believe it is essential to recognize that boys, too, have an inner emotional life, even though it may be difficult to get to. Some boys may need particular help in understanding and navigating that emotional world, and many may need guidance and practice to develop their emotional muscles that are weak from disuse or disregard.

We have stated that there are two strong, negative influences in the socialization of many boys: 1) they are "put in a box" that limits the range of their emotional and behavioral repertoires, and 2) their particular way of processing or responding to emotions is "misread" and we therefore distance ourselves and lose contact with them. Both of these influences challenge a boy's ability to directly address and discuss anything that might make him appear vulnerable in the company of others. How, then, do you set up a group experience for boys where it is okay to both feel and express vulnerability and, therefore, to make authentic contact with each other?

We have had to be thoughtful about this over time. We learned from early failures that boys in general were not comfortable with the traditional group counseling methods that we learned in graduate school, such as sitting quietly in a circle and discussing feelings face-to-face with others. We learned that traditional counseling processes and approaches were often, in fact, a "damned if you do, damned if you don't" experience for boys: They have learned to feel shame for showing vulnerability, now they are shamed if they aren't able to show it to us in counseling (Tannen, 1994).

What we discovered was that in order to help boys redress their relational constraints imposed upon them by our nurturing, we needed to support the way they make contact naturally. We learned from experience and research that boys, in general, had a biologically-influenced style of making contact that we had to understand and respect. In short, we learned that in order to help boys make better contact, we needed to make better contact with them. In the next section we detail the biological influences of what we have come to call a boy's "contact style."

The Biological Influences: A Different Kind of Contact for Boys

Earlier, we described what good interpersonal contact looks like: it involves an awareness of one's own emotional state and the ability to clearly communicate those emotions and needs. This clear communication involves verbal statements, congruent non-verbal communication – such as direct eye-contact – and an appropriately expressive physical presence that helps one be understood. We believe these types of contact skills are crucial if one is to meet the world appropriately in order to get one's needs met. These relational skills, in fact, have become even more important as the world has become more populated, with more of us living in crowded urban centers. In addition, over time, traditional gender roles have become more flexible: More women are in the business world, and more men are caring for the young and involving themselves in the difficult work of parenting. For these reasons, we believe that our work to help young boys develop their relational and communication skills is key.

The first few years we facilitated BAM! groups, we expected boys to practice and demonstrate these types of contactful behaviors right off the bat. It didn't take us long to learn that this was the wrong approach. One year early on, we started off the first session of our group by having the boys sit in a circle, face-to-face, and "check in" by telling us a bit about themselves. What we got instead of friendly sharing and warm contact in the group was a series of clipped, sarcastic, and critical comments accompanied by the non-verbal communication of cool and closed physical gestures and postures. Let's just say the temperature in the room and in the group dropped quickly and never really recovered.

We now see the failure of that early, opening exercise not only as a deficit in the range of social skills boys are able to demonstrate, but also as a deficit in our own understanding of what has been described as a boy's relational style (Kiselica, 2001, 2003) or what we will further define as a boy's "contact style." That is, we realized that both the boys and us, as leaders, had a new language to learn, The boys might need to improve their skills supporting good interpersonal contact, but we needed to learn about a boy's preferred style of communication, relationship and contact.

We now know that boys come into the world attending to – and making contact with – particular things in particular ways. We have learned that if we want to succeed in helping boys become more relational and contactful with themselves and the world around them, we need to have a better understanding of, respect for, and ability to work with these tendencies.

Like many professionals trained in the social sciences over the past 30 years, we used to think that boys and girls would reflect the same interests and develop the same social skills if we socialized them all equally. That is, we believed that boys would respond just as well to dolls and be less interested in wheels if we were just careful enough about which toys we chose for them to play with. As we will show, research over the past few decades has done much to debunk this myth that all behavioral, sex-related differences have roots in socialization.

As BAM! group leaders, we still maintain a hearty respect for the influences of socialization (spending a good amount of our time working with boys focused on helping them understand the limiting influences of traditional male socialization), but we have also come to see that ignoring a boy's natural "contact style" is dangerous: If we don't know how to make contact with boys, how do we expect them to make contact with us? Here is a story from Peter's own experience as a new father that highlights this point:

> *When my son Noah was just a few months old, I began to notice that he didn't make much eye contact with me. From all the reading I had done, I was expecting him to gaze deeply into my eyes as I gazed into his. But instead Noah seemed to prefer staring at shadows on the wall and was seemingly unaware of and indifferent to my presence. With my training in psychology, I was too quick to wonder if these were early signs of autism. I also couldn't help but notice that I felt like making less contact with him because he didn't seem to be that interested in making contact with me. Now that Noah is a smiling, talking, fully relational two-year old, I can laugh at the*

fears and concerns I had back then. But I also have learned that there was something about Noah – and about boys in general – that I needed to better understand.

What we have come to learn about boys is that they may not always make contact with us in the way we expect or want them to. After Peter's experience with Noah, for example, we learned that from the first day of birth onward, infant baby boys have shown a preference for looking at a mobile hanging over their crib rather than a human face that is gazing back at them (Lutchmaya & Baron-Cohen, 2002).

Throughout childhood, adolescence and adulthood, in fact, females have demonstrated much greater interest in and success with "reading faces" (Hall, 1984; Hall, et al., 2000; McClure, 2000; Woods, 1996). Women, for example, will take more time to consider what someone else's facial expression is communicating, and they will respond with more emotional arousal to that facial expression than a man will (Orozco & Ehlers, 1998). Additionally, watching a cartoon of two characters interacting, toddler girls will use more words to describe the mental and affective states of those characters, and they will also make more efforts to describe the intentions of those characters (Knickmeyer, et al, 2005). In these ways, girls tend to be better at the kind of "mindreading" that is essential for making good contact and empathizing with others (Baron-Cohen, 2003).

To underscore the contributions of biology in this discussion, consider the following: All human babies start out as female in the womb. In the first few weeks of development, some babies become boys by being "marinated" in testosterone and androgens. Researchers are now able to show that those baby boys who were influenced by higher levels of pre-natal testosterone show lower levels of eye-contact and produce less vocabulary by the time they are walking and talking toddlers (Lutchmaya et al., 2002a, 2002b).

The tendency for girls to have a larger vocabulary and be stronger in various aspects of language use has also been demonstrated across the lifespan, and importantly, estrogen is implicated in this strength

(Institute of Medicine, 2001). Estrogen is the hormone that most influences girls in the same way that testosterone is the hormone that most influences boys. When estrogen is at its peak influence at ovulation in the monthly female cycle, for example, females tend to be better at tasks related to retrieval of language from memory (Kuhlmann & Wolf, 2005). Interestingly, Koko, the female lowland gorilla famous for her use of sign language, also made more efforts at communication and produced more signs when she was at the peak of her cycle (Patterson, et. al., 1991). A similar finding related to the connection of language skills and language relates to menopause in women: When estrogen's presence and influence declines in menopause, so does the edge that women have over men in terms of verbal fluency, naming, and articulation. However, when a woman receives estrogen-replacement therapy, her verbal advantages over men returns (Kimura, 1995).

If boys tend to not read faces and emotions as well as girls, or use verbal communication as effusively or effectively, to what are they attending and how do they communicate? What does a boy's preferred contact style look like and how can it be seen from a strengths-based perspective rather than from a deficit model?

Like Noah gazing at the mobile in the story above, boys seem to attend slightly more to "effect" rather than "affect." Put another way, they seem to attend more towards the "motion" in the world and a little bit less towards the "emotion" in the world. From very early on in infancy, boys have shown a tendency to gravitate toward toys that move, rather than toys that have faces (Knickmeyer, et al., 2005). By the time they are toddlers, boys also have shown a strong tendency to prefer films about moving cars rather than films portraying faces that talk (Connellan, 2001).

Male Vervet monkeys have also been shown to have this same tendency to play with cars instead of dolls (Alexandera, 2002), lending support to the theory that early in our evolution as mammals, it became advantageous for males and females to attend to – to make contact with – differing aspects of the environment. That is, most female primates show strengths in attending to the relational and communicative aspects of mothering – paying close attention to the expressive faces and demonstrated needs of newborns in particular, while most male primates show strengths in attending to the visual and spatial aspects of the surrounding environment – i.e. things that move and that could either be a source of food or a potential threat (Wright, 1994).

As in our previous example regarding boys' tendencies to gaze at mobiles rather than faces, it is important to note the role of biology in this differentiation of toy selection and attentional differences in boys and girls. For example, girls born with Congenital Adrenal Hyperplasia (CAH) have experienced very high levels of testosterone in the womb. Although this hormone imbalance is usually corrected at birth, later in childhood girls born with CAH show strong preferences for what experimenters identify as "boy-typical" toys such as those involved in transportation and construction tasks (Berenbaum, 2000). Girls born with CAH also score unusually high on tests of spatial awareness and orientation which usually tend to be a strength for males on such tests (Berenbaum & Resnick, 1997).

Boys not only tend to pay more attention to things that move, but they themselves also tend to move more than girls do. As most parents of boys can attest, infant boys are more active than girls, especially when it comes to the activation of large muscle groups such as those involved in throwing and running (Junaid & Fellowes, 2006). These differences between boys' and girls' activity levels also have been shown to increase during childhood (Eaton & Enns, 1986).

In addition, Boys have demonstrated a strong preference for a more "rough and tumble" style of play than girls do (Maccoby, 1998). "Rough and tumble play," of course, is a euphemism for "aggressive play." In countries around the world, boys have been shown, in fact, to demonstrate higher levels of aggression (such as pushing, hitting, and grabbing) than girls do (Munroe, et al., 2000). And while it is true that the number of aggressive acts performed by boys tends to be greater in countries where boys are socialized in more traditional gender roles (thereby highlighting the influence of socialization on aggression) it is also true that this tendency for boys to be more aggressive has appeared in each country where it has been measured (thereby highlighting the role of biology in this tendency).

Let's summarize what we have stated so far regarding the biological influences on a boy's particular contact style: Boys seem to have a tendency to make contact with the world in a way that differs not only from girls, but also from adult expectations of what good contact should look like. That is, boys, when compared with girls, on the whole tend to use less direct eye contact, tend to not read emotions on faces as well, tend to use less verbal communication, and tend to be more physically active and even aggressive in the way that they engage in the world. In short, boys in general tend to not produce the kinds of contactful behaviors that we expect of children as they sit in classrooms or in the counselor's office.

On average, then, a boy's "contact style" with the world may not look like contact at all. That is, in a social situation where you hope to have his complete attention, a boy may tend to squirm and fidget, not looking you in the eye, and produce far fewer empathetic statements than you might hope. Spelled out in this way, it is easy to understand how boys are seen as having fewer relational and social skills and less ability to make good contact with themselves and others. Their contact skills are not only limited by their socialization as males, but their contact skills seem to also be particularized by their biology.

We think it is very important at this point, however, to assert our "boy positive" stance: We do not see boys as broken girls when it comes to relational and communication skills (Heesacker, et al., 1999). We do see that they have relational challenges – stemming from both biological and social influences – with which they need our help and encouragement. But we have also come to appreciate that a boy's contact style has its own strengths, as we describe in the next section. If we want to help boys make better contact, we have to learn to make better contact with them.

Seeing Boys' Strengths and Addressing Their Challenges

*"I note the obvious differences between each
sort and type, but we are more alike, my friends,
than we are unalike."*
Maya Angelou, Human Family (1990)

We have just highlighted the social and biological influences on what we have called a boy's "contact style." We have described the ways in which socialization limits a boy's relational capacities to make good contact and we have also described the ways that biology influences the particular kind of contact that a boy tends to make. We have summarized – and oversimplified – this difference by stating that boys tend more toward *effect* rather than *affect*. Having highlighted these differences, however, we now return to similarities.

As in Maya Angelou's quote, we think that boys and girls are actually more similar than they are different. All human beings around the globe share common characteristics that make us fundamentally human. We are all born needing the support of and attachment to significant adults, and, furthermore, we are born with the innate relational capacities to develop these attachments (Siegel, 1999).

Around the world, men and women share the same facial expressions that communicate essentially the same basic emotions of joy, sadness, fear, disgust, anger, and surprise – and multiple complex variations on those emotive themes (Brown, 1991). Affect theory (Tomkins, 1962), in fact, tells us that, for all of us, such emotions and their expressions are the manner with which we either reach out (e.g. feeling joy) or withdraw from the environment (e.g. disgust) in our ongoing process of regulating our needs.

We want to stress that boys as well as girls share all these basic capacities for relationship, emotion, and regulation (Kiselica & O'Brien, 2001). Furthermore, despite all the controversy over how different our brains may be, women and men share all the same basic cognitive functions as well as, on average, the same general levels of intelligence (Halpern, 2005). We state these similarities because we do not think that boys and girls should be treated or viewed as different kinds of animals. We see boys and girls, in fact, sharing nearly completely overlapping sets of skills and attributes with only slight differences at the edges of their skill sets.

It is just that by nature, boys tend to lean in one direction of interest and girls tend to lean in another. Baron-Cohen (2003) emphasized, as we do, that these differences are apparent "on average" in human populations and that variation and strengths may be different for any given individual, whether boy or girl.

In this way, we need to appreciate how boys and girls are mostly the same. We would be missing something important, however, if we did not recognize that boys and girls may have tendencies in contact styles that reflect both strengths and weaknesses. It is clear, for example, that a girl's tendency to be better at empathy and relational skills is a benefit to her in the complexly social and interpersonal aspects of our present-day world. It is also clear from research over the past ten years (Burr, et al., 2005; Crick, 1996), however, that a girl's edge in verbal skills and subtle relational understandings over boys in general can also present her with particular challenges. Crick and her colleagues (Crick & Grotpeter, 1995) have documented, for example the ways in which girls can and do use their verbal and relational acuity to, at times, act in clearly harmful and aggressive ways in their relationships with other girls. In these studies, girls report that they use such "relational aggression" because of how important it is for them to feel included, to have a sense of belonging and connectedness with their peers. In this way, a relational challenge for a girl may be to learn to stand more independently and, ironically, to care *less* about belonging to a group. We also know that girls suffer significantly higher rates of anxiety, panic disorders, and depression than boys do during adolescents (Hankin & Abramson, 1999). In this way, it may also be important for a girl to learn to be more assertive and externalizing (as opposed to the internalizing tendencies that these maladies represent) in expressing her independent wants and needs as well as being assertive about getting them met.

We know from the data presented earlier that a boy's relational and contact style brings different challenges. For example, many boys need to learn to be more cooperative and less aggressive, as well as less violent, in expressing their wants and needs. Additionally, they need practice in attending to and verbalizing their own needs, as well as attending to the expressed emotions of others.

We have found, however, that there is less affirmation as to the strengths that a boy's particular contact style may provide. In our work with boys in BAM! groups, we have seen these strengths at work in many different ways and in many different situations. Their tendency toward effect, for example, is demonstrated as a positive social skill in their quick readiness to work at solving problems both as individuals and in groups. Their high levels of activity (aka "squirreliness") in our groups also bring high levels of positive energy, eager participation, humor and risk-taking to our experiences together.

Even though the boys we work with may not be as comfortable with face-to-face communication as noted by Tannen (1990) we have found that when we create activities for them to do with each other, side-by-side and shoulder-to-shoulder, their natural styles of not appearing vulnerable disappear and they are able to literally hold and support each other in surprising ways.

We have also learned to reframe a boy's tendency to adore cars and trucks as reflecting a kind of social skill. We have pointed out in our work with boys, for example, the essential service to the community that the driver of a garbage truck provides. We have also talked about the intricate orchestration of communication with others that an operator of a large crane engages in on a daily basis. On a related sidenote, one boy we spoke to recently also described how much more important he felt after we helped him see his deep interest in software programming as actually reflecting the larger social skill of wanting to help people work together better on important projects.

As BAM! leaders, we have also come to realize that by honoring and channeling a boy's naturally high level of aggression, we can see a surprising social skill in what is normally viewed as pathology. Boys in our groups literally come into the room tumbling over one another, for example, and we have had to learn to reframe this as sometimes being a good thing. At the end of the first week of one new group, a ten-year-old boy named Mark expressed that one thing he liked about the group so far was that he had made a new friend in Nathan, another 10-year-old boy. As soon as the two of them came into the room for the second session the following week, Mark ended up on top of Nathan after a brief wrestling tussle, Nathan's smiling face literally being smashed into the foam mat we had thoughtfully provided. Although Mark's behavior clearly could be seen as aggressive, it was Nathan's smiling face that told us that Mark's way of making affectionate if rambunctious contact was being accepted, even appreciated. Sometimes, making and keeping friends looks different for a boy. We have learned that, unless someone is getting hurt, we need to honor that difference.

On a more serious note, we have also had moments in our groups where we find ourselves walking a fine line in supporting a boy's aggression – like when one boy described stepping in to break up a fight where his younger sibling was being pummeled by an older boy, for example – while at the same time taking a stand against the use of violence as a solution to problems. We have found, though, that boys are hungry to talk about such important distinctions and that our conversations and shared stories help them address these concerns.

What Boys Need to Learn, and What We Need to Learn from Boys: Three Ways to Make Better Contact

As we have described, we believe that there are many positive aspects of a boy's relational style – and about boys in general – that are often overlooked in our clamor regarding what they lack. In highlighting these strengths, we are not ignoring the clear needs and challenges that boys face regarding making better contact with themselves and others. By focusing on these strengths, however, we have found that we can harness and direct their natural tendencies and strengths in the service of shoring up their relational skill deficits. In this way, we get the best of both worlds: The boys learn new relational skills, and they, in turn, want to come to our groups because they are fun and engaging.

Based on the relational strengths we have been describing, we want to share with you three specific, strengths-based approaches to working with boys that we have found help us make better contact with them. We think of these approaches as our own goals as group leaders in working with boys. These three goals also serve to summarize what we have learned from the research we have described on both the social and biological influences on a boy's contact style, as well as how we have applied this knowledge in our practice with boys. Importantly, the three goals are two-sided: emphasizing not only what we need to learn about boys, but also what they need to learn to make better contact with others in the world around them.

1. Embracing a Broader View of Being Male.

Boys need to learn to broaden their conception of what it means to be male. We can help boys "out of the box" by contradicting the limiting social messages they hear.

Boys grow up hearing messages about what it means to be a man. These messages are often limiting and hurtful (e.g. "boy's don't cry" and "boys need to prove themselves through fighting"). We need to help boys learn that there are many ways to be a man, that it is okay to own and express vulnerable feelings, and that there are many ways to resolve conflicts other than through hurtful violence. Help the boys you know to feel valued and respected for who they are, whether they play football or dance ballet, whether they hunt or knit.

> We need to learn to see being male as something other than a problem. We can help by noticing the good in boys.

We tend to highlight the trouble boys get into and forget to support them for the good things they bring to us. Realize that part of the problem boys have in meeting the world has to do with the way that the world meets them. Take an active interest in what boys find interesting and find a way to value it. Help them to see that the trucks and tractors they love actually help build houses. Help them to see that football is also about being part of team, caring for your teammates, and doing something challenging and important together.

2) Learning to be Direct, Indirectly

> Boys need to learn direct relational and communication skills. We can help by encouraging understanding and expression of emotions and needs.

If boys tend to pay more attention to things like cars, wheels, and computers rather than faces, emotions, and relationships, they may need support and encouragement to develop and use their relational and communication skills: Teach the boys you know to look directly in someone's face to give or receive a compliment, help them understand what someone else is feeling and how their facial expressions show it, discuss how a character in a movie might have felt, help them see how important it is for them to understand their own feelings in order to discover, ask for, and get what they need.

> We need to learn to respect boys indirectness: We can help by "shooting baskets" with boys first, and talking later.

Because of both biological and social reasons, boys tend to not be as direct in expressions of certain emotions. Help boys attend to and express their more vulnerable emotions by approaching them indirectly: Let them fiddle with something in their hands while you talk,

Shoot baskets while having a conversation, tell them about your own experiences before expecting them to tell you about theirs.

3) Allowing and Inhibiting Physical Activity

Boys need to learn to regulate their levels of physical activity and aggression. We can help by actively teaching boys to romp respectfully.

Boys, on average, are at far greater risk than girls for being identified with ADHD and externalizing problem behaviors. Therefore, boys need to learn to "hold back" on certain impulses such as the desire to run around a classroom or engage in a physical fight. Boys need to learn to identify when they are feeling angry, for example, and how they can express that anger in a constructive and non-violent way.

We need to learn to allow boys opportunities for expression of both physical activity and healthy aggression in our work with them.

Boys, on average, are more physically active and aggressive than girls. They need to be given opportunities to engage in their environment in physically expressive ways. They need opportunities to engage, for example, in regular, active recesses at school, as well as being given permission to engage in "rough and tumble" play activities in which no one gets hurt. In order to help boys regulate their physical expressions of activity and aggression, we need to be actively engaged. It is not helpful to be "hands off" (i.e. "Oh, boys will be boys") nor over-controlling (i.e. expecting boys to sit quietly for extended periods of time). We need to actively provide boys opportunities to learn about their world, to practice wrestling respectfully and safely.

Conclusion

We believe in the ability of boys to be healthy and happy individuals as well as positive contributors to community and family life. To achieve this, we must recognize and support what is natural about boys' behaviors while helping them to be more relationally skilled and emotionally intelligent. This is not about making boys into girls. Whether boys are from urban, rural or suburban settings, what is important is that they are emotionally healthy. Whether they play football or dance ballet, whether they hunt or knit, what matters is that boys are relationally competent.

As we have described, in order for us to help boys make better contact with themselves and others, we must first be able to connect with boys ourselves. Knowing about boys' preferences for communication and contact help us to make better connections with them. Please refer to our book – BAM! Boys Advocacy and Mentoring (Routledge, 2008) – for more examples of our work with boys in group settings.

References

Alexandera, G. M. (2002). Sex Differences in Response to Children's Toys in Nonhuman Primates (Cercopithecus Aethiops Sabaeus). *Evolution and Human Behavior 23*, 467–479.

Angelou, M. (1990). *I Shall Not Be Moved*. New York: Random House.

Anderson, R. N. & Smith, B. L. (2003). Deaths: Leading Causes for 2001. *National Vital Statistics Report 52*(9), 1-52.

Baron-Cohen, S. (2003). *The Essential Difference: The Truth About the Male and Female Brain*. New York: Basic Books.

Barkley, R. A. (1998). *Attention-Deficit Hyperactivity Disorder: A Handbook for Diagnosis and Treatment*. New York: Guildford Press.

Berenbaum, S. A. (2000). Psychological Outcome in Congenital Adrenal Hyperplasia. In B. Stabler & B. B. Bercy (Eds.), *Therapeutic Outcome of Endocrine Disorders: Efficacy, Innovation, and Quality of Life* (pp. 186-199). New York: Springer.

Berenbaum, S. A. & Resnick, S .M. (1997). Early Androgen Effects on Aggression in Children and Adults with Congenital Adrenal Hyperplasia. *Psychoneuroendocrinology 22*, 505-515.
Brown, D. E. (1991). *Human Universals*. New York: McGraw-Hill
Buhrmester, D. (1996). Need Fulfillment, Interpersonal Competence and the Developmental Contexts of Early Adolescent Friendship. In W. M. Bukowski, A. F. Newcomb, & W. W. Hartup (Eds.), *The Company They Keep: Friendship in Childhood and Adolescence* (pp. 158-185). New York: Cambridge University Press.
Burr, J. E., Ostrov, J. M., Jnasen, E. A., Cullerton-Sen, C. & Crick, N. R. (2005). Relational Aggression and Friendship During Early Childhood: "I Won't Be Your Friend!" *Early Education & Development 16(2)*, 161-185.
Camarena, P. M., Sarigiani, P. A., & Petersen, A. C. (1990). Gender-Specific Pathways to Intimacy in Early Adolescence. *Journal of Youth and Adolescence 19*, 19-32.
Castellanos, F. X., et al. (2002). Developmental Trajectories of Brain Volume Abnormalities in Children and Adolescents with Attention-Deficit/Hyperactivity Disorder. *Journal of the American Medical Association* 288(Oct. 9), 1740-1748.
Chu, J. Y. & Way, N. (Eds.) (2004). *Adolescent Boys: Exploring Diverse Cultures of Boyhood*. New York:New York University Press.
Connelan, J. (2001). Sex Differences in Human Neonatal Social Perception. *Infant Brain and Development 23*, 113-118.
Crick, N. R. (1996). The Role of Overt Aggression, Relational Aggression, and Prosocial Behavior in the Prediction of Children's Future Social Adjustment. *Child Development 67*(5), 2317-2327.
Crick, N. R. & Grotpeter, J. K. (1995). Relational Aggression, Gender, and Social-Psychological Adjustment. *Child Development 66*(3), 710-722.
Diller, L. (1999). *Running on Ritalin*. New York: Bantam.
Eaton, W. O. & Enns, L. R. (1986). Sex Differences in Human Motor Activity Level. *Psychological Bulletin 100*, 19-28.
Hall, J. A. (1984). *Nonverbal Sex Differences: Communication Accuracy and Expressive Style*. Baltimore: The Johns Hopkins University Press.
Hall, J. A., Carter, J. D., & Horgan, T. G. (2000). Gender Differences in Nonverbal Communication of Emotion. In A. H. Fischer (Ed.), *Gender and Emotion: Social Psychological Perspectives* (pp. 97-117). Paris: Cambridge University Press.
Halpern, D. (2005). Sex, Brains, & Hands: Gender Differences in Cognitive Abilities, *Skeptic 2*(3), 96–103.

Hankin, B. L. & Abramson, L .Y. (1999). Development of Gender Differences in Depression: Prescription and Possible Explanations. *Ann. Med. 31*(6), 372-379.
Heesacker, M., Wester, S. R., Vogel, D. L., Wentzel, J. T., Mejia-Millan, C. M., & Goodholm, C. R. (1999). Gender-Based Emotional Stereotyping. *Journal of Counseling Psychology 46*, 483-495.
Holmgren, D. (2007). The Essence of Permaculture. [on-line] http://www.holmgren.com.au/html/Writings/essence.html#Footnotes.
Institute of Medicine (2001). *Exploring the Biological Contributions to Human Health: Does Sex Matter?* Wash DC: National Academy Press.
Junaid, K .A. & Fellowes, S. (2006). Gender Differences in the Attainment of Motor Skills on the Movement Assessment Battery for Children. *Physical & Occupational Therapy in Pediatrics 26*(1/2), 5-11.
Kimura, D. (1995). Estrogen Replacement Therapy May Protect Against Intellectual Decline in Postmenopausal Women. *Hormones and Behavior 29*, 312-321.
Kiselica, M. S. (2001). *A Male-Friendly Therapeutic Process with School-Age Boys*. In G. R. Brooks & G. E. Good (Eds.), *The New Handbook of Psychotherapy and Counseling with Men* Vol. 1 (pp. 41-58). San Francisco: Jossey-Bass.
Kiselica, M. S. & O'Brien, S. (2001). Are Attachment Disorders and Alexithymia Characteristic of Males? In M. S. Kiselica (Chair), *Are Males Really Emotional Mummies: What Do the Data Indicate?* San Francisco, CA: Symposium Conducted at the 109th Annual Convention of the American Psychological Association.
Kiselica, M. S. (2003). Transforming Psychotherapy in Order to Succeed with Adolescent Boys: Male-Friendly Practices. *JCLP/In Session 59*(11), 1225-1236.
Knickmeyer, R. S., Wheelwright, S, Taylor, K., Raggatt, P., Hackett, G., & Baron-Cohen, S. (2005). Gender-Typed Play and Amniotic Testosterone. *Developmental Psychology 41*(3), 517-528.
Kraemer, S. (2000, December). The Fragile Male. *British Medical Journal 321*.
Kuhlmann, S. & Wolf, O. T. (2005). Cortisol and Memory Retrieval in Women: Influence of Menstrual Cycle and Oral Contraceptives. *Psychopharmacology 183*(1), 65-71.
LaFrance, M. & Hecht, M. A. (2000). Gender and Smiling: A Meta-Analysis of Sex Differences in Smiling. In A. H. Fischer (Ed.), *Gender and Emotion* (pp. 118-142). Cambridge: Cambridge University Press.

Leffert, N., Benson, P. L., & Roehlkepartain, J. L. (1997). *Starting out Right: Developmental Assets for Children.* Minneapolis, MN: Search Institute.

Lutchmaya, S. & Baron-Cohen, S. (2002). Human Sex differences in Social and Non-Social Looking Preferences at Twelve Months of Age. *Infant Behavior and Development* 25(3), 319-325.

Lutchmaya, S., Baron-Cohen, S., & Raggat, P. (2002a). *Foetal Testorone and Vocabulary Size in 18- and 24-Month-Old Infants. Infant Behavior and Development* 24(4), 418-424.

Lutchmaya, S., Baron-Cohen, S., & Raggat, P. (2002b). Foetal Testorone and Eye Contact at Twelve Months. *Infant Behavior and Development* 25(3), 327-335.

Maccoby, E. E. (1998). *The Two Sexes: Growing Up Apart, Coming Together.* Cambridge, MA: Harvard University Press.

Manstead, A. S. (1992). Gender Differences in Emotion. In A. Gale & M. Eysenck (Eds.), *Handbook of Individual Differences: Biological Perspectives* (pp. 355-387). New York: Wiley.

McClure, E. B. (2000). A Meta-Analytic Review of Sex Differences in Facial Expression Processing and Their Development in Infants, Children, and Adolescents. *Psychological Bulletin* 126(3), 424-453.

McNelles, L. & Connolly, J. (1999). Intimacy Between Adolescent Friends: Age and Gender Differences in Intimate Affect and Intimate Behaviors. *Journal of Research on Adolescence 9(2),* 143-159.

Merrell, K. W. & Popinga, M. R. (1994). Parent-Teacher Concordance and Gender Differences in Behavioral Ratings of Social Skills and Social-Emotional Problems of Primary-Age Children with Disabilities. *Diagnostique 19,* 1-14.

Mortola, P. (2006). *Windowframes: Learning the Art of Gestalt Play Therapy the Oaklander way.* Hillsdale, NJ: GestaltPress/Anal. Press.

Mortola, P., Grant, S., & Hiton, H. (2008). *BAM! Boys Advocacy and Mentoring: A Leader's Guide to Facilitating Strength-Based Groups for Boys, Helping Boys Make Better Contact by Making Better Contact with Them.* Routledge Series on Counseling and Psychotherapy with Boys & Men. New York: Routledge.

Munroe, R. L., Hulefeld, R., Rodgers, J. M., Tomeo, D. L., & Yamazaki, S. K. (2000). Aggression Among Children in Four Cultures. *Cross Cultural Research 34(1),* 3-25.

National Center for Education Statistics (2005). *Gender Differences in Participation and Completion of Undergraduate Education and How*

They Have Changed Over Time. [on-line] Available: http://nces.ed.gov/pubsearch/pubsinfo.asp?pubid=2005169.

Oaklander, V. (1978). *Windows to Our Children: A Gestalt Therapy Approach to Children and Adolescents.* Highland, NY: The Gestalt Journal Press.

Orozco, S., & Ehlers, C. L. (1998). Gender Differences in Electrophysiological Responses to Facial Stimuli. *Biol Psychiatry 44*(4), 281-9.

Patterson, F., Holts, C., & Saphire, L. (1991). Cyclic Changes in Hormonal, Physical, Behavorial, and Linguistic Measures in Female Lowland Gorilla. *American Journal of Primatology 24*, 181-194.

Perls, F., Hefferline, R., & Goodman, P. (1951). *Gestalt Therapy: Excitement and Growth in the Human Personality.* New York: Dell.

Pollack, W. (1998). *Real Boys.* New York: Random House.

Pope, H. G., Jr., Olivardia, R., Gruber, A., & Borowiecki, J. (1999). Evolving Ideals of Male Body Image as Seen Through Action Toys. *International Journal of Eating Disorders 26*, 65-72.

Reynolds, C. R. & Kamphaus, R. W. (1992). *Behavior Assessment System for Children: Manual.* Circle Pines, MN: American Guidance.

Siegel, D (1999). *The Developing Mind.* New York: Guilford.

Soifer, D. (2002). *Special Education Reform 2002: Where to Begin?* VA: Lexington Institute.

Tannen, D. (1994). *Gender and Discourse.* New York: Oxford Uni. Press.

Tannen, D. (1990). *You Just Don't Understand.* New York: Morrow.

Tomkins, S. (1962). *Affect Imagery Consciousness: The Positive Affects (Vol. 1).* New York: Springer.

Vaishnav, A. & Dedman, B. (2002, July 8). Special Ed Gender Gap Stirs Worry. *Boston Globe.* Retrieved July 8, 2002 from http://www.boston.com.

Wester, S. R., Vogel, D. L., Pressly, P. K., & Heesacker, M. (2002). Sex Differences in Emotion: A Critical Review of the Literature and Implications for Counseling Psychology. *The Counseling Psychologist 30*, 629-651.

Wheeler, G. (1991). *Gestalt Reconsidered: A New Approach to Contact and Resistance.* New York: Gardner Press.

Woods, E. (1996). Associations of Nonverbal Decoding Ability with Indices of Person-Centered Communicative Ability. *Communication Reports 9* (1), 13-22.

Wright, R. (1994). *The Moral Animal: Why We Are the Way We Are: The New Science of Evolutionary Pychology.* New York: Random House.

Editors' Note:
In the historical and social field of Northern Irish society, passions surge and are blocked in accordance with the survival realities of the area and times. Life, death, loyalty and faith carry particular meanings and weight. Sensitivity to the local vagaries and challenges of life for adolescents is necessary to be able to be an effective therapist. Bronagh Starrs brings four young Northern Irish people to life as she describes her work with them. She is a vibrant presence, reaching out to her clients, yet measured and considered as she frames their issues using McConville's developmental stages of adolescence. The sense of the young people's edginess, riskiness, and the shame they carry and provoke in others is vivid in her writing, yet she meets it head on, with courage, commitment and always carrying hope. In the process there is much for us all to learn about recognizing and responding to trauma in a relational manner, irrespective of the setting.

10

Working with Adolescents from a Catholic Background in Northern Ireland:

A Generation-Long Accumulation of Shame

Bronagh Starrs

The bloody conflict is over. We hope. As we move into times of peace, today's adolescents are living with the legacy of many centuries of oppression and dispossession. Our painful and complex political history continues to directly impact adolescent development, as teenagers here grow up in an environment where trauma and shame have become ground conditions of the field of experience. Adolescence is a process of intrapsychic and interpersonal boundary development; and the therapist works to support the growth and integration of these realms of experience. McConville's model of development and therapy is essentially a model of contact boundary development. He recognises that the adolescent develops by breaking away from milieux (physical, social, cognitive, philosophical, romantic, religious etc.) in which she finds herself already embedded, and in the process reorganises, simultaneously or sequentially, both the interpersonal and the intrapsychic. Using McConville's model and Robert Lee's conceptualisation of shame, this paper explores how trauma affects adolescent development by exploring how the trauma and shame of Northern Ireland's culture impedes the very business of disembedding, making it more dissociative than healthy boundary-making, and how then interiority can usher in overwhelming and unbearable pain.

(It is important to note that having been raised in an Irish Nationalist Catholic family and community, in an acutely sectarian society, and having worked predominantly with adolescents from a similar background, I am aware that my account of the historical context and of the experience and behaviour of adolescents is not representative of the entire society. The Catholic/Nationalist/Republican community in general possess tremendous resilience, empowerment and agency; I am reporting cases in which young people were experiencing particular hardship. There are other voices and other stories. This is mine.)

Rites of Passage

Rites of passage into adulthood are a culture's way of telling its emergent citizens who they are and how to think of themselves, their roles and possibilities. Traditional initiation practice includes preparation for transition of boy into warrior and girl into homemaker and childcare provider. Today this same process through rites of passage continues to powerfully influence the consciousness of the developing individual during adolescence – as strongly in Western as in indigenous culture, and it is certainly alive and flourishing in Northern Ireland.

Traditional initiation ritual often involves mutilation of the body and the phases of separation, transition and reintegration. Seán aged

17 and from West Belfast, was the youngest of three siblings. He lived with his mother and two sisters in a poor Catholic housing estate where unemployment and crime levels are high. His father died when he was 3 years old. Seán had been joyriding for four years and was involved in criminal activity. He received numerous threats regarding his behaviour from the IRA, who essentially policed the estate in which he lived.

When I first met Seán, he knew that a punishment shooting or beating (or both) was imminent for him. He felt terrified of experiencing the pain and was living in fear of the day he would be targeted. As he spoke I also noted his eager anticipation at the respect he would gain from his peers for his bravery. After being kneecapped he could stand shoulder to shoulder with the others, proud of his new status – having arrived in the world of men. He did not have long to wait for the ritual to be performed. A group of 3-4 men approached him one evening after dark. He was blindfolded, beaten with studded hurling sticks and was shot in both knees and ankles. He recognised the voice of one of his assailants – it was his uncle. Seán took his own life by hanging two years later.

Deirdre, also 17, was referred by her doctor because she was depressed. She had an older and a younger brother and they lived with their parents on a small farm in the country. Her father was alcoholic and regularly violent towards his wife when he was drunk. Deirdre was studying for her A level exams and had applied to several Universities where she hoped to study a degree in engineering. She was a bright student and had been predicted to receive excellent grades by her teachers. Her father communicated clearly to Deirdre that he believed the desire to pursue third level education was a pointless exercise for a girl. Instead she ought to get a job and settle down with a husband. Over recent months Deirdre had lost her enthusiasm and motivation to study and began to feel that she wouldn't be capable of undertaking a degree. Her mother told her that she believed Deirdre would fail her A level exams.

Deirdre wanted to leave home although she felt she was not capable of surviving without her family. Her mother worked long hours and in the evenings Deirdre was expected by everyone in the family to cook dinner. She was disappointed at being a girl and felt that she would have been more supported and more interesting to others in her family had she been a boy. She felt that nothing was ever good enough about her and sensed that boyfriends only used her for sex although she felt she could never challenge them on the issue. She ate little – nothing until 3pm each day and was developing a strong dependency on alcohol. With encouragement, Deirdre received adequate grades in her exams and proceeded to college. Within the first semester she became pregnant, left college and returned home to live on the farm.

Ideally, the adolescent's family and society create an experience wherein the adolescent is recognised precisely as a self, and where s/he may take the first tentative steps toward feeling that s/he has a unique, authentic and meaningful place in the world. However, both Seán and Deirdre's stories exemplify and underscore the potential challenges and implications faced by young people in Northern Ireland as they make their way towards adulthood. For some in the Catholic community of Northern Ireland, the symbolic transmission of what it means to be an adult male or female has, through the generations, developed into a malignant expression of this natural cultural mechanism.

History as Context

In describing life experience for adolescents in present day Northern Ireland it is necessary to contextualise their experience. This context is a very old and very troubled one. Celts, Normans, Vikings and others arrived as they made their way westward through Europe. The political involvement of England in Ireland began in 1171 when Henry II, King of England declared himself overlord of Ireland. In the 16th Century England made a second conquest with Henry VIII declaring himself King of Ireland. After unsuccessful rebellion by the Irish, the country was run by an English central Government. Protestantism was imposed; although only in Ulster did it become firmly established. Here, Scottish Presbyterians colonised the area. The land owned by the Catholics was confiscated and they were forced into the poorer bogland. The Protestant settlers had virtually all political power. The Protestants were in the minority throughout Ireland, but in the northern Province they were the majority and had considerable power and all the good land.

Since British involvement in Ireland commenced hundreds of years ago, there has been a heavy price to pay for the Irish through loss of our identity. Anything of value had to be relinquished – the most obvious losses being land and language. The land was taken from the Irish speaking Catholics by the British Protestants. These wealthy landlords made up 10% of the population. Catholics, who made up 75% of the population, were not permitted to vote, stand for Parliament, be a member of a learned profession, teach in a school, carry a firearm, own a horse worth more than £5, manufacture or sell books or newspapers, to name just a few of the Penal Laws which were passed by the Protestant Parliament of Ireland. These laws ensured the limiting of political and economic power on the basis of religion. In 1641 Catholics had owned 60% of the land. Disenfranchisement of the majority of the population meant that by 1776 ownership of land by Irish Catholics was estimated at 5%.

Life for those who belonged to the dominant Protestant Ascendancy was luxurious. They lived on large estates, pursued professional careers in military, government, law or education and lived off the rents they demanded from the peasant Irish tenants who had previously owned the land. Life for the majority of dispossessed Irish Catholics consisted of living and working on rented land and as servants in the big houses (landlord's estates). They lived their lives in abject poverty on a diet almost exclusively of potato.

Although these events were experienced many generations ago, their impact is still felt; and the Irish memory strong. Recent conflict between Catholics and Protestants has its origins in this time of history.

Much of our cultural identity was relinquished, repressed and shamed through contact with the British. Ours was a fiercely strong oral tradition – folklore, culture and traditions were preserved and handed down the generations through the art of seanchas (storytelling). Children learned about their heritage, their family and community history and were taught the great Irish legends, the songs, dances and poetry of the people through their native tongue. Sadly, as so much of our identity was held within the language, something immeasurable was lost when a language shift was imposed on the Irish people within one generation. In the 1800s children were educated through English and were forbidden to speak their own language in school. The children were made to wear tally sticks around their necks whilst in school. Each time a child spoke Irish a notch was carved in the stick. At the end of the school day, due punishment would be given (most often beatings) according to how many notches had been accumulated.

Understanding that in order for their children to survive in an English dominated economy and achieve better quality of life, parents urged and encouraged their children to speak English. Mothers and fathers communicated minimally with their children as they did not want to encourage Irish – now seen as an inferior, redundant language. The Irish language, and with it, a people's expression of identity which had been preciously preserved within the language, had all but vanished in most parts of Ireland. (Still today, the use of language can be a delicate and sensitive art: words here are weighted and can often be a trigger because of connotations which are politically, historically, emotionally and culturally nuanced e.g. we have never agreed to the naming of this place – Northern Ireland? The North? The Province? Ulster? The Six Counties? The Occupied Six Counties?)

The 1800's saw a marked campaign by the Catholic majority to fight for national independence and overthrow British rule. During this century the Irish also experienced the Great Hunger. Two million people were lost through starvation and forced exile. The struggle continued and intensified for freedom and for Home Rule, culminating in the Easter Rising of 1916 and the War of Independence. The Irish Free State was established in December 1921. An Anglo-Irish Treaty was signed and 26 counties gained independence. Six of the nine counties of Ulster remained within the United Kingdom, under British Rule. Northern Ireland came into being.

One third of the population of Northern Ireland was Nationalist and these were a people diminished and demeaned in every way possible by the powerful Unionist majority. A campaign for social justice and an end to discrimination and lack of civil rights for the Catholic Nationalist population got under way in the sixties. Clashes between the police and protesters became a regular feature of marches. British soldiers were drafted in and internment was introduced in 1971 with adolescent boys and men being arrested, often tortured, and imprisoned without trial. The response from the outraged Nationalists was increased support for the IRA. One of the protests arranged by the Northern Ireland Civil Rights Association took place in Derry on January 30th 1972. Thirteen unarmed demonstrators (six of whom were minors) were shot dead by British troops. That day became known as Bloody Sunday. It remains one of the most significant and controversial experiences of the last 40 years and is associated with the commencement of The Troubles. Since then there have been over 3600 deaths as a result of the conflict. 53% of those who lost their lives were young people under 30 years of age; 274 of them aged 17 and under. (Smyth, et al., 2004)

There has been an ongoing attempt to end the conflict which has, over time, involved all political parties from the north, paramilitary organisations, the Irish and British Governments, and international support and encouragement, notably from the United States. For the past ten years or so we have been moving cautiously into a time of peace. Ceasefires have been declared by the major paramilitary groups and are being upheld for the most part. Communication between what was thought to be two entirely disparate groups – the Protestant/Unionist/Loyalist/British community and the Catholic/Nationalist/

Republican/Irish community continues and each side appears increaseingly capable of tolerating the other for the sake of progress and of peace. People seem tired of the fight and hope is stirring.

Irish-Catholic Adolescence

At a cultural and political level, today's young people are living with the legacy of The Troubles in Northern Ireland and are the transition generation as we move tentatively and with a good deal of scepticism into a post-war era. Our adolescents are being asked to trust the process, both politically and psychically. Many of today's adolescents have not directly experienced the Troubles. Bombings and shootings are unusual occurrences now. Police barracks and British army bases are being demolished, military patrols and checkpoints are virtually a thing of the past, towns and cities have been rebuilt – there remains little evidence that these children were born into a war zone. The Irish-Catholic teenage population here navigates and negotiates the core, universal tasks and experiences of adolescence – like teenagers the world over. However, these children *were* born into a war zone and that has had an often subtle, yet tremendously powerful impact on their developing sense of self and relationship to the surrounding world. It is so important to be mindful of the context of their experience.

The adolescent's journey is a process of evolution from the child's introjected sense of self and environment and the relationship skills of childhood, towards the emerging adult's ability to relate to and engage with the world of other whilst having developed a relative degree of comfort and familiarity with who she is within herself. Her emerging capacity for contact moves in the direction of becoming increasingly differentiated and self-authored over time. Of course this is an intersubjective process. The experience of adolescence leaves a powerful legacy in her abilities and limitations for making contact in adult life: how solidly she stands in a reflective relationship of ownership to herself and the quality of contact she makes with her environment are directly contingent on how she has or has not been received by the people who have been close to her; and on how her environment has or has not supported her in experimenting to discover her own boundaries as she attempts to find her place in the world.

When generation after generation come to be so disempowered and dispirited, the expression of frustration, anger and despair is turned on the area that is safest, namely the family. The external struggle becomes internalised and ritualised, and the result can be so devastating. Fear and mistrust of authority has become deeply ingrained in our experience. Those in positions of authority and power have abused and betrayed those in their care: The British Government, Security Forces, Judicial System, Catholic Church and indeed families. More than 800 years of humiliation and displacement has brought profound loss and engendered much shame in the experience of the Irish Catholic/Nationalist community of Northern Ireland. So much unspeakable and often unacknowledged hardship has been experienced through the centuries. The result is that trauma has become a condition of the field. All of the oppression and violence has left its mark on the people and I recognise a familiar posture of shame and dispiritedness in today's generation of adolescents.

Shameful, self-propagating interactional patterns have been established and sadly, as a result, people have learned not to expect to be received or supported by their environment. Each generation, by virtue of its experience of being humiliated and intimidated, has shamed the next. Today's adolescents have been born into a culture of isolation, secrecy, repression and fear. Shame has become part of the ground of their experience: the same disparaging and undermining patterns which have been experienced at a cultural and political level, have occurred within the family system, and inevitably also, at an intrapsychic level for these adolescents – such is the influence of culture on the developmental process.

Ground Shame & The Adolescent's Journey

I want to show how McConville's (1995) stages of adolescent development are shaped by the specific context of Northern Ireland's past history and current state, by using case vignettes of young people I have met and worked with. Although the stages do appear in a progressive order generally, all three stages are recursive and adolescents will recycle through them as new material arises. There is one dominant stage through which the adolescent organises his/her experience, and within that there is a perpetual movement through all of the stages. I will show also how the subtleties of what Robert Lee calls *ground shame*, which is a creative adjustment in which the individual attempts to protect him/herself or someone else in the field, in the face of harsh conditions, can impact the adolescent's journey in a destructive manner. I have changed names and details to ensure anonymity.

1. A First Stage: Disembedding

In healthy development there is a psychological impulse to liberate oneself from the embedded experience of childhood and move towards the establishment of a more grounded, embodied sense of self. The central theme of the disembedding stage is the emerging and heightening of boundaries, which facilitates the adolescent's psychological segregation from the familiar world of childhood and family. Typical adolescent behaviour, including not letting parents know exactly what he is doing, reluctance to participate in aspects of family life, engaging in forbidden activity etc., is powerfully effective in generating an experience of boundary between teenagers and adults. It is behind this boundary that the adolescent's relationship to himself and to the world will be reworked and reorganised. This reworking and reorganising is also dependent on the extent to which relational connections are possible from behind this boundary. Disembedding can be complicated if the emerging adolescent is discouraged from separation in the first place:

David

David, a pseudo-mature and articulate 13 year old, self-referred recently. The presenting problem was his fear of the wind and I could see that the process of disembedding for this teenager was problematic. David described an underbounded relationship with his mother; they were 'best friends' and had no secrets – characteristic in a friendship between two teenagers, inappropriate and destructive for a young teenager and his mother. His mother shared details of many aspects of her adult life with David, including details of the marital relationship, actively discouraged David to develop peer friendships or new interests and assured him that her chronic depression would require hospitalisation for a lengthy period if he attempted to challenge parental dominion.

David told me what it felt like to be in the wind. He described his fear of being swept off his feet and blown away, together with a pervasive sense of despair and anger at his engulfment by the wind. After making a quick sketch of himself in the wind, he sat in silence for a few moments staring at the image and then said, 'The wind's a bit like my mum'. From that moment, the disembedding and self-definition process gathered momentum and over the course of therapy, with support, challenge, the acquisition of a skateboard, baggy jeans and skater friends, a teenager emerged. And as he found his ground, his fear of the wind dissolved.

When an adolescent's development and presenting symptom issue is tangled in the family, it is helpful to meet with other family members, particularly parents. Working with David's parents, offering support and educating them about their role in the dynamics of the relationship was a central feature of the work and infinitely more effective than meeting with David alone.

David's mother came to see me herself and it emerged that she had grown up in a quiet rural community, well known as a Republican area. Her family was repeatedly intimidated by British troops and she grew up expecting that one day these soldiers' threats to kill her father and brothers would be realised. She feared for the lives of the men in her family and knew there was little they could do to protect themselves from the occupying forces. This mother was terrified that her son would come to danger if she were to let him out of her sight and so she was determined not to ever do that. This mother's experience of trauma throughout her childhood was considered normal by her, as it was the experience shared by so many others. Until she began to tell her story she had not been aware of how painful this experience was for her, nor had it ever occurred to her that it might be directly impacting on David's attempts to develop as an adolescent. The mother's need for support seemed to me, in effect, much deeper than David's.

Drug and alcohol experimentation, a tongue piercing, refusal to visit grandparents on Sunday afternoon, angry and seemingly unreasonable outbursts, intense and secretive conversations with peers which immediately cease when an adult enters the room etc. – These behaviours, some of which are understandably bewildering and alarming for parents and other adults, are how the adolescent supports himself in risking the attempt at developing a more authentic sense of self. The adolescent begins to create and organise meaning in his world, which includes reinterpretation of his view of parents and family history from his own perspective. Sometimes he discovers deeply upsetting realities that he would prefer to ignore and this is too much for him. Often the impact of this awareness remains firmly bounded off from the adolescent's awareness and development of an inner world becomes too threatening a possibility, particularly where there is inadequate environmental support. The young person becomes caught in acting out through blatantly self-destructive behaviour patterns, choosing a lifestyle which is often dangerous, involving high-risk and/or criminal activity.

For these adolescents, the heightening and expansion of boundaries leads neither to growing contact between the parts of self, nor to a richer contact boundary between self and others, although the psychological impulse is to do just that. With these young people it is necessary to create sufficient environmental support so that they can begin to tolerate their painful reality and move out of this frozen way of being in the world.

Conor

Conor, age 16, was referred by his father. He is the middle child of nine siblings and was placed in care aged 8 when it emerged that his uncle had been sexually abusing him and other members of his family. Conor was separated from most of his family and spent the next seven years in care, often running away, getting into trouble with the police and vandalising property. Conor's parents separated and his mother lives abroad. He has not seen her since he was eight. He has supervised contact with his younger siblings and occasionally sees his older brothers. Around 18 months ago Conor came to live with his father who referred him to me because of his 'out of control' behaviour. He had been joyriding, then bashing up the cars and setting them alight. During arguments, Conor would inevitably threaten to set his father's car alight, which understandably alarmed the dad who was concerned about the sincerity of the threat.

It is difficult to imagine the extent of hurting which Conor has experienced in his young life. It also quickly became clear that I was merely the next in a long list of professionals he had encountered along the way. He had no expectation of being met with understanding or respectful interest. When Conor first came to see me he was drinking heavily and getting into trouble. After a while he told me about getting drunk and stealing cars. He would drive into walls at around 30/40 mph wearing no seat belt. He loved the buzz and feeling of being alive that it gave him, which, according to him, was well worth the pain of the injuries he suffered. Often he would then smash up the cars and set them on fire.

He was surprised that I didn't lecture him or call the police but rather became interested in trying to understand the meaning of his behaviour. He talked of feeling dead or asleep in his body most of the time and it seemed he could only feel alive whilst engaging in high risk activity. He felt extremely angry when he watched the flames of cars he had set alight and felt there were flames inside him too. We worked with embodying the flames and Conor began to attend to the fire which was raging within.

On his 17th birthday I decided to send Conor a text to wish him a happy birthday as I guessed my wishes might be the only ones he received. Sadly I was right. This however marked a significant turning point in the work with Conor as texting became an important means of relating for us – it is safer and less threatening than the face to face encounter and afforded him the space to articulate the unspeakable. He began to tell me about the deep sadness and loneliness he felt at not seeing his mother and having little or no contact with his siblings. He described his anger and shame at having been sexually abused and his shame of having been placed in care. Sometimes during sessions we would talk about the texts and sometimes we would not, although it has become easier for Conor to articulate his experience to me face to face. He brought a cd of his favourite song to the session once (at his request) and we explored the meaning of the lyrics for him. It was a useful device for helping him articulate his own experience and further appreciate his struggle:

The Rose that Grew from Concrete

You try to plant somethin in the concrete, y'knowhatImean?
If it GROW, and the rose petal got all kind of scratches and
    marks, you not gon' say,
"Damn, look at all the scratches and marks on the rose that
    grew from concrete"
You gon' be like, "Damn! A rose grew from the concrete?!"
Same thing with me, y'knahmean?
I grew out of all of this
Instead of sayin, "Damn, he did this, he did this,"
just be like, "DAMN! He grew out of that? He came out of
    that?"
That's what they should see, y'knowhatImean?
All the trouble to survive and make good out of the dirty,
    nasty
y'knowhahatImean unbelievable lifestyle they gave me
I'm just tryin to make somethin..
When no one even cared
The rose it grew from concrete
Keepin all these dreams
Provin nature's laws wrong
It learned how to walk without havin feet
It came from concrete

The flower's struggle bore a striking similarity to his own life experience and he often uses the flower's symbolism in our conversations. (Imagine the experience of being rooted in and attempting to disembed from concrete!) Conor needed someone to believe in him so that he could begin to believe in himself. Gradually the car theft ceased and realising that alcohol fanned his flames and ignited his anger, he began to moderate his drinking. He became more and more relaxed within himself. He became more reflective, stopped stealing cars, changed his friends and went back to school. He was frozen in the impulsive acting out, denial and projection of disembedding and the work was to support his emerging interiority in a way that was not shaming or overwhelming. The work with Conor is ongoing and he is gradually and tentatively developing a sense of himself as an acceptable and worthy human being.

Working with disembedding-stage adolescents requires patience and sensitivity. It is important to be mindful of their limitations as they struggle with the dilemmas of separation and individuation. Unlike more mature adolescents and adult clients, they do not have access to an observing ego. Often when adults are trying to be helpful, their assistance is received as an attack and the adolescent feels that some aspect of the self is being criticised.

2. A Second Stage: Interiority

This development of a new sense of self and way of contacting the world which unfolds initially at the external, interpersonal level is initially tenuous and crude in form. However, it is the first important stage in the development of a mature, differentiated and interdependent style of relating to self and to the world. The next and often challenging stage along the developmental path for the adolescent is the opening up of an interiority. The adolescent now has to come to grips with a naturally expanding and deepening inner world of private experience – trying out and testing new internal boundaries in the experience of self.

The stage of interiority is not a whole experience, rather it becomes more the foreground as the disembedding and projection still continues, but with less intensity. The central issue for the interiority stage adolescent is the struggle within herself for authenticity. She embarks on an intense search for meaning and integrity – working to develop inner strength, a sense of personal worth and an individuality which will in time enable a richer experience of connection and relationship with self and others. The adolescent becomes highly self-conscious and keenly attuned to whether or not she is taken seriously. There is a tendency to assign highly self-referential significance to interpersonal contact and although relationships become more reality based, she may struggle to regard issues with balanced perspective.

It is as if there is a lack of internal differentiation between observing and experiencing aspects of the ego, which makes it easy for the adolescent to drown in her interiority. What can become interiorised is a sense of not belonging – a sense of shame. The therapist's role is akin to that of the life-guard: teaching her to swim and lose her fear of the water, yet at the same time, ensuring she does not get out of her depth and become lost at sea.

Carolyn

Carolyn, age 17, self-referred because she was unhappy at school. My first impression of her was that I had seldom seen anyone who looked so afraid and vulnerable. In the beginning we would often sit on the floor opposite each other, with Carolyn huddled behind a bundle of large cushions. She never, ever made eye contact with me, but said she wanted me to sit with her and not talk. She said she had a box inside her with 'bad stuff' in it. She had a dream one night that we were standing at the top of a staircase. She was too afraid to descend the staircase alone. She didn't know what she might find when she got to the basement and it helped to have me there to accompany her. I had my hand on her back. My touch felt gentle and supportive, but she was afraid that I might push her down the steps. She needed me to stay a little behind her and we must move at her pace. Her dream has been a helpful guide for me in the work. It has also been an effective way for Carolyn to manage the rhythm of what happens between us and continue to find the safety and support she needs from me. (She will often tell me how she is experiencing me and the work by using the imagery of the dream.)

We have been working together for almost three years now and about ten months into therapy she started to open the box and disclosed that her father had been sexually abusing her for as long as she could remember. Her mother knew about the abuse taking place – she walked into a room when Carolyn was being raped by her father and silently exited again. The incident was never spoken of. Carolyn also disclosed to me that her father's friend raped her when she was eleven years old. She is sure her father consented to this and memories are emerging of others being involved in her abuse. It appears likely that she was 'passed round'.

I intuitively sensed that the abuse by her father was ongoing, although Carolyn assured me that it wasn't. Several months later, when she left home to go to college, she confided that this had indeed been the case. She does not go home unless she feels it is absolutely essential and that, thankfully, is a rare occurrence. During these short visits, which are never overnight, we stay in close contact. She is learning to protect and support herself in the world. I have watched her journey from wanting to be and feeling that she was dead, to finding fulfillment and enjoyment in her life (although she is still convinced that she will die soon). It has been a moving and often very difficult experience to bear witness to her unfathomable pain and support her in discovering her humanness and sense of self.

Carolyn has found creative expression particularly helpful at times in the attempt to articulate her experience. The following is a description in her own words of her experience:

"I'm neither male nor female; I don't have a gender or sexuality. I don't exist below the waist. I'm essentially pointless and dead. I don't feel much anymore. I don't fit with the category of "female" because I don't fit the definition in my mind – I'm not very feminine. At the same time I'm not masculine. It's like I'm stuck at an age before puberty and adolescence... like I'm a child walking around in an adult world and that is scary because I spent too much time in a bad part of the adult world when I was a child. I have a space inside – it's empty because someone got inside and damaged it. I don't have a face because I don't really know who I am – other people have eroded that... Sometimes my thoughts take on a life of their own – I feel almost separate from them but they are so real and so strong that I feel like I'm living in a nightmare. I cannot control these thoughts; I can't silence them and they really affect life. These are physical thoughts too. My body remembers things my head has managed to hide. Sometimes my body just has a bad day. Sometimes the memories are so horrible I wish I could stop them – physically on days like these banging my head off a wall seems like a good idea."

Carolyn had not so much disembedded from her family field as dissociated from herself and the world during her childhood. So, working in an embodied way has been important. She is learning to trust and care for her body and has developed well the capacity to be present in her encounters with others. Supporting Carolyn in creating a meaningful and enriching life for herself has been an important aspect of the work, as she comes to terms with and transcends her years of abuse. She is only now beginning to stop blaming herself for what happened and is experiencing a new freedom which is exhilarating for her. The co-creation of a safe and respectful connection between us both has unquestionably been the most significant and most healing feature of the work. The world of relationship is becoming safer for her now and she is finding more and more empowerment in her life. An extremely bright and capable young woman, Carolyn is studying a subject which she loves. She has made some good friends at college and for the most part, enjoys her life.

Carolyn's family is staunchly republican. For her, raids on the family home by British troops where she was subjected to terrifying and degrading behaviour by police and soldiers was a regular feature of family life. Often, during these raids, her father would be arrested and detained, returning home days or weeks later having been beaten, interrogated and humiliated. It was at these times that Carolyn experienced the most painful, aggressive and demeaning times of being abused. It seems that Carolyn's father vented his aggression and resentment at the situation he found himself in (both personally and politically) by brutalising his daughter sexually.

3. A Third Stage: Integration

As the adolescent develops a more solid presence in the world and establishes a growing sense of ownership of experience, he can risk a more mature style of contact without threat of the self's disintegration. He becomes more engaging whilst maintaining a sense of himself. His quality of contact is enriched and he is able to relate to others and to himself in more differentiated ways. The adolescent's journey is from embeddedness within a family field and an introjected sense of self and his world, towards ownership of his life and appreciation of his unique place in the world. The adolescent's reorganisation of self and of his relationships with family, peers and his wider environment, culminates in a sense of personal agency and an essential security in who he is in himself and in the world.

Some of the young people I meet have moved through the earlier stages of disembedding and interiority and are struggling with the integration of the two in the final phase of adolescent development. They require additional support in adopting personal responsibility for their lives and there is often a conflict between what they want and obstacles to attaining it.

Niall

Niall, age 17, self-referred because he was stressed about schoolwork and exams. He grew up in a 'wholesome' (as he described it) family and was the youngest of three boys. His older brothers had both won scholarships to prestigious colleges and their academic achievements were a source of pride for the family. When Niall came to see me he was beginning his final year of secondary school and had begun the application process for third level education. He was a bright student who lacked the motivation and inclination to study. He was a gifted singer-songwriter, though he sensed his family's disapproval – his time would be better spent sitting at his desk studying. He didn't actually want to go to college but instead had dreams of becoming a rock star. He would own a farm and in the evenings his friends would come round, they would play some guitar and drink beer. Niall felt pressured by his parents and older brothers to succeed academically. They wanted him to attend a fine college and become a scientist. They frowned upon his creative endeavours and he felt a strong sense of inadequacy when he was in their presence. It appeared as if they were supportive of him, but their support was experienced as expectation.

One morning I had a phone call from Niall's mother. She wanted to respect her son's confidentiality and certainly did not want to intrude in the therapeutic process. The reason for her call was to ask me how she and Niall's father could best support their son in his final year of school. I was struck by her depth of caring and concern for Niall. The family had noted that, despite Niall's ability, he appeared to lack confidence when it came to schoolwork. He seemed to freeze in terror when the subject of college arose. I heard no expectation in her voice. I told Niall about the conversation and about how I experienced his mother as concerned – not about his academic performance, but about Niall himself. She seemed as supportive a mother as I had met.

We began trying to figure out whose expectation Niall was experiencing. It emerged that Niall was having difficulty identifying himself as either creative or academic – he could not possibly be both. Rock stars don't study physics. He was also silently fearful that he would not be as successful as his older brothers – so opting out of academics and college was an attractive and safer option. Niall was projecting his concerns about himself and his future onto his parents. It was *their* need for him to be responsible and realise his potential as a capable student. And so long as he projected this aspect of his life, he could identify with the more fun part of himself who sat up most of the night getting drunk and smoking pot with friends as they played music and discussed their philosophies on life.

As Niall developed a more encompassing view of his situation he drew back his projections and worked towards integration of the composite parts of himself. He let go of his expectation and found a way to honour these diverse aspects of himself. He dropped biology and took on music instead. He was more thoughtful and empowered regarding his choice of college subjects and he began to see the possibility of guitars and physics playing equally important, fulfilling parts in his life. Niall became less defensive and withdrawn with his family and felt that he didn't have to fight for his place so much now.

Two Potential Pathways of Experience

I do not meet many adolescents who have reached the stage of integration. Niall's experience did not include generations of oppression and shame. His family is Protestant and he has not grown up in Northern Ireland. Fortunately for this adolescent, trauma has not been a condition of the field of his experience. Niall was affirmed and supported by his environment in developing a self and our time together was focused on refinement and fine-tuning of the self-formation process. Most adolescents I make contact with have a much more brittle sense of self and sometimes no real sense at all. The work of integration is often a long way off – finding someone home inside is the principal focus. These adolescents need to be supported in discovering that they are more than their pain and that support, connection and belonging is possible in their experience.

McConville (2006) postulates that when we make contact with another person we are attuned, either consciously or unconsciously, to at least four possibilities: (1) objectification and condemning judgment, (2) neutral disinterest, (3) neutral interest or curiosity, and (4) enthusiastic embrace. Certainly the first and possibly the second are shaming encounters. There is a quality of support within the latter two experiences of relating. My contact with adolescents informs me that the first two possibilities are most familiar for them. To be met with neutral interest or curiosity is quite unexpected; enthusiastic embrace is treated with contempt and suspicion. We are a sceptical, cynical people and our standard mode of contact is to shame and be shamed. We have developed appropriate behaviour strategies to make others the reciprocals for our shame. For us, personality has shaped itself around this enterprise and we have become known for our sharpness and sarcasm.

Many people do not expect to be supported here and I believe that is because experience in the family informed us that support was unavailable. Robert Lee (Lee, 1996, 2001; Kanner & Lee, 2004) speaks of our inherent wisdom in using shame as a regulator of the field. We experience shame when we perceive that our yearnings for connection and belonging might not be, are not, or have not been met in our environment, and we do not have sufficient support. Shame's function is to have us pull back from and hide our yearning when we sense that we are not received. Hence, every experience of shame is a natural attempt to protect, although the effects of shame can be very destructive.

When an entire people have been shamed to such a profound extent by another nation, that shame becomes part of the ground of our experience. For centuries we have been treated as second-class citizens by the occupying forces and stripped of our land, our identity and often our dignity. And because of this political history, there have not been a lot of human and other resources that people could count on. Supportive relational connections have not been possible; and so the way to survive in the face of this climate of isolation that has existed has been for people to learn to rely on themselves.

I suspect that there might be two potential pathways of experience for adolescents: a model of adolescent process for the child who emerges from a relational field and another suitably adapted blueprint for the child who emerges from a field of isolation, the latter essentially to do with survival. The relational field provides the necessary support and resistance from which to disembed and begin to move off into the world. A field in which trauma is part of the ground of experience often seems to result in more dissociation than healthy boundary making at the disembedding stage. The development of interiority, as well as bringing the adolescent into deeper contact with the self, may, for the traumatised adolescent, prove overwhelming as s/he confronts directly and personally, the impact of many generations of shame. In a spirit of integrity and self-preservation, the adolescent dissociates from various components of experience.

So many adolescents growing up in Northern Ireland find themselves without relational connections and resources. They do not feel appreciated and valued for who they are, which makes their journey through adolescence a lonely and difficult one. Some do not make it and many of those who do, arrive at adulthood having had their experience of the emerging self disconfirmed and diminished. Such a shame!

References

Kanner, C. & Lee, R. G. (2004). The Relational Ethic in the Treatment of Adolescents. In R. G. Lee (Ed.), *The Values of Connection: A Field Approach to Ethics* (pp. 113-134). Hillsdale, NJ: The Analytic Press/ GestaltPress.

Lee, R. G. (1996). Shame and the Gestalt model. In R. G. Lee & G. Wheeler (Eds.), *The Voice of Shame: Silence And Connection In Psychotherapy*, (pp. 3-23). San Francisco: Jossey-Bass

Lee, R. G. (2001). Shame & Support: Understanding an Adolescent's Family Field. In M. McConville & G. Wheeler (Eds.), *Heart of Development: Gestalt Approaches to Working with Children and Adolescents. Vol II - Adolescents* (pp. 253-270). Hillsdale, NJ: Analytic Press/GestaltPress.

McConville, M. (1995). *Adolescence: Psychotherapy And The Emergent Self*. San Francisco: Jossey-Bass.

McConville, M. (2006). Shame *In Adolescent Development And Psychotherapy*. Paper presented to the Cleveland MetroHelath Conference

Song: *The Rose That Grew From* Concrete Album: The Rose That Grew From Concrete Artist: 2pac with Nikki Giovanni. November, 2000. Interscope Records .

Editors' Note:

Therapists working with adolescents, and particularly those working with young women, will be aware of the increasing recognition, and likely increase in frequency, of eating problems and disorders in the younger section of our population. There is a long and healthy tradition in the literature of seeing the family context in which these situations emerge. Marlene Blumenthal shows us how relationship is paramount in developing this theme, recognizing the multiple strands of connection that become interwoven in the tapestries of the lives of the young women she works with. We experience the thoughtfulness and warmth which she brings to her work, as well as her preparedness to be flexible and not hold fast to limiting viewpoints. She introduces concepts from attachment theory and the issue of shame, to build a fully relational rationale for therapy with these patients. She illustrates how therapy is, in essence, the relational context in which the entrenched patterns, the creative adjustments from the past, can be acknowledged, shared and healed.

11

Disordered Eating:

A Tapestry of Relational Themes and Creative Adjustment[1]

Marlene Moss Blumenthal

Imagining

It's nighttime and I'm crying myself to sleep, again. I don't know *why* I cry. I just feel awful. I've been a good student since elementary school. I have lots of friends, but no best friend. I did everything just right, today. I do that every day. I even made dinner and put my younger sisters to bed – like I

---

[1] The author thanks Neil Harris for his infinite wisdom, creativity, and dialogical approach to editing.

... 285

always do. My mom needs me to manage. She's always down. Sometimes she drinks a lot, but she works hard.

Now I'm in college...I've been getting good grades but that's not enough. Sometimes I feel like I'm going crazy...I feel so upset. I tried sticking my finger down my throat and threw up. I felt better. Now I do it every day. Even when I eat too much junk I can throw up and feel better. But just for a little while. The pain in my stomach is getting worse...it never goes away. I am starting to lose it... can't study, my grades are coming down. I feel so down all the time... I can't stand being alone.

This familiar narrative evokes nearly unbearable pain as I listen to grown women, young women, and adolescent girls share their stories, their pain and their shame. For many, they are telling their stories, speaking the unspeakable, for the first time. The narratives come in fragments... a few now, a few later, and we engage with each other in our attempt to weave a coherent story. We labor to bring the strands together as a meaningful tale that can help us understand and to appreciate this creative adjustment, the underlying strength and determination to live an undersupported, developmentally challenged life. Many have had life saving medical interventions, have learned life skills to manage their emotional ups and downs. Yet, the ongoing felt experience, the "emptiness in my core", the "never ending tightness in my chest," the "feeling like I'm 'no body'" continues to be part of everyday existence.

Identifying and Illuminating the Threads

My experience in working with adolescent girls and women with eating disorders is that we are holding a large, multi-dimensional tapestry and together we are working to identify and illuminate various threads and patterns. Consistent intertwining threads emerge as we sit together. These threads include relationship patterns, shame and isolation, culture and gender, and the development of social skills. The threads are often tightly layered and intertwined and we need to look closely to tease them apart.

Early Relationships

The core issues in these cases that have so often been under attended to in some treatment programs were boldly underscored in the words of a fourteen year-old client. Her parents had sent her for treatment of her eating disorder to a well-respected group whose treatment, both family intervention and skill training, is guided by research. I had worked with the girl and her family a few years before on some family decision making. Recently, the parents decided that they wanted me to see their daughter in a supportive role in cooperation with the eating disorder intervention group with whom I have a working relationship. As the fourteen year-old brought me up to date on the intervention – or rather, as she raged about how the treatment was the wrong one for her – my curiosity heightened. She went on to say, "Don't they know… it's not about someone making me eat the right foods – it's about my relationships. I have trouble with the relationships in my family."

When we engage, I find that clients who have experienced, or continue to experience anorexia, bulimia, or other repeated patterns of eating difficulties, usually talk about difficulties in their early relationships, and in other significant relationships. And what often emerge are their feelings of shame and isolation. At times these feelings are accompanied by descriptions of disconnection, being missed by significant others. Frequently, they describe early relationships as being fraught with anxiety or inconsistency.

Holmes (2001) cites studies of eating disordered patients who show a mixture of insecure attachment patterns. He suggests that by mastering the longing for food, the anorexic individual is "no longer at the mercy of the need for a secure base over which she has no control." (p. 9). Cozolino (2006), a psychologist and author of *The Neuroscience of Human Relationships*, posits that "securely attached children successfully use other people to modulate their stress and do not produce an adrenocortical response when attachment figures are available. In contrast, those with insecure attachment schema do show HPA stress reaction in the same situations" (p. 147). The latter is translated into the development of enduring patterns of arousal with poor coping strategies. When there is a "failure of the secure base providing caregiving to alleviate anxiety, the capacity to develop both intimacy and autonomy is inhibited" (Holmes, 2001, p. 97).

Lynne Jacobs might say that our stance as therapists is to "hold the hope" (2008). I remind myself as I sit with a young adult client who tells me repeatedly, "I try to do everything right, but on my own -- I can't count on others. Yet nothing goes right, never has, never will... the only thing I can control is what I eat or don't eat, and I can't even manage that. I eat too much and feel awful, I vomit and feel awful..." In experiencing her cycles of hope and dread, we have noticed the familiar, underlying lived pattern in this capable young woman's experience. It is only my belief in her determination to weather her experience of dread and live for the next period of hope that supports me to hold space and hope for this bright, creative individual. Our progress is slow but memorable. Her perseverance inspires me.

I am recalling another bright high school student who described herself as never having *fitted* in socially. She feared her developing body – almost as if she would lose the opportunity to be a child and find the love from her mother that she had never felt. In her mother's presence, she seemed to disappear as her self-absorbed mother made little space for her to exist. So she starved herself. After recovering with medical intervention, she seemed stuck – wanting to be healthy yet terrified of getting bigger. Her adoring father felt as helpless as his daughter. In order to avoid the terror of feeling her own shame and pain, this bright and creative young woman became a perfectionist, excessively careful, with an aversion to experience her own sensations and emotions. This young woman, who after fainting and being rushed to the hospital was astounded and reassured when her parents remained consistently by her side, giving up a vacation, so that they could watch over her. Her need to consistently be reassured of her intimate connection to both parents, and her learning to explore her wants and needs in relation to them and to her environment in a safe, therapeutic setting, was essential to her healing.

Working with a 14 year old who was struggling to meet her father's and stepmother's expectations required holding space for her parents while staying consistently present for this young person. Her question, "Where do I belong, where do I fit?" emerged from her perceived differences between her step siblings and herself, and the differences in parenting styles between her biological parents and their respective spouses. The underlying pain seemed to emerge from her yearning for connection with her biological mother, whose good intentions toward her daughter were undermined by competing interests. This made it difficult for her mother to have a sustained intimate connection with her. Perhaps the 14 year-old's restrictive eating, while living with her father was her way of rebelling against his requirement for her to achieve scholastically as modeled by her stepsiblings. Perhaps, at some level, she believed that her mother would rescue – making time and space for her – if she starved herself.

Another example of an insecure attachment pattern emerged in a well meaning family. The daughter, now in her twenties, had significant learning difficulties in her early years that made space for her parents to intervene promptly and consistently. Rather than allowing their daughter the opportunity of learning to manage her frustration, these loving parents became her rescuers, while criticizing her for her inability to follow through and organize herself. In many ways, she grew into a competent late adolescent. However, she failed to develop a capacity to self-soothe and began to binge and purge and enjoy the calming effect of alcohol. Her shame at her inability to manage her feelings and difficulty in eating a nutritional diet without excessive weight gain led to her pattern of binging and purging. Her bulimia served as a distraction, giving her a temporary sense of feeling soothed and then offering her a temporary release from uncomfortable and unmanageable feelings. Somehow, this pattern of behavior brought on a brief feeling of security and protection – feelings that had sustained her in her early years. When life's challenges exceeded her capacity for organizing and managing, when relationships soured and criticism came her way, she felt that she was unable to tolerate the anxiety and started the cycle of binging and purging as well as drinking. In the safety of a healing therapeutic relationship, the family began to organize differently. The parents made arrangements for their daughter to be in charge of her own finances, while they began to spend more time alone as a couple. This mother and daughter are healing their relationship, and the daughter is taking charge of and managing the vicissitudes of her own work and intimate relationships, sparing her mother the intimate details and setting an appropriate boundary. This family continues to work at organizing differently.

Shame and Isolation

It is not the stories that are so devastating, but the isolation surrounding the stories – there is no one to tell, to help hold the pain. These girls are alone in their felt experience of shame. And consistently, I hear the themes of emptiness, of missed connection, of absence, and of insecurity about being loved.

Several girls have told me, "My mother is strict, tough, and unavailable", or, "She should get a life, instead of micromanaging mine." "She's always telling me what I feel and what I should do... and what to wear." "Doesn't she know that I KNOW what I want... guess not, 'cause she NEVER asks ME, NEVER listens..." and (in a whisper) "doesn't care." Sometimes I hear stories about Aunt Sarah "who told me I was getting fat," or Uncle Jack who said, "Oh, my, you were such a beautiful little girl, what happened?" or about "... my father (or my boyfriend) who is always telling me to exercise... *if you did you'd be so pretty.*"

Often, the insecurity about being loved is hidden, deep down under. One talented and very bright high school senior insisted that her family was fine, her parents were good, relationships were okay. After an incident when both parents dropped everything to be with her in the hospital, she remarked with surprise and exhilaration, "They really DO love me." This was a watershed experience of knowing that she was loved in a newly felt way.

Professional parents with an overweight, academically and socially successful daughter brought their daughter in to talk with me. The pictures woven into this tapestry by the parents and daughter suggested that social acceptance was a high priority in the family. In a teary interchange between this young woman and her father, she told him how important it had been for her as a child to be adored by him. She shared that she now felt ugly and didn't think he loved her anymore, as she had gained a lot of weight (and had grown more than a foot). She showed him the picture that she carried in her wallet. It was one of herself at the age of 11. She had long, wavy, blond hair, huge eyes and was very thin. She began sobbing as she told him of her experience of his becoming critical toward her as she began to develop. He seemed to be the spokesman for two generations of the family when he cautioned her about becoming fat, and began to demand that she exercise more often, more vigorously, and for longer periods of time at a workout session. The father cried and apologized for anything that he might have said to bring this on, and for his actions. The father had grown up in a family where his mother was obsessed with being thin, and criticized anyone who, in her eyes, was 'fat.' He rarely missed a day at the gym, himself. However, the generational pattern of relationships had been established. The apology was an essential beginning, but not sufficient.

Shame, Enduring and Recurring

Gillie (2000) has named shame as a fundamental aspect of bulimia. She argues that "it is very likely that the bulimic client has experienced insufficient support in the field for important needs, and consequently, has experienced a significant rupture in the intersubjective field" (p.103). In my experience, shame is also a fundamental aspect of anorexia and other eating disorders. Perhaps, as Kaufman (1996) indicates "individuals suffering from these disorders typically experience themselves as inherently deficient, worthless, or disgusting – as failures" (p. 129).

Shame has to do with the experience of disconnection and isolation. If shame, a natural, and as some believe necessary part of development, becomes repeated, with no empathic other of the field to support healthy contact, the ground is ripe for a lifetime of constriction and pain in an attempt to relate by avoiding the dreaded feelings connected to the shame experience (Figure 1.)

It helps in thinking about this as a therapist, to understand how we may develop our felt sense of self. Damasio helps us to understand the early influence of relationship on brain development. Demasio, known for his research on the neurology of emotion, memory, and language writes about the emergence of consciousness (1999). His interest is specifically "about the sense of self and about the transition from innocence and ignorance to knowingness and selfness" (p. 4) and the biological circumstances that permit this early and critical transition. He posits that there is first an imaged nonverbal account of relationship that allows for a "subtle image of knowing, the feeling essence of our sense of self" and for "the enhancement of the image of the causative object" (p. 171). He elaborates by describing the feeling of knowing that then springs to life in a nonverbal account inherent in a newly constructed neural pattern. This early sense of self is the neural foundation on which additional information accrues as the infant develops. So it is in relationship that we develop our felt sense of self. And with repeated relational interactions the neural pathways relating to memory of this felt sense of self are developed. And, it would seem that the manner in which a felt sense of self is experienced, the ground of relational experience, is dependent upon the kind of early relational experiences one has had. It would follow, then that new experiences would continue to influence neural pathways, throughout our lives, with our earliest experiences providing the ground for us to explore in therapy.

Figure 1. Being Hard Wired for Relationship Patterns[2]

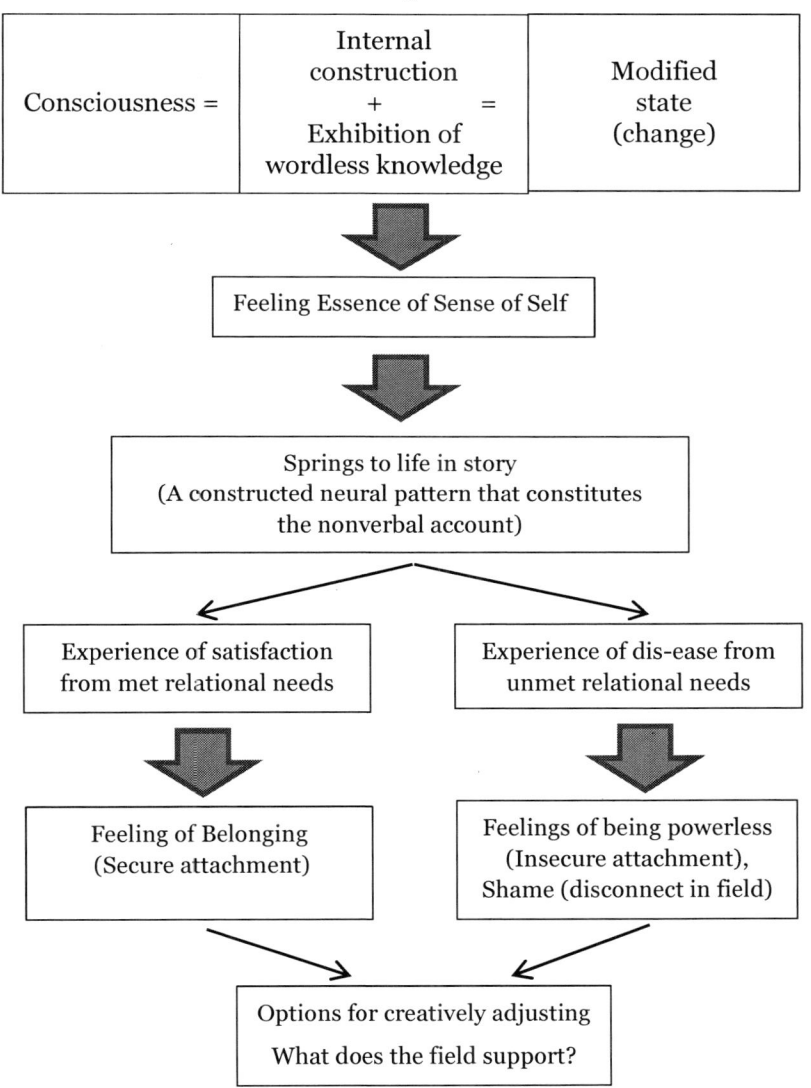

[2] From Damasio, 1999

Lee (2007, and Chapter 2) has examined some of the neurobiological research literature that addresses the role and importance of relationship in structuring neural circuits during our first years of life. He has made some important connections between our early relationships, factors shaping a child's developing sense of shame and belonging, and the meaning for us as Gestalt therapists and theoreticians. Lee cites Trevarthan, referring to his research on mother-infant interactions and states that Trevarthan "concludes that infant neurological growth literally requires brain-brain interaction occurring in the context of an intimate (positive) relationship between caregiver and infant" (p.40.) Lee continues to suggest, citing additional research, that "the attach-ment relationship is essentially a regulator of arousal"... and "that the regulatory process is the precursor of psychological attachment and its associated emotions" (p.40). Schore, a neuropsychoanalyst who has done extensive research on the neurobiology of emotional development, is another one of the theorists that Lee has drawn upon in relation to addressing, the importance of attachment styles when exploring development (2007). Schore proposes that when a child's active bid for attunement has been unsupported shame is produced (1994). And the tapestry frays.

When our environmental supports are insufficient, when our sense of belonging (Lee, 2007) is threatened, our neural patterns develop in such a way that our sense of equilibrium, of 'all is okay in our world' is absent. We may develop that felt sense of dis-ease, questioning at a sensory level, 'where do I fit?' The experience that 'I don't belong' or even more powerfully, 'I feel like dirt, or garbage – I don't belong anywhere' is a common theme articulated by girls and women with eating disorders.

Feelings of shame and isolation, as well as difficulty in relationships are themes that form the impetus for bringing most of my clients into therapy. What piques my curiosity, however, are the field conditions supporting an eating disorder as a creative adjustment.

Culture and Gender

In the US, and perhaps in Europe and elsewhere, the cultural impact on vulnerable girls is paramount in determining the *chosen* creative adjustment. By culture, I mean not only the larger world context, what is valued in the media, but also what is supported in one's family. Many of the girls and women who come to me with disordered eating have mothers who have either struggled with their own eating issues in the past, are currently doing so, or are frequently directing negative verbal comments about their daughters' bodies to their daughters.

Whether it is the biological underpinning that predisposes girls toward being interpersonally oriented (Gurian, 2002) or cultural expectations or both, the end result is that external appearance is emphasized for girls. "Beauty" and "being attractive" as culturally defined, is embedded as a standard to which a girl aspires from a very young age.

Cultural determinants are cited, with girls talking about the importance of being thin as a way of being competent and fitting in. Pipher, in her book *Reviving Ophelia* (1994) writes, "Attractiveness is both a necessary and sufficient condition for girls …Girls feel an enormous pressure to be beautiful and are aware of constant evaluations of their appearance" (p.55). And, to illustrate how scary the influence of culture on girls' aspirations can be, the standards of beauty have changed. In one of many examples, Pipher draws our attention to the drastic difference between the measurements, from 1959 to 1983, of Miss Sweden who has become taller and thinner over the years. According to Pipher, Miss Sweden was 5'7" and weighed 150 pounds in 1959. In 1983 she was 5'9" and weighed 109 pounds! Yet, average women are heavier today than they were at the middle of the last century, expanding the difference between the real and ideal.

The changes at puberty call for acceptance of one's physical attributes by those in the field when a culture values "thinness." Girls with early menarch who have a higher percentage of body fat become at risk. These early maturing girls consistently run counter to the cultural norms and can be at greater risk than late maturing girls. Myrna Frank (1996, 1999) found that the cultural impact on girls can be mitigated for vulnerability to eating disorders by parents' teaching their daughters to question cultural norms.

In families where the parents are culture-wise, questioning the dominant culture, and demonstrate "good enough parenting" girls fare better by having adequate body image and ability to voice resistance to the immediate pressure to conform that comes from peer and media culture (Frank, 1996). In Frank's study, communication between mothers and daughters was both nonverbal and behavioral. In this respect, not only is it important to support the young girl in questioning her peers' behaviors, but it is essential to support parents to do so, as well. This usually allows parents to restory their own narratives in the service of their daughter's development.

Often, well-meaning parents fail to support their daughter's emerging voice. One articulate high school senior with whom I had worked expressed a relational pattern. "Even if I handle the situation in school, and I do it right, if my mother gets word of it she has to interfere, call the school, call other parents and try to control. She'll come to the school and get the principle involved or call a bunch of parents and start the whole thing all over again. I don't know why I bother... if she would only get a life and stop trying to run mine. I am okay with my body...whenever I eat something she gives me a look... you just know she wants me not to eat that...she thinks I'm too fat...and, doesn't she get it that I am really good at managing my social life!"

In families where the culturally mandated concerns about the body are transmitted and amplified, the risk for girls to develop an eating disorder is increased. The vignette describing the father-daughter interaction in an earlier section, illustrates how embedded historic messages are transmitted across generations. Additionally, just as when the yearning for intimacy or security in relationship is unmet, the experience of being criticized for being hungry or wanting to eat results in an overwhelmingly shame based experience.

Creating the Tapestry

In summary, we encode relational patterns from our earliest moments. As we develop, our nonverbal constructions are implicated in our essential experience – our sense of self. We non-verbally construct a narrative of our relational experiences.

These relationship experiences are organized into experiences of well-being or of yearning. When our relationships are predominantly supportive, we experience satisfaction or well-being. If our relational needs are wanting, we experience a lack of satisfaction, or yearning. Again, Lee has illuminated the biological underpinnings of this shame experience (2007). The search for belonging is what leads us to find solutions – to resolve the field in creative ways. And we develop creative adjustments that are field supported. These creative adjustments may or may not contribute to our health and well-being. Disordered eating is one category of creative adjustment (Figure 2 – on the following page).

Skill Deficits, Family Context, and Developmental Themes

Girls who haven't been taught to question perceived authority, who automatically introject or ingest others' wants may be described as having "skill deficits." I would say that these girls have a limited range of contact styles. Many are lacking the ability to push back against mandates or suggestions that do not contribute to healthy growth, and well-being. They have been undersupported in their development of a range of choiceful behaviors, ways of meeting the world.

The work with these young people and their families is to demonstrate the necessity for acknowledging and accepting feelings that emerge, and to build the support for these girls so that they can become sensitized to their feelings, fears, and desires. This requires supporting the families to make room for the expression of these feelings so that they can be expressed in a receptive field.

Figure 2. Creative Adjustment

Relational Failures in Human Environment

Creative Adjustment

What does the field support?

for Eating Disorders
(which could also include, Aggression, Hyperactivity, Rage, Withdrawal, Addictions, Other)[2]

Bulemia

Craving to be admired, respected & loved

Hungry to feel a part of someone, held close

Feelings of emptiness

Binging

A substitute for shamebound, unmet interpersonal needs

Shame (disgust, nausea)

Can no longer swallow (such shame)

Purging

Emotional cleansing from shame, temporary release, but magnifies shame

Anorexia

Desensitization of needs for nourishment

Experience of sense of control over shame

---

[3] Basic concepts adapted from Kaufman (1989).

When a depressed 15 year-old finds her voice to tell me that she no longer wants to be a competitive figure skater, but that her parents refuse to allow her to skate at all if she won't compete, I see this as an opportunity to explore the developmental processes taking place within the family field. How available are the parents to hearing their daughters "I want"? How able is the daughter to speak her "I need," or "I want"? The image that comes to mind is that of the turtle emerging from its shell to peek around, and asking, "How safe is the environmental field?"

If I can support the young woman bound for college to speak directly to her father and be received in her need to suggest a mutual activity rather than to swallow her want in deference to his choices, and can secure his support in her communicating to her mother that she will decide what she will eat for breakfast, rather than to have her mother dictate the menu, and, concurrently support the parents in communicating their caring, respect, and confidence in their daughter's choices in return, we have begun to heal some dysfunctional patterns.

In working with adult clients, it is the healing therapeutic relationship that allows the client to make meaning of deceased parents' rules and lifestyles, values and expectations and to examine their own meaning making and experience in light of these expectations. It is the compassionate, healing relationship that slowly but surely supports our clients in softening some of their own self-criticism, perfectionism, and self-expectations thereby allowing them to have compassion for their own parents and for themselves.

I worked with a wonderful adult client whose childhood years were embedded in a family field where her father was a warm and explosive man with a tendency toward uncontrolled spending and mother was thrifty and focused on housekeeping. With the exploration of her immediate experience as well as the way in which she made meaning in the present, she began to make important decisions around her eating patterns and choices. The holding relationship allowed for her to explore her own conflicted spending, her deeply ingrained feelings that vacillated between feeling loved and terrified, and most of all allowed her to feel accepted, normal, and be able to get out of bed in the morning.

Implications for Therapy

A relational Gestalt approach to working with girls and women with disordered eating offers what is missing in so many other approaches – a healing relationship and an opportunity for clients to restory their narratives, both of which contribute to a more spontaneous, creative, lived experience.[4]

Beginning with our earliest moments our neural circuits are structured through our relationships with others. Siegel (1999) encourages us to learn about "the emotional communication inherent in attachment" as a guide to understanding "the nature of emotion regulation within interpersonal relationships." He calls the aggregate of research supporting this assumption "interpersonal biology."

When our earliest relationships are those in which attunement and mutual self regulation predominate, we develop a sense of comfort and security. We move into life from a secure base. Our internal processes, those that hold the memories of our earliest relational patterns are consistent with a felt sense of being okay in our world.

When there is insufficient support in the environment and the creative adjustment is disordered eating, capacity for contact is constrained. Eating disorders are marked by less flexibility, or more rigidity in the capacity for contact. In a healthy relationship and in therapy, we have the opportunity to expand our capacity for contact. Stern (2002), in his new introduction to *The First Relationship* suggests that "the change that occurs in psychotherapy arises from the implicit knowledge evolving within the relationship between the therapist and the patient..." (p. 12). Furthermore, Stern and colleagues have found that the implicit knowledge about their relationship "that becomes

---

[4] Of course, in cases where medical stability is required, it is essential that medical intervention precede therapy.

intersubjectively shared" between client and therapist "is a potent mechanism for therapeutic change".

The power of gestalt therapy emerges in the experience of being met by another whose presence, sensitive attunement, and full humanity allows for the possibility of dialogue. It is within this therapeutic relationship offered in the gestalt therapy approach that girls and women attempting to recover from eating disorders can find a healing relationship, begin to heal, and take their place in the world of relationships.

References

Cozolino, L. (2006). *The Neuroscience of Human Relationships: Attachment and the Developing Social Brain*. New York: Norton.

Damasio, A. (1999). *The Feeling of What Happens: Body and Emotion in the Making of Consciousness*. San Diego: Harcourt.

Frank, M. (1996). The Contribution of Culture-Wise Good-enough Parenting to Resistance to Eating Disorders in Girls at Early Adolescence. Ann Arbor, MI: UMI Microform 9717541 (1997).

Frank, M. (1999). Raising Daughters to Resist Negative Cultural Messages About Body Image. *Women and Therapy* 22(4), 69-88.

Gillie, M. (2000). Shame and Bulimia. *British Gestalt Journal* 9(2), 98-104.

Gurian, M. (2002). *The Wonder of Girls: Understanding the Hidden Nature of Our Daughters*. New York: Atria Books.

Holmes, J. (2001). *The Search for the Secure Base: Attachment Theory and Psychotherapy*. Philadelphia: Taylor & Francis.

Jacobs, L. (2008). Traumatized States of Mind. Lecture. PGI Residential, Santa Barbara, CA.

Kaufman, G. (1992). *Shame: The Power of Caring* (3rd ed.). Rochester, Vermont: Schenkman Books.

Kaufman, G. (1989, 1996). *The Psychology of Shame:Theory and Treatment of Shame-Based Syndromes*. (3rd ed.). New York: Springer.

Lee, R .G. (2007). Shame and Belonging in Childhood. *British Gestalt Journal* 16(2), 38-45.

Pipher, M. (1994). *Reviving Opheia: Saving the Lives of Adolescent Girls*. New York: Ballantine Books.

Siegel, D. J. (1999). *The Developing Mind: How Relationships and the Brain Interact to Shape Who We Are.* New York: Guildford Press.

Stern, D. N. (2002). *The First Relationship.* Cambridge, MA: Harvard University Press.

Schore, A. N. (1994). *Affect Regulation and the Origin of the Self: The Neurobiology of Emotional Development.* Hillsdale, NJ: Erlbaum.

Editors' Note:
In the following chapter Jon Blend takes us into his work and we meet the young people he sees, as a member of a Child and Adolescent Mental Health Team in the National Health Service in the United Kingdom. The setting is specific, but the issues are universal and are those of the art of engagement, and the skills of supporting and helping adolescents as a Gestalt therapist. Jon's is a resourceful and lively presence, bringing his background in music and in drama into his work whenever that takes the relationship forward, as part of his wide range of ways of being and the interventions that makes possible. More than that, he conveys how his authentic presence invites contact and meeting and how he encounters the complex worlds and lives of his patients. The wider relational field, of families and peers is alive in the individual work as Jon helps his patients equip themselves to live fuller, richer lives.

12

Am I Bovvered?

A Gestalt Approach to Working with Adolescents

Jon Blend

I *can't be bothered to miss you anymore*
Month twelve, day thirty-one and hour twenty-four
I used to think if missed hard enough you'd come back for sure
I can't be bothered now to miss you anymore
                                                Miranda Lambert

Bovvered?

I have chosen to use the surly teenage character Lauren, made famous by British TV actress Catherine Tate, as a *leitmotif* for this article about some of the troubled and troublesome young persons I work with. Lauren readily picks quarrels with everyone. When confronted about her behavior she begins her long, haranguing reply with the retort:

"Am I bovvered? Does my face look bovvered?" (In other words, 'do I give a damn?')

Lauren strikes a chord with many because she represents contempory, disaffected youth, whose acerbic manner often leads to awkward, uncomfortable exchanges, particularly with adults. In her mouthy assertions Lauren demonstrates machismo rather than cool. As this article shows there are male equivalents of Lauren and Laurenites can be found in other cultures. Meanwhile in England the term 'bovvered' has entered the vernacular.

As a social worker I counsel children and their families at an NHS Child and Adolescent Mental Health Service (CAMHS) in the South of England. This is a specialist multi-disciplinary team that blends psychiatry, nursing, family therapy, social work, art therapy, and psychology and psychotherapy services. Our task is to assess and treat troubled under 18's referred by doctors. These youngsters present with a range of emotional, and behavioural difficulties of varying complexity and risk, including self-harm.

This article describes some of my work in the CAMHS setting. I work with children and adolescents individually, sometimes in groups or with their families. I also see parents and offer consultation to school nurses.

I originally trained in social work and worked in adult psychiatry for fifteen years. I joined the CAMHS team in 1995 and simultaneously began training as a counsellor and subsequently as a psychotherapist. As a Gestaltist I bring to the team my understanding of contact and field, a process model of self and a dialogic phenomenological stance (Yontef, 1993). From Violet Oaklander I learnt to incorporate expressive and projective techniques from creative arts media into my Gestalt work with young persons. Some of my clinic work is brief; a timely intervention may be short involving a dozen or fewer appointments. In other instances, for example working with abused or traumatised children, a longer time frame is required to help youngsters remedy complex difficulties, recover self-esteem and acquire self-regulatory coping strategies.

What does it feel like to work with seriously troubled adolescents? There appear some similarities with borderline clients; youngsters may engage awkwardly, often manifesting rage or despair; some seem guarded whilst clearly hoping for a 'quick fix'. A few protest noisily, even walking out – often following an impasse; others flip between idealising and hating me. A sense of humour helps me survive, and a thick hide! Remembering that adolescence has a developmental function that drives the beginnings of differentiation and personal autonomy is important too. Likewise, I recall with compassion my own turbulent teenage years, and the field supports I needed to emerge safely through them. Working with adolescents sometimes feels like riding on a rollercoaster, veering between the everyday and the profound as we explore the meaning of life and love or identify social exclusivity according to clothing brands. Yet it is the process of being engaged empathically as a 'Thou' (Buber 1970) that most adolescents find validating and life-affirming: the experience of a co-created inclusive Gestalt relationship. As a therapist my role with teenagers is far from purist; at times I function as mentor, cheerleader, advisor and parental substitute. Without such flexibility many troubled teenagers might never engage.

I want to illustrate my work with adolescents, and introduce a perspective from Gestalt theory, using a series of vignettes drawn from my practice.

Syreeta: the challenge of contact

Syreeta, who had just turned 16, sought counselling after being suspended from her school for swearing and lewd behaviour. Her Iranian parents, who attended the initial assessment with her, spent long hours working at their respective businesses. Each had a different idea about setting boundaries with Syreeta. Their marriage was marred by domestic violence and they had raised a thuggish elder son who now mixed with criminals. Syreeta had been copying his behaviour in part, drinking hard and having underage sex. I was taken aback by her parents' harsh litany of complaints against her yet was equally shocked by the force of her profanity, showering her parents with curses. The interview left me feeling heavy hearted and exhausted. Taking in the high level of aggression and chaos within the family field I thought: 'this is going nowhere'.

Given the preponderance of constraints in the field simply offering a therapeutic space for Syreeta would not suffice. I suggested that parents consider embarking on marital therapy as well, and they agreed to let me refer them on for this.

Building a therapeutic alliance with Syreeta and her parents was difficult and took time. I needed to show my ability to remain open-minded and impartial, without directly challenging how they organised their lives, which might polarise the situation, shutting off communication. I was aware of cultural differences between us and the need to respect the values and behaviours within the family field, whilst ensuring that I neither colluded with the denigration of Syreeta, nor with her putting herself 'at risk' [1].

I began somewhat warily, when Syreeta arrived for her first session, half expecting her to behave in a foul way with me too. She swaggered in late, with the top buttons of her blouse undone, heavily made up, pulling her chair close and fluttering her eyelashes. I commented on her dramatic entry and asked if she was flirting with me – ' Just being friendly!" she replied with a bright smile, removing her chewing gum.

She hungrily took the space to talk as she described her fear of the family enmity rising. She despaired of managing to

---

[1] Whilst in terms of local child protection practice Syreeta at age 16 was regarded legally as a young adult, I was concerned that the family's dysfunction and her own behaviour left her vulnerable.

talk at home without being judged and criticised. Syreeta was as yet unaware of a frequent intersubjective dance that could emerge between her and others – how she could become triggered as well as her role in provoking others. In particular she was unaware that this occurred within a relational context. Yet her mapping or knowledge of her emergent sense of 'self' was intrinsically linked to her mapping an 'other'. Syreeta's behaviour did not take place within a vacuum; whilst she tended to disown her actions, others such as her parents experienced her as provocative. This led to reprisal and counter reprisal, as distrust spiraled, neither side giving in. Whilst occasionally they might connect, their exchanges quickly deteriorated, descending into arguments.

Nonetheless I began to warm to Syreeta, listening to her talking rapidly about her disillusionment with family life and her fury towards her parents for papering over their dysfunctional relationship. Finding myself getting `flooded', I shared this with her, commenting, `What a lot you are telling me in such a short time!' When I enquired how she felt after saying so much she smiled broadly and told me how wonderful it was to be listened to, without judgment.

I smiled back in acknowledgement. I later added that I could offer her feedback about her dilemmas if she wished; either way she was free to consider or reject this. She nodded assent. 'If you're willing, I'd like to teach you some more effective ways of expressing angry feelings, that won't get you or anyone else hurt I continued.

'Suppose you tell me what you've tried and I'll tell you what I've found – we can compare notes.'[2]

Zahm (1998) has commented on the merits of using self-disclosure judiciously, in the service of the client. Certainly

---

[2] I am grateful to Mark McConville whose original version of this intervention appears in his book on Adolescence.

Syreeta seemed soothed and yet encouraged to talk when I responded towards her with openness. I sought to bring to our encounter an attuned way of relating, meeting her pain with compassion, addressing her angry feelings respectfully, providing support when she felt vulnerable, offering space to withdraw when she felt overwhelmed. Syreeta continued to let down her guard and to share more of her process. She described in detail her frustrations at home and school and owned her difficulty trusting people. This latter, coupled with her short temper led to difficulty in maintaining relationships: 'When I get so suspicious, right, I go and fuck it up... honest, I don't mean to!'

Within the privacy of the therapy session such candor contrasted with the 'face' she presented to her social world, a dimension of the field where 'coolness' and external validation mattered. I empathized with her struggle over competing relational needs – the tension between maintaining 'face' and owning her shortcomings – without sinking into shame. As I took in her communications and got to know her better, I understood more of her thoughts and feelings, letting them resonate inside me. Sometimes I used my own responses to track, comment on and augment her musings. For Syreeta, long accustomed to 'I-It' relating (Buber, 1970), this provided a rare experience of being received as a "Thou" (ibid) working in collaboration with an adult. As Safran, Greenberg and Rice put it:

"Working with the client, rather than working on the client, makes the client a partner in the therapeutic enterprise. Resistances and dead ends become problems to solve jointly." (Safran et al 1990, p30).

The more Syreeta experienced my interest in her as genuine, the more her capacity to reflect on her actions, thoughts and feelings deepened. She developed the beginnings of a relationship between a self-scrutinizing part of herself and another self-accepting part, starting to review and critique her experience without becoming devastated. When Syreeta was able to own her guilty feelings, e.g. of having caused hurt to others by her actions, she found this useful. It launched a process of internal dialogue that helped her better understand and manage 'unfinished business', moving with greater awareness towards resolution.

Syreeta's narrative revealed how she was used to controlling outcomes by manipulation in her dealings with friends, family and authority figures. But I decided to allow contact to happen by not confronting this prematurely. In the sessions that followed I worked with her on noticing how she lashed herself with retroflective fault finding. I taught her to track her breathing as a means of managing strong feelings. I had a sense that she was finding in me, an adult who could offer some of the gentler father qualities of care and respect. Clearer, vital figures of interest began to emerge from her; there was a sense of ease as our relating became more contactful.

In week six she gave a confusing account of feeling responsible for her aunt Fawzia's miscarriage the year before. Syreeta had been with her aunt when the latter's toddler had kicked Fawzia in the stomach. "I was there – I could have stopped him!' Syreeta lamented. I shared my own responses of feeling touched by her pain, and also surprise at her readiness to assume responsibility for Fawzia's miscarrying. Syreeta began a 2-chair dialogue with her aunt within which she started to question her former assumption of responsibility. I offered to help her find a way of beginning to mourn the dead child, which she gratefully accepted. Two weeks later, as she hadn't mentioned the topic, I sought an update. Syreeta told me that she felt 'much better' as she no longer felt responsible for the tragedy. She told me that our work had however brought up reminders of a good friend who had been killed in a road accident whom she missed greatly.

Syreeta continued to work on issues of loss in our next two meetings, reflecting on 'the real me – underneath the hell-raiser'. To develop her sense of self I encouraged her to make lists of her likes and dislikes, attitudes and beliefs. We examined how some of her values differed markedly from those of the family field, whilst others converged. We discussed family loyalties and the choices that Syreeta could exercise independently herself. She learnt to focus her awareness on her breathing, reducing her hyper-arousal sufficiently to become more responseable and less eager to fight. A quieter and calmer Syreeta began to emerge, exchanging micro-skirts and plunging necklines for more modest apparel. When I commented on the 'grown up' nature of her new appearance she blushed then deflected, complaining about some local lads who had leered at her and called her 'slag'. 'I'm not some piece of meat!' she concluded: 'I'm not having sex anymore, doc – until I meet someone nice!' I commented that her statement sounded important, a maturer revaluing of herself and what she wanted out of life. When I fed back how her manner seemed softer too, less defensive, she beamed.

Whenever I imagined myself stepping into Syreeta's shoes and then into those of her immigrant parents I experienced the helplessness on both sides. Most likely her parents had started out well intentioned (Lee, 2007) but became embarrassed and stymied by Syreeta's insubordination. Yet draconian attempts to curb her and restore order consistently failed. In relocating her internal struggle between autonomy and self-responsibility at the interpersonal boundary Syreeta ensured her parents remained closely involved. In this way her actions served as a creative adjustment.

During a review meeting the following week however Syreeta's parents were critical of me for not having 'changed her enough'. Sadly they vetoed any further engagement with our service. Syreeta was dependent on her parents for transporting her from school to clinic; under the circumstances she and I discussed referring her on to the nurse or counsellor at her new school.

Mark McConville describes many families as being either 'underbounded' or 'overbounded' in their contact process. The former type foster connectedness at the expense of differentiation and the latter conversely favour separateness over merger. (McConville, 1995 p135) Within Syreeta's 'underbounded' family parents were unclear about how their children's roles and responsibilities varied from their own; they struggled with accepting that Syreeta's personal autonomy was growing and that she was entitled to her own thoughts and feelings.

The Phases and Tasks of Adolescence

McConville describes the pre adolescent child as 'embedded' in the family (McConville, 1995, p 15). The child-self is unreflective; her experience is lived not known, without an observing ego. The child-self progressively 'disembeds' as she begins to experience having an inner world that is separate from her outer existence (ibid). As she spends less time with family, turning to friends and other adults, the teenager forges her identity from peer culture. In place of family values shared teenage tastes in food, appearance, music, ideals and attitudes begin to inform her emerging sense of self.

Much young adolescent behaviour appears deliberately aimed at creating a boundary between themselves and adults (ibid). Often anger and projection serve to keep such 'uncool' emotions as guilt and shame at bay. Battles fought at the boundary between self and other keep the pressure off the still fragile, internal self. Yet the teenager's experience of this divide can also be painful and lonely.

Middle adolescence is characterised by an interior focus during which inner life becomes more richly experienced and the boundary with the external social world becomes clearer; here relationships assume more of a reality-based quality.

In later adolescence the experience of self is consolidated. The young person becomes increasingly less defended and migrates to the outside world - now regarded as a source of mastery and of pleasure. The proto-adult takes charge of herself, emerging as a whole entity, ready and able to make her own way in life.

This sketches the growthful tendencies of the adolescent experience. But without sufficient environmental support, as Syreeta's vignette shows, things can go seriously awry. McConville (Mc Conville, 1995, p88) talks about "frozen protective polarity dynamics " – one of two dysfunctional types of child-self versus teenage-self polarities. In the "frozen" pattern the teenage-self is predominantly identified with, whilst the former child-self (where the vulnerability may lie) becomes disowned.

In the second type, known as 'interrupted polarity dynamics', the child-self emerges in awareness whilst the teenage-self is disowned. (The vignette of Stef, below, illustrates the 'frozen' dynamic whilst the example of Kris portrays the 'interrupted' dynamic.)

Working with Anger

Violet Oaklander describes anger as the most misunderstood of the emotions. (Oaklander, 2006; Oaklander, 2007). It receives 'a bad press': as children we are often told that it's wrong to be angry. Consequently we learn to avoid that feeling, albeit often at considerable personal cost. Yet, as Oaklander reminds us: 'Anger is an expression of the self, and the self is reduced when one inhibits anger.' (ibid)

When an adolescent encounters a therapist, often at the behest of parents, she may perceive such meetings as potentially dangerous, leading to exposure of her vulnerability (McConville, 1995, p 195). Many teenagers who experience anxiety and discomfort during this engagement stage attempt to self-regulate by seeking to wrest control of the situation, often by trying to polarize the field. Adolescents may resort to anger, silence or provocation as strategies for this purpose (ibid); the therapist's initial aim becomes simply to 'traverse the minefield' keeping the field intact. Many adolescents assume they will not be liked or taken seriously; they may behave rudely or absurdly, seeking to replace uncertainty within the relational field with structure, testing out the rules of engagement, so to speak. Some do so by inviting rejection. The therapist who harnesses her presence, insightfulness, steadfastness and fortitude to acknowledge and validate a teenager's anger without interpretation extends the possibility of a new and powerfully bonding experience. She may need to manage provocation gracefully, sidestepping the trap of replaying old 'parent-versus-child' conflicts if an effective working relationship is to be formed (ibid).

Anger serves other functional purposes during adolescence. It protects the younger teenager who lacks the capacity to reconcile her contradictory attitudes and beliefs, which may otherwise leave her feeling overwhelmed. At this stage young teenagers often need to skew reality to support their fragile emergent selves. Projecting inner conflicts onto the field, the family, or others, enables personal dilemmas to be reworked at the interpersonal boundary. For example, Mary experiences conflict over her wish to attend a party and her need for sleep before next day's exams. Her desire to stay out late is counterbalanced by her mother's telephoned reminder of Mary's promise to come home early. Here the dialogue between Mary and her mother creates a field within which Mary's needs for play and rest are supported, sharing out matters of power and responsibility. Sometimes there is insufficient support for dialogue and co-regulation within the family field (see the example of Stef later in this chapter). Then those agencies within the wider community – hospital, police or school whose remit includes a regulatory or public safety function may take up the responsibility polarity in dealing with adolescents.

Anger provides a physical sense of personal solidity for the adolescent whilst supplying propulsion for her to venture away alone. This allows her an experience of brief separation from parents, whilst showing her peers, 'I can do this myself!' (Otherwise the adolescent who retroflects his anger risks remaining confluent with parents and therefore unable to differentiate). Generally, experiments with gaining autonomy continue whilst private inner experience increases until the adolescent becomes able to consolidate his or her new self (ibid).

Addressing the Family System

To a much greater extent than is the case in adult psychotherapy, counselling children and adolescents involves working with social issues such as poverty, marital breakkdown, alcoholism and mental illness. Misatuned rigidity in the parent leads to reactive rigidity in the child; a lack of environmental support in the family field curtails the adolescent's developing self-support. Accordingly disembedding is either premature or delayed. Supporting parental functioning clears the way for the children to continue on their path of healthy growth (Oaklander, 2000). Meeting with parents or caregivers en route is therefore an important staging post (Reynolds, 2005). I usually assess adolescents together with their families; this models transparency and avoids triangulation.

Parents may also need separate help with thinking through developmental issues, reflecting on marital difficulties or setting boundaries. The multi-disciplinary nature of CAMHS facilitates this, enabling co-working arrangements.

McConville notes that adolescents present the clinician with a vexed complex interpersonal situation rather than symptoms, (McConville, 1995). Certainly the toughest challenge is getting teenagers to engage. It helps to clarify whether s/he is concerned about his behaviour, will the family support change, and is there stability and safety in the present living situation. Many adolescents feel embarrasssed about agreeing to have therapy and 'saving face' can be vital. I adopt Mc Conville's informal approach; casually asking whether s/he could 'live with our meeting for a few sessions' (ibid).

My initial aim is to convey trustworthiness, a non-judgemental attitude, empathy and congruence. I also need to check out the situation using my own phenomenology. Attending carefully to my co-transference helps me assess the client's sense of agency, intent and motivation to change whilst also gauging our likely support needs. For example, if I feel fearful in response to a threatening, previously violent teenager standing before me, perhaps referred with 'anger problems', impulsivity and a history of making false accusations, I need to pay due attention to my fear. Equally I need to remind myself that the field or context in which these eruptions took place, perhaps ratcheted up through provocation, goading or humiliation in the home, school, or institutional care setting were probably quite different from those that this client might be experiencing with me now in a therapy consultation. That said, for some young persons who have been severely mistreated by adults my dialogic attitude alone may be insufficient to counter painful memories of such betrayal; going on the offensive may seem the best form of defence against feeling vulnerable, faced with a novel, unfamiliar situation such as entering therapy. Weighing all these factors helps me decide whether it is wiser to work on a one-to-one basis or in some other configuration – e.g. dyadic work or working with the family in the clinic setting (Blend, 2009). In extremis I will ask a colleague to join me during initial sessions: I am likely to be more effective when not overly preoccupied about safety concerns. Thereafter one can usually establish whether there is sufficient goodwill, mutuality and respect for our work to proceed, risking the occasional intersubjective rupture and establishing healing through its repair (Hughes, 2008). On rare occasions where establishing a basic working alliance proves unsuccessful, referral on to another agency, perhaps for groupwork or 'wilderness' type therapy may appear a safer option and more useful to the client.

Getting Started

The experimental attitude that characterises a Gestalt approach often works well with young persons. Early on, many projective exercises (Oaklander, 1988) serve a dual function as 'ice breakers', and experiments, helping to further dialogic relating (Buber, 1970). Many of the adolescents I see enter therapy feeling disconsolate and disempowered: their relationships with key adults have often deteriorated becoming exclusively 'I-It' based (ibid). During the initial phase of therapy I may use questionnaires or construct a genogram or friendship map together to help chart their field. Other teenagers prefer to draw their own 'timeline', a graph that maps the high and low points of their lives (Sunderland & Engleheart, 1997). Whilst their attention is frequently on the content or story, my interest lies as much in the process – how are they engaging with me, how do I feel about them, and how do I imagine they feel about me?

Sometimes I use sentence completion tasks, simple prompts that elicit attitudes and values: Boys..., A Mother..., I feel angry about...., My biggest worry is...., I'm good at..., etc. I may set a kitchen timer for ten minutes. Many enjoy the challenge of 'beating the clock'; others slump or perseverate; some find moving to the next item inordinately hard. How a youngster responds to such tasks often provides early clues as to how she functions in the world, indicating what is lacking in her field that may require our attention. Fifteen-year-old Damian, whose parents had just separated, wrote: Marriage is... 'for fools who lie'. When I finished reading his answers aloud he spoke bitterly about his parents breaking up: 'I should have seen it coming – the signs were there' he said. Fourteen-year-old Cheryl, who self-harmed, wrote: 'I hate my life – I'm good at ... nothing.' Unpicking this painful self observation helped Cheryl become aware of her difficulty getting noticed within her family where attention frequently focussed on her learning disabled brother.

"You want me to do what?!!"

For every second teenager who enjoys using arts-based activities and projective fantasy work (Oaklander 1988), I encounter another who dismisses it as 'childish': 'I just want to talk' they say, exasperatedly, seeking short cuts 'to get started'. Often these are youngsters who have grown up in a hurry; many are survivors of abuse or trauma.

Instead, borrowing an idea from Violet Oaklander (Oaklander 2000), I may use a book of astrological sun signs with some to explore character traits. Jamahl, 14, was fascinated to learn what was written about Gemini – his sign: "Yeah – that's me man, clever, sarky, always on to the next thing." Others recoil from the descriptions – " No way that's me!" 'What is the real you like,' I ask – and they join the dance, co-creating a new relationship.

Some adolescents feel self conscious in the early stages of therapy and may avoid experiments unless the therapist provides environmental support by joining in. Armed with old newspapers and standing by the waste bin, gawky depressed Khalid (15) and I take turns at naming the sources of our annoyance that day. Earlier he's told me 'something went wrong' at school. I feel empathic though notice how he deflects and shuts down when I express interest.' Sensing that something more active may rouse his energy I've suggested an experiment.

'I don't get this feelings stuff' he complains so I model tuning in to my awareness, closing my eyes and focussing on my breath. I supply a short commentary, detailing how my body tightens as I recall receiving a parking ticket earlier today. On hearing this Khalid nods, wide eyed: 'Man, bet you was angry!' In turn he remembers receiving a detention for fooling around in class. Khalid begins to feel 'hot and tense' in his chest: 'Its like springs bursting'. We continue the experiment, naming each 'annoyance' and tearing off a strip of newsprint to signify it, screwing this into a ball and hurling it into the bin. Afterwards Khalid's eyes are shining and the tingling in my arm confirms that I'm feeling more present; as we compare notes he reports feeling 'so much better'.

This experiment can be reviewed in terms of the Gestalt contact cycle (Clarkson, 1989, p27). Khalid feels 'hot' (sensation/fore contact), moves to the bin (mobilisation), names his frustrations (action phase), throws the paper into the bin (final contact), feels 'better' (satisfaction/post-contact) and relaxes (withdrawal).

I find Tudor's adaptation of the Gestalt contact cycle for children is helpful when working with younger adolescents. Tudor substitutes the following names for phases of the cycle: feeling, knowing, thinking, doing/acting, making, enjoying and letting go (Tudor, 2002, p157). Sometimes these younger teenagers experience confusion about using words like 'feeling'. However most understand what thinking means. If a therapist asks what the youngster is thinking, the reply they receive often contains feeling language (Oaklander, 2000, personal conversation). So I ask, 'Gemma, what do you *think* about being grounded by mum?' Gemma replies: 'its not fair – I hate it!' Likewise, helping Khalid clarify what he needed (knowing) enabled us then to consider together what options he had for managing his feelings.

Roberto: 'bothered about my body'

Roberto was an isolated, depressed 16 year old with a congenital muscle wasting condition. This had left him with one arm thinner than the other and reduced motor skills, affecting his ability to dress, write and catch a ball. The school matron referred him after Roberto complained to her repeatedly about persistent teasing from fellow pupils who mocked his appearance and his clumsiness. At the initial meeting Roberto presented as a shy, sensitive lad. His mother appeared anxiously protective and talkative whilst Roberto's highly decorated squadron leader father looked uncomfortable and said little.

At first Roberto was highly ambivalent about attending clinic, dismissing my attempts to engage him with shrugs of his shoulders, looking away. As Oaklander observes, in therapy: 'without the thread of a relationship nothing much will happen' (Oaklander, 2007). During this rocky start I wondered if Roberto might become sufficiently bothered to risk showing me his vulnerability?

In session five I commented on how wary he seemed of getting to know me; that my efforts to engage him felt to me 'like pulling teeth' (!) I speculated however that this wariness might serve an important protective function for him, and suggested that he remain on his guard unless and until he felt he could trust me. Roberto mumbled angrily to himself – about not wanting to be quizzed by 'idiot adults' and rose suddenly to leave, reaching for his coat. He attempted in vain to shove his arm into the sleeve, cursing quietly. I expressed sadness at his choosing to leave early, though confirmed that he was free to do so. I also offered to help him into his coat. This surprised Roberto; he insisted he might still leave early though he allowed me to assist him. I accidentally brushed his 'skinny' hand and he shrank back in embarrassment. Noting his response I asked him how his 'grip' was, offering to compare handshakes with both hands. To my surprise he proffered his 'good' hand which I shook and then, hesitantly, his 'skinny' hand. When I shook the latter firmly, commenting favourably on the amount of grip he retained, even in this hand. Roberto burst into tears and sat down again.

He began to sob, whilst recalling how others withdrew from his deformed hand and treated him as an outcast. Roberto said that he had come to hate his image when he looked at himself in the mirror. Worse still, in the showers after PE or games, Roberto's inept performance and his 'useless' arm drew sarcastic, ribald remarks from peers that left him feeling crushed and lonely. I had a sense that his attitude to himself had become one of disgust. Whilst I do not commonly use touch in my practice as a therapist it seemed important for me not to shrink from so doing here.

I offered an experiment whereby Roberto could hold or grip my hands with his until he had 'had enough'. Gingerly he opted to try this though instantly retroflected, apologising profusely for having 'sweaty hands'. When I confirmed that this was ok too we sat holding hands silently across the table for three minutes, exploring the dance of contact and withdrawl also through mutual gaze. Little needed to be said afterwards though something had clearly shifted in our relating; it was as though Roberto understood that I was concerned enough to want to understand what was bothering him. Hereafter he engaged more fully in therapy and made use of 2-chair work to confront those who mocked his appearance. He developed a swagger, began dressing with attitude and started to hold his head higher. At a family review three months later all agreed that Roberto's confidence had increased considerably; the teasing had stopped, he had become friends with another boy and he was no longer depressed.

Shame is a regulator of the social field (Lee, 2001). Roberto yearned to be met with support rather than with ridicule. Yet the ground of his expectations, based on his history of not being received with support hitherto triggered a shame response with me. This left him with a desire to pull away from contact and to hide. (ibid). Through the 'safe emergency' of our experiment Roberto experienced the possibility of healing, that his support needs could be met. His sense of feeling inadequate began to shift accordingly to one of self-acceptance and pride.

Stef: 'why should I care about me?'

Stef, 16, had lived alone with her mother for years since her father died. Her paediatrician referred her for counselling because of a congenital skeletal disorder whereby she would repeatedly dislocate her limbs. Yet from the outset the figural issue appeared to be her difficult relationship with her mother whom she complained 'treats me like a child.' Stef played up to this by acting immaturely by accompanying friends to London without money or adequate clothing. On these trips Stef spent what funds she had on beer or trinkets, pretending not to be hungry when her friends went off in search of food.

Stef was angular and androgynous, severely dressed in contrast to her mother's ultra-feminine appearance. She sat awkwardly during assessment, picking her nails, eyes downcast, whilst her mother berated her for forgetting to eat when out with friends. Over the summer holidays Stef had passed out in the street three times and had been taken by ambulance to hospital and admitted overnight. I ruled out an eating problem, as it was clear that Stef ate regularly at home and school.

Stef elected to attend fortnightly sessions after school 'to get my mother off my back'. Initially our engagement was difficult; 'I don't know why I come here,' was her usual opener, though as I pointed out, she brought herself to the clinic independently and on time, indicating she must be getting something out of coming for herself. 'I dunno – you're the expert!' she retorted. 'Well come on; fix me then!' Stef found managing silences hard; when we unpacked this she owned her fear that I was judging her then and finding her lacking. My reassurance did not help; for two months Stef remained constantly on her guard. I shared my feeling of mild frustration that she seemed to be constantly fending me off – often through verbal 'fencing'. Stef muttered agreement; 'It's not just you', she responded, though had trouble finishing the sentence.

Remembering my touchiness in my own adolescence gave me the patience to maintain a sense of creative neutrality. My interest lay in helping Stef stay longer with her figural experience instead of her continued deflections.

'What's wrong with doing what I do?' She demanded of me, rolling her eyes.

'You tell me!' I countered '... anyway, what's good about doing what you do?'

'Wel – I don't have to think – mum'll collect me, bales me out'.

'And what's not good about doing what you do?'

'I'm always depending on her – she never trusts me ... so why the hell should I care anyway – so the ambulance came. Big bloody deal – that's what you pay taxes for, right? God's sake!'

A feature of adolescence is the tendency to organise experience by polarising (Mc Conville 1995). Stef dealt with her tension between new urges and old child-self introjects (like obeying authority) by reworking the conflict through the interpersonal field. She avoided her own intra-psychic conflict by successfully provoking her mother into assuming the responsible (introjected) side of the polarity – e.g. collecting Stef from hospital. Stef began to show similar behaviour with me. In session five, having casually mentioned another fainting episode, Stef walked out of the clinic in response to my expressing concern about her behaviour. 'I'm grown up now – don't be so wet!' was her parting shot. She returned to her session afterwards, muttering 'Sorry'. 'Apology accepted', I replied softly – 'so what happened there?'

Stef began to cry. Through tears she spurted gobbets of anger about her lack of physical robustness – her bodily collapses secretly frightened her – and her ambivalent feelings about 'looking dowdy'. I empathised with her fright and her frustration, offering to help her 'tune in closer', to develop greater awareness of her responses. This she accepted for the first time. I shared my enjoyment too at the spirited nature of her responding and said I imagined her father would have been proud of her. Stef wept openly as she recalled her loneliness as an only child growing up without her father, a topic that her mother felt uneasy about discussing. As this aspect of the family's confluent contact style became differentiated, she became better equipped to organise her private experience and manage it in her interactions with those around her. I used visualisations, drawing and structured writing exercises with Stef to explore what she did and didn't like about her body. These helped her undo the retroflections of shame she experienced at needing to ask for support (Lee, 2001).

After three months Stef trusted me sufficiently to attend clinic weekly. What I was able to provide for her was the holding of boundaries, negotiating, listening and being gentle but not a pushover. Having to manage an illness myself – asthma – I was able to put myself in her shoes. She learned to receive my male attention without becoming overwhelmed. Her 'Laurenite' rebellious projection shifted to a more ambivalent response, able to own the contradictory pulls within her. Her fainting ceased and she developed an interest in clothes and makeup, reflecting a newfound acceptance of her body. As she began acting less impulsively, her relationship with her mother improved.

Striking a Chord

Zinker reminds us: "Gestalt Therapy is really permission to be creative" (Zinker, 1977, p18). The discipline of improvising as a musician with a Playback Theatre Company helps me stay creative in my nonverbal communicating (Solas 1993; Solas 2007, Blend, 2005.Blend 2009) Gestalt therapist and saxophonist Hana Dolgin writes about how improvising in music, as in therapy, involves learning to stay constantly in the moment, accepting imperfections in one's playing without dwelling on them (Dolgin, 1995).

Music was a lifeline for me in adolescence; it gave me an outlet for expressing complex and intense feelings through playing piano and guitar. Nowadays in my work I encourage teenagers to bring in their CDs or lyrics that express something important for them. After listening to a track or reading the words together we discuss the sentiments evoked. This informal, inclusive approach helps many an isolated or alienated teenager who is depressed and struggling to verbalise, to feel that someone else understands them.

As humans we can be powerfully affected by the resonances of sound; when embarking on a visualisation exercise I sometimes pluck harmonics on a Cimbala (Polish harp) or pick out a particular chord progression on the guitar. This often helps restless or hyper vigilant teenagers ground their energy, and engage more deeply. Few adolescents actively dislike music. Some teenage lads attempt to strum my guitar, gyrating their hips in a tacit display of emerging sexuality. Others are drawn to the percussion. Many withdrawn teenagers gravitate to quieter instruments like bells or triangles though really find their metier when encouraged to try out the louder drums.

Music making, drawing and using clay proved important means of expression for Kris in my final vignette:

Kris: From Collapse to Confidence

Kris, aged twelve, was referred by his GP with a year's history of 'school phobia'. He had found the transition to secondary school difficult and had dropped out during the first term after developing panic attacks. Depressed and clingy, he had become electively mute in the presence of strangers. I first met Kris and his family together with a colleague. Kris's parents appeared stiff and reserved, seemingly unused to straight talk. The family style appeared confluent and depressed with parents appearing unable to provide Kris with the requisite support and challenge to help him with disembedding. In contrast to the 'Laurenites' above Kris appeared quieter, withdrawn rather than disruptive. Yet underneath he suffered, 'bothered' by the challenges of decision-making, asserting himself and managing relationships.

Kris began therapy sitting with his legs tightly crossed, head bowed, and his breathing shallow. Mostly silent, he tutted at my invitation to write things down. When I commented on this, asking if he was angry about coming to therapy, he withdrew. I mirrored his retroflective posture, which felt uncomfortably constricting to me; I sensed this served as a creative adjustment, allowing him to anaesthetise overwhelming feelings. (Oaklander, 2007) When I acknowledged how tough it had seemed for him to get through last week's interview he nodded, muttering – 'too bad' and later: 'See, I can't do it!' When I fed back how miserable and furious he seemed, he screwed up his eyes and sank low again. I bracketed a twinge that my observation might have been too blunt. Reconnecting with my own breathing rhythm helped restore my dialogic attitude, enabling me to commit to 'clearly knowing and accepting the given' (Yontef, 1993, p187) that comes with adopting the Paradoxical Theory of Change (Beisser, 1970). I felt determined to stay with him if possible. Eventually Kris looked at me to break the silence. As he appeared to lack sufficient self support to allow his figures to form, let alone engage in verbal dialogue here and now, I suggested he survey the room to see what took his interest.

His gaze settled on a large drum. He reached for it and began to tentatively tap it. I responded using another drum, copying the sounds he made, quiet and louder, fast and slow. I suggested he use the drum to convey his panic to me. At this he widened his eyes and straightened his posture, looking more alive. When I asked what he was experiencing, he pointed to his heart, indicating his sense that it was accelerating. I asked: 'Where are you now? Are you approaching the school gates?'

I asked if he could show me the different phases of his panic, like the movements of a symphony and hesitantly he obliged (I was aware of his interest in classical music). Witnessing his efforts I sensed our contact level increasing. At the end when Kris looked up I suggested we play his three 'movements' together and for the remainder of the session we continued to drum in unison, playing the sounds of his panic rising, overwhelming him and falling away. In subsequent sessions Kris began to explore polarities of his experience using various tones and textures of drum, xylophone and guitar: loud and quiet, hard and soft, tentative and assured. Through our music making I sought to extend his awareness and acceptance of the range of different feelings inside him (Oaklander, 2000), suggesting: 'Play what's going on inside you now". Kris responded with enthusiasm and began his shift from "Shouldistic Regulation" to "Organismic Self-Regulation" (Yontef, 1993, pp 212-214) through dialogic music-making

Often I 'met' Kris through 'doubling', i.e. adding unison notes that emphasised his figures of interest. (Lousada, 1998, p. 210) At other times I provided accompaniment to his figural rhythms and melodies. Our work assumed a symphonic style; sessional themes like 'I can't be bothered', 'leave me alone', 'what if I never', 'I want to move forward' would appear, rise to a crescendo or die down suddenly, to be dredged up and reworked later or the following week. Sometimes I sang in counter harmony, adding ground to his figures, which he listened to intently. Of course these responses were my projections, though working in this way seemed to help him gain self-support I felt moved by his struggle and enjoyed the experiential nature of our work together. For Kris, playing solo, duetting, withdrawing and playing together again appeared to strengthen his self and contact functions. I felt alive, in touch with my own passion for communication through music and the lifesaving role it had played in my ado-lescence.

Throughout the following term Kris struggled with warring introjects about talking versus not talking, fearing that talking about his panic would exacerbate matters. His separation anxiety increased and he withdrew, alluding enviously to his brothers' 'easy life' at the village primary school. I noticed that he broke off contact when conflict loomed. Though he sorely missed his close friend Oliver (who was now attending the new school) he equally feared 'panic' would return if he got in contact with him. He drew himself surrounded by a bomb which represented 'the panic going off' whilst he attempted in vain to phone Oliver.

Recognising his terror and shame I continued to focus on building our I-Thou relationship, sometimes sharing my here and now sensory responses and my own experiences of feeling frightened. I did not want to rush this important stage of our work. Through various experiences of drawing, role-play and guided fantasy (Oaklander 1988) Kris's level of verbal communicating increased. As our contact deepened he began to express his dread of the inquisition he might face from classmates concerning his prolonged absence.

Once, Kris sought to leave the session early after becoming distressed at my directing him to draw how he perceived his dilemma about school. He cried, sulked and demanded his mother collect him. I felt slightly cruel at my insisting that he stay and finish the hateful task, saying it might be helpful for him 'in the long run' to persevere a little longer rather than give up. I wasn't going to give up on his emerging adolescent self. I feared that if I acceded to his impulse to do so at this point he would leave, filled with panic and shame, in a parallel manner to the way he had left school – a double sense of failure. Nor did I want to collude with his notion that when the going gets tough, one should simply abandon ship. Kris appeared snared in a 'shame bind'. (Kaufman, 1985; Lee, 2001) He secretly longed to confront his 'inquisitors' though feared being exposed to their contempt. I thought of the paradoxical theory of change: change happens when we allow ourselves to surrender to 'what is' (Beisser, 1970). I imagined that Kris would fare better were he to stay with his shame experience assisted by my support, albeit delivered in this challenging way. I recalled times in my own therapy when the witnessing of my experience by another, though uncomfortable for me, had been crucial and enabled me to stay in dialogue. Kris agreed to stay.

In the following session he announced his readiness to confront his terror. I suggested he draw his 'panic'. Kris deflected: 'I'm no good at this stuff you know'. Assuming that he feared my judgment I reminded him that drawing here didn't need to be 'great art', just an experiment to see what we might learn together about 'panic'. I sensed my need to become directive – 'just see what you can do'. Kris hunched, and began drawing an amoeba-like shape, naming this 'Sly- because it creeps up on me slyly, suddenly'.

'How do you feel about Sly?' I asked

'I'd like to kill him!', Kris replied, flushing.

'Show me how! I invited.

Kris straightened up and with relish began drawing the many stages of 'Beating Sly Up'. These included him kicking, squeezing and standing on Sly, then cutting him into ' pepperoni pizza slices'. Breathing deeper and with stronger voice Kris sat back, pronouncing himself 'well pleased' with his drawing.

I continued to observe and mirror Kris's breathing and bodily stance, sharing my own self-observations concerning 'Sly' as experienced at a sensory and feeling level. Kris became more aware of how his hunching, tight posture shut off many feelings, especially his unspoken rage against Sly. Wanting to sustain the momentum and keep with physical expression, the following week I introduced clay into our session. Clay is a flexible, sensual, easy to handle medium that allows the expression of creative and destructive urges. I took Kris through a series of warm up exercises, which included slapping, and punching clay. (Oaklander, 2000) Whilst Kris told me that he was 'imagining Sly getting his comeuppance' he gently squeezed the clay, holding back his energy.

'Let him have it!' I suggested.

Kris gleefully placed Sly between two boards and jumped on 'him' triumphantly.

'He doesn't look so powerful now' I observed; ' What's it like, doing this?'

'Great!' Kris replied grinning: 'now he's really nothing!'

'And you- how do you feel inside?'

'Great - like I'm ten foot tall – like a mountain!'

I encouraged Kris to really hold and own his power suggesting he embody this new stance. Kris stood on my desk as 'mountain', looking down on Sly: 'I'm powerful and you're tiny now!' he crowed.

Kris gradually stopped retroflecting as he continued to externalise his feelings about 'Sly', finding sufficient self-support to abandon his former mutism. We continued exploring the polarities of his experience – feeling competent and feeling helpless, using various arts modalities, which he selected. He grew two inches and started to feel more at home in his body with an enhanced sense of self. In 'Laurenite' terms his transition from 'bothered' to more "bovvered' was important; by developing a more pugnacious, devil- may-care stance his anxiety about what others thought of him became less figural. As we concluded a year's work he started a rap – 'this is the story of Confident Kris!' inviting me to join him. We became human 'beat-boxes', moving in rhythm around the room, swapping improvised stanzas that described his heroic conquest of the mighty Sly.

Family in Flux

Whilst Kris was attending clinic his parents explored some marital difficulties assisted by my colleague. Following a period of unemployment Kris's father had lost considerable self-esteem and perceived himself as unable to support his family. He had become caught in a shame bind (Lee, 2001) yearning to know that he still mattered to his family yet feeling unable to ask for such validation. He hid his shame by withdrawing into silence. As Kris's mother took on extra work to increase the family income her resentment grew and she erupted in rages. Through couple therapy, Kris's parents learned to give and receive support and affection. They became more effective in their interactions with Kris, attuning to his needs and allowing the children more differentiation within the family field. My colleague and I held joint reviews, which the family attended, in liaison with Kris's school. I encouraged father and son to spend regular time together pursuing an activity they both liked, which proved mutually affirming. Following a consolidating summer en famille Kris made a successful return to school.

Conclusion : Can We be Bothered to Father Adolescents?

"How can I try to explain – when I do he turns away again."

'Father and Son' lyrics Cat Stevens

I want to conclude this chapter with a brief focus on a relatively neglected aspect of the family field, the influence of the relationship between adolescents of both genders, and their fathers.

In contemporary UK society, children are increasingly brought up in the absence of any paternal figure. Yet fathers have a positive psychological role, which combines emotional passion, moral restraint,

Blend – Am I Bovvered? ... 333

and physical presence. This is important in the erotic development of daughters and the aggressive development of sons (Wheeler, 2001; Samuels, 2001). As a male therapist, I am aware of many of my young clients lacking committed, effective, authoritative fathers. I also encounter many caught up in adjusting to stepfamily relationships[1] where the family field contains multiple parents, bringing additional loyalty conflicts, which challenge self-regulation. As Robert Lee points out, parents need holding too; in his view there are not 'child development problems' as such, rather there is a need for 'field development' that enables parents to own and receive support with areas in which they hitherto felt unsafe to confide (Lee, 2007).

Gordon Wheeler (2001) cites a 'paradigm of individualism' in the West, a traditional, gender-typed authoritarian style of fathering. It is the 'grow up and stand on your own two feet' notion of manhood. Wheeler and other writers on contempory masculinity (Biddulph, 1999; Lee, 2007; Mortola, Hiton and Grant, 2005; Samuels, 2001) have similarly sug-gested that, for many men, the very idea of receiving support from another person is fundamentally challenging, if not fraught with difficulty. Those whose internalised notions of masculinity and father-hood are authoritarian in origin may dismiss sharing, working co-operatively and accepting uncertainty or helplessness as effeminate and shameful.

Wheeler (2001) proposes a range of relational possibilities for fathering:

1. teaching – providing – directing – taking charge
2. nurturing – caretaking – listening – accepting
3. joining – sharing – playing – enjoying
4. depending – needing – asking – receiving.

---

[3] See the organisation called 'StepIn' – Advancing Stepfamily Awareness through Psychotherapy: www.stepinasap.co.uk

The presence or absence of any of these has important consequences in adolescence. Development takes place along the paths that are supported – through inner capacities and creativity, according to the way that young people are received in the social/relational field (ibid). A Gestalt Therapy model requires the self to integrate and fashion itself out of the whole field. As therapists we are well placed to see where intervening in the external world of relationships can alter the support network from which the self-process seeks its course and draws sustenance.

In such cases, as Wheeler points out, there can be a role for adolescent mentoring. This could involve a teacher, therapist or other interested adult who is able to mediate the process of supporting the teenager in navigating a world of hopes, disappointments, fears and dreams, who understands the coded messages of longing and shame that elude an unreceptive father's awareness, There is a particular need for 'receiver' style fathering (category 2 above) to augment other, more 'doing' focussed roles (3 and 4). Mentoring offers substitute companionship; sensitively conceived it may also help the father-son dyad through rocky patches in their journey of mutual self-discovery, providing respite if not reparative glue.

Fathering-by-proxy is an important component of the therapeutic work I undertake with many adolescents. There is considerable need for good, male relating to discourage disaffected youngsters from going completely off the rails. There is also a danger from the way the popular press portrays teenage culture of demonizing adolescence. Rather, adolescence is a transitory process often characterized by stormy behaviour that later gives way to integration. As the self consolidates, family alliances can be re-worked such that the emergent young adult becomes responsible for his or her own life choices.

One could imagine a different kind of 'Lauren', given the right male support and guidance. To remedy the deficit, as Wheeler observes, the prevailing traditional Western ideology of masculinity needs reconstructing. In other words we may all need to get bothered!

References

Beisser, A. (1970). The Paradoxical Theory Of Change. In J. Fagan and I. L Shepherd (Eds.), *Gestalt Therapy Now: Theory, Techniques, Applications* (pp.77-80). Palo Alto, CA: Science & Behaviour Books.

Biddulph, S. (1999). *Manhood – An Action Plan For Changing Men's Lives*. Trowbridge, Wiltshire, UK: Hawthorn Press.

Blend, J. (2005). Playback Theatre: A Dialogic, Phenomenological Approach To Therapeutic Work In Community Settings. (Unpublished MA dissertation).

Blend, J. (2009). I Got Rhythm : Music–Making with Children and Adolescents. International Gestalt Journa l 32(2), 165-181.

Buber, M. (1970). *I and Thou*. New York: Scribner and Sons.

Clarkson, P. (1989). *Gestalt Counselling in Action*. London, Sage Publications.

Dolgin, H (1995). Jazz and Gestalt Therapy: The Art of Being in the Moment. (on line) http://gestaltforlife.com/gestaltjazz.htm.

Hughes, D. (2008). Safe Relationships: The Road to Emotional Recovery from Trauma in Fostered and Adopted Children. Presentation delivered to Psychological Trauma and the Child Conference. London.

Kaufman, G. (1985). Shame: *The Power of Caring*. Cambridge,MA: Schenkman Books

Lee, R. (2001). Shame and Support. In G. Wheeler & M. Mc Conville (Eds.), *The Heart Of Development:Gestalt Approaches To Working With Children, Adolescents And Their Worlds*. Vol. 2 – Adolescence (pp. 253-270). Hillsdale, NJ: Analytic Press/GestaltPress.

Lee, R. (Feb. 2007). Presentation delivered to "Relational Child, Relational Brain" conference. Esalen, California (Chapter 2 of this book).

Lousada, O. (1998) The Three-Layered Cake, Butter with Everything. In M. Karp, P. Holmes, & K. B. Tuvon (Eds.), *The Handbook of Psychodrama* (pp. 213-236). New York: Routledge.

McConville, M. (1995). *Adolescence: Psychotherapy and the Emergent Self*. San Francisco: Jossey-Bass.

Mortola, P., Hiton, H., & Grant, S. (2008). BAM! Boys Advocacy and Mentoring. New York: Routledge Publications.

Oaklander, V. (1988). *Windows To Our Children: A Gestalt Therapy Approach To Children And Adolescents*. Moab, UT: Real People (original work published 1969).

Oaklander. V (2000). A Gestalt Approach to Working with Children and Adolescents. Summer training intensive.
Oaklander, V. (2006). *Hidden Treasure: A Map To The Child's Inner Self*. London: Karnac.
Oaklander, V. (2007). Informal address to "Relational Child, Relational Brain" Conference: Esalen, California.
Playback Theatre (on line) www.playbacksouth.org.
Reynolds, C. (2005). Gestalt Therapy With Children. In A. L. Woldt & S. M. Toman (Eds.), *Gestalt Therapy: History, Theory, And Practice* (pp. 153-178). Sage, London.
Safran, J., Greenberg, L., & Rice, L. (1990). Integrating Psychotherapy Research and Practice: Modelling the Change Process. In R. G. Erskine, J. P. Moursund, & R. L. Trautmann (Eds.), *Beyond Empathy: A Theory of Contact in Relationships*. New York: Routledge Press.
Samuels, A. (2001). *Politics On The Couch – Citizenship And The Internal Life*. London: Profile Books.
Solas, J. (1993). *Improvising Real Life. Personal Story In Playback Theatre* (3rd edition). New York: Tusitala Publishing.
Solas, J. (2007). *Do My Story, Sing My Song: Music therapy and Playback Theatre with Troubled Children*. New York: Tusitala Publishing.
Sunderland, M. & Engleheart, P. (1997). *Draw on Your Emotions*. UK: Speechmark.
Tudor, K. (2002). Integrating Gestalt in Children's Groups. In G. Wheeler and M. McConville (Eds.), *The Heart Of Development: Gestalt Approaches to Working With Children, Adolescents and Their Worlds*. Vol. 1, Childhood (pp. 147-162). Hillsdale, NJ: Analytic Press/GestaltPress
Wheeler, G. (2001). The Self In The Eye Of The Father: A Gestalt Perspective On Fathering The Male Adolescent. In G. Wheeler & M. McConville (Eds.), *The Heart Of Developmen: Gestalt Approaches To Working With Children, Adolescents and Their Worlds*. Vol. 2, Adolescence (pp. 122-152). Hillsdale, NJ: Analytic Press/GestaltPress.
Yontef, G. (1993). *Awareness, Dialogue And Process. Essays On Gestalt Therapy*. Highland, NY: Gestalt Journal Press.
Zahm, S. (1998). Therapist Self Disclosure in the Practice of Gestalt Therapy.. *Gestalt Journal 21*(2), 21-50.
Zinker, J. (1977). *Creative Processes in Gestalt Therapy*. New York: Brunner/Mazel.

Editors' Note:

Who better to introduce this interview, than Violet Oaklander herself, a hugely respected senior member of the child therapy field, and a major influence on all Gestalt therapists who work with children.

Violet Oaklander:

Peter Mortola is exactly the right person to interview me about my work. Since we worked together for ten or more years, and he wrote his PhD dissertation at UC Santa Barbara on how I train adults to work with children, he knows my work more than anyone else.

We met in 1987 when I first moved to Santa Barbara and later he came to many of my summer training programs, observing, documenting, analyzing. At some point he became my co-trainer, bringing to the trainings a depth that was amazing. (He also helped with a lot of the schlepping.) Besides the training, Peter came to many of my one and two day workshops. A high point was working together in South Africa in three cities, involving 500 therapists. Peter has written extensively about my work adding his own voice and interpretations. I might add that his own work has gone well beyond my own.

Peter teaches my work in some of his classes at Lewis and Clark College in Portland, Oregon, and to my delight often sends me papers that his students have written.

Recently I moved to Los Angeles, CA to live near my family, but I can see that I will never be able to retire completely.

October, 2009
Violet Oaklander

13

●●●●●●●●●●●●●●●●●●●●●●

You, Me, and the Parts of Myself I'm Still Getting to Know:

An Interview with Violet Oaklander on the Role of the Relational Triangle in her Approach to Therapeutic Work with Children and Adolescents

Peter Mortola

Overview

Much of what has been written regarding relational practice has focused on the quality of the two-way relationship between the therapist and the client. In Violet Oaklander's approach, this aspect of relational practice is clearly important, that is, much of what she is able to help the client achieve in therapy is based first on the establishment of trust, support, guidance and fun between the adult therapist and the child client.

Another and less focused upon aspect of Dr. Oaklander's relational practice, however, involves what I will define in this chapter as a three-way relationship, or a relational triangle, that is also key to the work that is accomplished in her therapeutic approach. Although the relational triangle will be more specifically defined later in this chapter, in brief, it implies that there are three parties involved in her relational, therapeutic work: there is the child that sits before the therapist, there is the therapist, and there are also parts of the child's self, previously undifferentiated and unexpressed, that emerge and become present in the room. These emerging aspects of the client's self are brought into awareness through a three-way dialogue between and among the child, the therapist, and those emerging aspects of the child's self. Through these three-way dialogues, new relationships are established and the self becomes both better differentiated and better integrated, or, in other words, both projected and owned.

In the following sections, I will first contextualize and then define this relational triangle before then providing an example of it from Violet Oaklander's practice. To close the chapter, Dr. Oaklander will join me in a conversation to discuss how and why she facilitates the relational triangle with the children she sees.

The Relationship Triangle

Awareness has long been noted as a cornerstone of a Gestalt approach to therapeutic work (Perls, et al, 1951; Polster & Polster, 1973; Wheeler, 2000). In *Windows to our Children* (Oaklander, 1978), Violet Oaklander also focuses on this theme as being central to her own work combining a Gestalt approach to working with children and adolescents: "My goal is to help the child become aware of herself and her existence in her world" (p. 53). In Oaklander's view, this awareness of the self develops through experience into a helpful and necessary contact with the self. Through this enlivening contact with the self, the child is better able to understand herself and her own needs and to then be better able to meet the environment in a healthy and an engaging/contactful way:

> Awareness is so tied in with experiencing that they are one and the same. Similarly, as the child in therapy experiences her senses, her body, her feelings, and the use she can make of her intellect, she regains a healthy stance toward life…As she learns who she is and accepts who she is in her differentness from you, then she will contact you, and you will know it. (p. 59)

Oaklander stresses that the way she helps a child become both more self-aware and in contact with herself is through the kind of relationship she establishes with her young clients. In her training with adult therapists, Oaklander has stated: "You are working first on the relationship and then on contact… finding creative ways to make the connection" (p. 33).

As mentioned above, the quality of relationship that Oaklander establishes with the client is much richer and more complex than just the dyadic quality of the therapist/client relationship. The following paragraphs illustrate in more detail and definition how Oaklander establishes and develops the relational triangle with her young clients.

The first side of this three-way relationship is between Oaklander and the "sentient client." By sentient client I mean the client who sits before Oaklander and is aware of him/herself to some extent, but who is also limited, as we all are, in this self-awareness. Oaklander develops this first part of the relationship through her kind and respectful presence, her "I/Thou" attitude toward the client (Buber, 1958), and in the engaging and light tone of voice she uses with young clients that lets them know that this thing they are doing together is very much like play (Mortola, 2006).

The second side of this three-sided relationship triangle is between Oaklander and the "emerging client." By emerging client I mean the parts of the client that the client has not necessarily differentiated, been aware of, or been in contact with. Oaklander develops this part of the relationship through the use of projective exercises. In these exercises, as in the sand tray example below, Oaklander has the young client create a scene or drawing inhabited by multiple characters or characteristics (for example: a scene in the sand tray involving pretend water and three cake-decoration surfers). She then has the client speak "as if" they were those different aspects of the scene (for example: "I am this surfer."). In this second aspect of the relational triangle, Oaklander asks many questions of the client that deepen the client's involvement in the character/projection (for example: "Okay, well what are the waves like? How's the water? Is the water cold?").

There is something significant here, but a bit paradoxical, at this stage of Oaklander's work: We normally speak of the qualities of the helping relationship between the therapist and client as being those akin to trust, sincerity, honesty, etc. However, in Oaklander's approach, the qualities of the relationship in this second side of the triangle are more akin to make believe, pretend, and goofing around. To be sure, this playful relationship would probably never have been established if trust and sincerity hadn't been present in the way that Oaklander addressed the client in the first side of the relationship triangle. Still, to me it has always been a fascinating aspect of Oaklander's work, and the relationship she builds with her clients, that such "real" work emerges out of such "unreal" approaches (more on this later in the interview).

The third and final side of the relational triangle that Oaklander establishes is between the "sentient client" and the "emerging client," that is, between the client as she presently sees herself and those parts of the self that she is not fully aware of. Oaklander will often facilitate this third side of the relational triangle by having the "sentient client" speak directly to those aspects of the "emerging client" (In the example below, Dr. Oaklander asks the boy she is working with to dialogue between the characters he has created in his sand tray: "Well what about you, could you help him?"). She may also facilitate this kind of dialogue a bit indirectly by asking the "sentient client" if there is anything he or she said as the "emerging client" that fits for them (for example: "Is there anything about this story that reminds you of your life?"). In either case, the sentient client is engaging with aspects of the self that have not been as much in the foreground, and the result is usually some kind of greater awareness of both the self and of possibilities.

Theoretically speaking, Oaklander's effort here is to engage different and overly differentiated aspects of the self in a kind of dialogue so that better contact and integration can occur. In her approach, dialogue between and among these three sides of the triangle leads the client to a greater awareness of and experience with the self. Through this process of dialogue and discovery, the rich diversity of the aspects of the self becomes both more differentiated and more integrated by the client as the work progresses. This work of dialogue and discovery with the client is important because, as Wheeler (1991) has stated, "The problem may lie in the missing connections between the *pieces* themselves – the formation of significant wholes of purpose, of commitment, of meaning" (pg. 98).

In this next section, I provide a transcript of Oaklander (Mortola, 2006) telling the story of her work with one particular teenage boy using the sand tray. Following this example, Violet Oaklander discusses with me, in an interview,` her approach to this relational triangle I have described.

Sand Tray Example with Tommy

> I was working with a fourteen-year-old boy named Tommy whose parents were going through a bitter divorce, and he was an only child. The parents were having terrible arguments. They really disliked the way the other one was parenting and they were fighting for custody of this child. The courts insisted that the parents take Tommy to therapy and that they go too. I could not see both parents in the same

room because they were so difficult. I don't mind couples fighting and arguing, but this was extremely bad.

So Tommy comes in alone the first time I saw him and his attitude was, "I don't care about the divorce, it doesn't bother me." Pretty typical of his age. But his grades were falling and he was showing other symptoms that something wasn't right. He was also pretty resistant. He didn't say anything, but his manner was like, "What am I going to do here with this lady? I'm not going to talk, I have nothing to say."

Anyway, this is not necessarily what I always do the first time that I see a child. I can't remember why I said this, maybe because he walked over to the sand tray and was fooling around with the sand. I said, "I'd like you to make a sand scene, anything you want." And he says "Okay." He finds a basket of cake-decoration figures and takes these three little surfers and he puts them in the sand. Then he moves the sand around a little bit to represent the waves, and says, "That's it."

So I said, "Tell me about your scene." All he says is, "There are three surfers," which is typical of the way children will respond. They just don't know what else to say. So I said, "Well I'll tell you what, you be one of the surfers. Which one are you?" So he says, "All right, I'm this surfer." And I began to dialogue with him. I said, "Okay, well what are the waves like? How's the water? Is the water cold?" He is reluctantly answering these questions, and as he's talking one of the other surfers falls over. So I said, "What happened to him?" And he said, "He fell." And I said, "Well what's going to happen?" And he kind of got into the spirit of it and says, "His surfboard is going to hit him in the head and he's going to drown."

It's interesting because at that point he sort of began to pull in again emotionally. He had been kind of playing with me, but now he began to pull away again. But I kept going on because he hadn't quite closed down yet. I said, "Well what about you, could you help him?" He said, "No, and then it'll probably be my fault that he drowns."

I could see at this point that he wasn't going to go any further with this. So I said, "Is there anything about this story that reminds you of your life?" And he said "No." But I said, "You know, you kind of said it was your fault that the surfer drowned. I'm just wondering if, in your own life, there's anything you think is your fault?" At this point Tommy bursts into tears and said, "Everything that is happening with the divorce is my fault."

Interview with Violet Oaklander

Peter: Thank you, Violet, for exploring this idea of the "relational triangle" with me. I just spent a summer teaching and thinking about your work: it occurred to me that your work, and much of Gestalt work in general, is premised on the notion that there is always more to ourselves than our conscious mind can hold at one time.

Violet: Yes, and in my approach it is through fantasy and projection that the child comes back to herself, to more of a sense of herself.

Peter: So therapeutic exercises like creating a sand tray scene allow us to project and contact parts of ourselves so that we can then become aware of them, dialogue with them, and integrate more of ourselves.

Violet: Yes, but it's all based on the therapeutic relationship, the contact, that I make with a child. It's not the same if they are playing with the sand tray by themselves. The therapist guides the work and provides support. There is the element of play in that relationship. If it gets too heavy, they break contact. And anything is so much easier to deal with when it's not obvious that it is an aspect of the self.

Peter: In that way, the projective process allows and supports a discussion, a dialogue, between the client and herself in which the therapist is engaged as well. So the difficult thing seems to be how to get started...

Violet: Well, first of all, like in the sand tray example, he is using something that he likes and feels comfortable with. He knows the beach, the sand, surfing. So I start with the surfer: "Be the voice of the surfer." I dialogue and guide or facilitate the beginning of story or a metaphor, and whatever issue is present comes out of the metaphor because of the projection. I have no idea where it's going to lead.

Peter: That reminds me of something that a participant said in your summer training years ago after working with the sand tray. She said, "I don't think I would have had that insight if I had not become the pieces in the sand tray. It really got to the underlying issues of what was going on for me."

Violet: Right, the fantasy is kind of a bridge into aspects of the self that they don't even know are parts of the self. The child begins to relate to those parts and gets to the point where they can own them. It's like they're looking into a window of the self.

Peter: "Window to the self"...I see the connection to the title of your first book. There's been a lot of discussion about the importance of the relationship that the therapist establishes with the child that helps them internalize the strengths of that relationship. But one thing that is so particular about your work, and seems so important to me, is the way that you help children learn how to have a relationship with not just others, but also with themselves.

Violet: The important part of this work is about that relationship: The more they know themselves the stronger they are. It has to do with relating to themselves: "Yes, that's part of me..."

Peter: So at the end of the work, the child is stronger because he has access and ownership of more of himself. He has been strengthened not only through better contact with the environment, you, but also through better contact with himself.

Violet: If there is something we don't know exists then we can't have a relationship with it. When the child creates a story or fantasy or drawing or form in clay or whatever it is, she can let herself go, she is not talking about herself at first because there is this aspect of fun, of play. As therapist, you are using materials that are intrinsic to the child...pastels, clay, puppets... that are so nurturing and gratifying to the child's very being. If you're just talking to the child, it isn't going to happen. You are leading them into a fantasy, it's going into another realm.

Peter: I think this is so interesting that the other realm you lead them into is where you are having a conversation with parts of the client that they don't even know are them. You are instigating a relationship with parts of the self that they don't necessarily have a relationship with.

Violet: I think it's so important that the therapist is there, that there is a safe container. That contact is so important, it's not the same if they do it by themselves.

Peter: Thank you, Violet, for having helped so many of us who work with children learn so much that is both theoretically and practically valuable. I really appreciate you talking to me about this important work!

References

Buber, M. (1958). *I and Thou.* New York: Scribner.
Mortola, P. (2006). *Windowframes: Learning the Art of Gestalt Play Therapy the Oaklander Way.* Hillsdale, NJ: The Analytic Press/ GestaltPress.
Oaklander, V. (1978). *Windows to Our Children: A Gestalt Therapy Approach to Children and Adolescents.* Highland, NY: The Gestalt Journal Press.
Perls, F., Hefferline, R., & Goodman, P. (1951). *Gestalt Therapy: Excitement and Growth in the Human Personality.* New York: Dell.
Polster, E. & Polster, M. (1973). *Gestalt Therapy Integrated: Contours of Theory and Practice.* New York: Vintage Books.

Wheeler, G. (1991). *Gestalt Reconsidered: A New Approach to Contact and Resistance*. NewYork: Gardner Press.

Wheeler, G. (2000). *Beyond Individualism: Toward a New Understanding of Self, Relationship, and Experience*. Hillsdale, NJ: The Analytic Press/GestaltPress.

Appendix

∙∙∙∙∙∙∙∙∙

We are honoured that the folowing chapters in this book have been or will be co-published in journals:

A version of Chapter Two, "Shame & Belonging in Childhood: The Interaction Between Relationship and Neurobiological Development in the Early Years of Life," by Robert G. Lee, appeared in the *British Gestalt Journal*, 2007, *16*(2), 38-45.

A version of Chapter Two, translated into French by Danielle Poupard, "Honte et attachement dans l'enfance: L'interaction entre le développement neurobiologique et la relaltion dans les premières années de vie," by Robert G. Lee, appeared in *Revue québécoisede Gestalt, 2010, 12*, 51-67.

A version of Chapter Four, "Something in the Air: Conditions that Promote Contact when Meeting Young People Who Have Stories of Early Trauma and Loss," by Neil Harris, appeared in the *British Gestalt Journal*, 2011, *20*(1), 20-28.

A version of Chapter Six, "The Adolescent Male: Shame, Support, and Developmentally Effective Psychotherapy," by Bronagh Starrs, appeared in *Inside Out*, 2009, *59*(3), 40-49.

A version of Chapter Seven, "Relational Modes and the Evolving Field of Parent-Child Contact: A Contribution to a Gestalt Theory of Development," by Mark McConville, appeared in the *British Gestalt Journal*, 2007, *16*(2), 5-12.

Appendix ... 351

A version of Chapter Eight, "Zig Zag Flop and Roll: Creating an Embodied Field for Healing and Awareness when Working with Children," by Denise Tervo appeared in the *British Gestalt Journal*, 2007, *16*(2), 28-37.

A version of Chapter Eleven, "Working with Adolescents from a Catholic Background in Northern Ireland: A Generation's Long Accumulation of Shame," by Bronagh Starrs appeared in the *British Gestalt Journal*, 2008, *17*(1), 5-14.

A version of Chapter Thirteen, "Am I Bovvered? A Gestalt Approach to Working with Adolescents," by Jon Blend appeared in the *British Gestalt Journal*, 2007, *16*(2), 19-27.

Selected Titles from GestaltPress

Organizational Consulting: A Gestalt Approach
    Edwin C. Nevis
Gestalt Reconsidered: A New Approach to Contact and Resistance
    Gordon Wheeler
Gestalt Therapy: Perspectives and Applications
    Edwin C. Nevis, editor
The Collective Silence: German Identity and the Legacy of Shame
    Barbara Heimannsberg & Christopher J. Schmidt
Community and Confluence: Undoing the Clinch of Oppression
    Philip Lichtenberg
Becoming a Stepfamily
    Patricia Papernow
On Intimate Ground: A Gestalt Approach to Working With Couples
    Gordon Wheeler & Stephanie Backman, editors
Body Process: Working With the Body in Psychotherapy
    James I. Kepner
Here, Now, Next: Paul Goodman and the Origins of Gestalt Therapy
    Taylor Stoehr
Crazy Hope Finite Experience
    Paul Goodman, edited by Taylor Stoehr
In Search of Good Form: Gestalt Therapy With Couples and Families
    Joseph C. Zinker
The Voice of Shame: Silence and Connection in Psychotherapy
    Robert G. Lee & Gordon Wheeler, editors
Healing Tasks: Psychotherapy With Adult Survivors of Childhood Abuse
    James I. Kepner
Adolescence: Psychotherapy and the Emergent Self
    Mark McConville
Getting Beyond Sobriety: Clinical Approaches to Long-Term Recovery
    Michael Craig Clemmens
Back to the Beanstalk: Enchantment and Reality for Couples
    Judith R. Brown
The Dreamer and the Dream: Essays and Reflections on Gestalt Therapy
    Rainette Eden Fants, edited by Arthur Roberts
A Well-Lived Life: Essays in Gestalt Therapy
    Sylvia Fleming Crocker
From the Radical Center: The Heart of Gestalt Therapy
    Erving & Miriam Polster

The Gendered Field: Gestalt Perspectives and Readings
Deborah Ullman & Gordon Wheeler, editors

Beyond Individualism: Toward a New Understanding of Self, Relationship, and Experience
Gordon Wheeler

Sketches: An Anthology of Essays, Art, and Poetry
Joseph C. Zinker

The Heart of Development: Gestalt Approaches to Working with Children, Adolescents, and Their Worlds (2 Volumes)
Mark McConville & Gordon Wheeler, editors

Body of Awareness: A Somatic Developmental Approach to Psychotherapy
Ruella Frank

The Unfolding Self: Essays of Jean-Marie Robine
Jean-Marie Robine; edited and translated by Gordon Wheeler

Encountering Bigotry: Befriending Projecting Persons in Everyday Life
Philip Lichtenberg, Janneke van Beusekom & Dorothy Gibbons

Reading Paul Goodman
Gordon Wheeler, editor

The Values of Connection: A Relational Approach to Ethics
Robert G. Lee, editor

WindowFrames: Learning the Art of Gestalt Play Therapy the Oaklander Way
Peter Mortola

Gestalt Therapy: Living Creatively Today
Gonzague Masquelier

The Secret Language of Intimacy: Releasing the Hidden Power in Couple Relationships
Robert G. Lee

CoCreating the Field: Intention & Practice in the Age of Complexity
Deborah Ullman & Gordon Wheeler, editors

Aggression, Time, and Understanding: Contributions to the Evolution of Gestalt Therapy
Frank-M. Staemmler

Relational Approaches in Gestalt Therapy
Lynne Jacobs & Rich Hycner, editors

Relational Child, Relational Brain, Development and Therapy in Childhood and Adolescence
Robert G. Lee & Neil Harris, editors

Transforming the way we live and work in the world

Gestalt International Study Center

GISC is a diverse worldwide learning community based on trust, optimism and generosity. We study and teach skills that energize human interaction and lead to action, change and growth, and we create powerful learning experiences for individuals and organizations.

- **Leadership Development**
    - Leadership in the 21st Century
    - Leading Nonprofit Organizations
    - Graduate Leadership Forum
- **Professional Skill Development**
    - Cape Cod Training Program
    - Introduction to the Cape Cod Model
    - Executive Personality Dynamics for Coaches
    - Applying the Cape Cod Model to Coaching
    - Applying the Cape Cod Model in Organizations
    - Finding Your Developmental Edge
    - Women in the Working World
    - Advanced Supervision
- **Personal Development**
    - The Next Phase: A Program for Transition & Renewal
    - Optimism & Awareness Essential Skills for Living
    - Couples Workshop
    - Building Blocks of Creativity
    - Nature & Transitions
- *Gestalt Review*

Launched in 1977, Gestalt Review focuses on the Gestalt approach at all systems levels, ranging from the individual, through couples, families and groups, to organizations, educational settings and the community at large. To read sample articles, or to subscribe, visit:

www.gestaltreview.com

For more information about any of GISC's offerings or to read our newsletter, visit:

www.gisc.com